on track ...
The Moody Blues

every album, every song

Geoffrey Feakes

on track ...
The Moody Blues

every album, every song

Geoffrey Feakes

sonicbondpublishing.com

Sonicbond Publishing Limited
www.sonicbondpublishing.co.uk
Email: info@sonicbondpublishing.co.uk

First Published in the United Kingdom 2019
First Published in the United States 2019
Reprinted 2020, 2025

British Library Cataloguing in Publication Data:
A Catalogue record for this book is available from the British Library

Copyright Geoffrey Feakes 2019

ISBN 978-1-78952-042-2

The right of Geoffrey Feakes to be identified as the author of this work has been asserted by him in accordance with the Copyright, Designs and patents Act 1988.
All rights reserved. No part of this publication may be reproduced, stored in a retrieval system or transmitted in any form or by any means, electronic, mechanical, photocopying, recording or otherwise, without prior permission in writing from Sonicbond Publishing Limited

Typeset in ITC Garamond & ITC Avant Garde
Printed and bound in England

Graphic design and typesetting: Full Moon Media

This book is dedicated to the memory of Ray Thomas (1941 – 2018)

Acknowledgements

A big thank you to Stephen Lambe and all at Sonicbond Publishing for their support and encouragement in putting this book together.

Thanks to the Dutch Progressive Rock Page who have published my reviews and interviews since 2005 and provided the inspiration to write this book.

Gratitude to all the members of the Moody Blues, past and present, and everyone associated with the band.

I would also like to thank all the researchers, journalists, archivists and fans that have gone before and made available a wealth of information.

A special thank you to my wife Margaret and her gracious support through five months devoted almost entirely to the band and their music.

Finally, a fond farewell to the Classic Rock Society who sadly closed their doors in 2019. Since I joined in 2001, they've been a treasured source of entertainment and information.

on track ...
The Moody Blues

Contents

1 Foreword 9
2 Introduction 11
3 The Key Players 14
4 The Magnificent Moodies 20
5 Days of Future Passed 29
6 In Search of the Lost Chord 38
7 On the Threshold of a Dream 46
8 To Our Children's Children's Children 53
9 A Question of Balance 59
10 Every Good Boy Deserves Favour 65
11 Seventh Sojourn 71
12 Blue Jays 77
13 Octave 82
14 Long Distance Voyager 88
15 The Present 93
16 The Other Side of Life 98
17 Sur la mer 103
18 Keys of the Kingdom 107
19 Strange Times 113
20 December 119
21 Live Albums and Videos 124
22 Compilation Albums 129
23 Tribute Albums and Bands 136
24 Solo Albums 139
25 Seventeen (Almost) Forgotten Songs 154
26 Top Twenty Moody Blues Songs 156
27 Bibliography and Online Resources 157

Foreword

Like many fans of a certain age, my introduction to the Moody Blues was the 1965 UK number one single 'Go Now' (or 'Go Now !' as it was written on the label). I was just ten years old, and the soulful singing and infectious piano hook left a lasting impression. They were virtually written off as one-hit wonders until almost three years later a song called 'Nights in White Satin' appeared on the radio. The song's singer and writer just happened to be from my hometown of Swindon in the South West of England. The yearning lead vocal, ethereal backing voices and orchestra (which I later discovered to be a Mellotron) were a revelation. And this was 1967, the year of classics like 'A Whiter Shade of Pale', 'Penny Lane', 'Strawberry Fields Forever', 'Waterloo Sunset', 'Silence is Golden' and 'I Can See for Miles'. These songs, along with many others, were the soundtrack of my adolescence.

In 1970 after leaving school, I followed in the footsteps of Graeme Edge, becoming a trainee draughtsman, and John Lodge, studying engineering at a local college. Most importantly, I had money in my pocket to fund what was becoming an insatiable appetite for music. Fuelled by the weekly music press, which I read avidly, and late-night radio, especially *Radio Luxembourg*, I discovered the delights of what was commonly known as 'Underground music'. The Moodies 'Mark Two' had already released five albums at this point and following a recommendation, I purchased *On the Threshold of a Dream*. By the end of the record, I was hooked. From the quirky charm of 'Dear Diary' to the cinematic 'The Voyage', the sheer range of the band's sound was awe inspiring.

In 1971, I started attending gigs on a regular basis, and there were strong releases from Jethro Tull, Yes, Pink Floyd, David Bowie, Elton John, Deep Purple, Emerson Lake & Palmer, The Who and Led Zeppelin. My record collection grew at a rapid rate. In those pre-internet days, there was something very special about walking into a record shop and buying an LP on its first day of release. *Every Good Boy Deserves Favour* was no exception, my first brand new Moody Blues album. To say I played it to death would be an understatement. From the overly ambitious 'Procession' to the haunting 'My Song', I absorbed every note and every word. It was ambitious, and it was tuneful, I couldn't wait for the next album.

Although my loyalty has been tested over the years (the bouts of inactivity, the departure of Mike Pinder, the synthetic sounds of the '80s and '90s) my affection for the band has remained. While the post-1970s albums may not scale the heights of the earlier classics, every release has something to recommend it. In short, the Moody Blues were the obvious subject for a book of this kind.

Following the 'Introduction' which includes a brief history of the band, I introduce the 'Key Players'. We are then into the main body of the book, a chapter dedicated to each album where every track and related non-album track is individually discussed. As the band have always been attentive to presentation, I also cover the album artwork. This is followed by the chapters 'Live Albums and Videos', 'Compilation Albums', 'Tribute Albums and Bands' and 'Solo Albums' which are all self-explanatory. While I neither endorse nor dismiss bootlegs, they are not part of the remit of this book. I round things off with 'Seventeen (Almost) Forgotten Songs'.

As a music reviewer, I spend a good deal of time listening to new albums and bands. One of the positive aspects of writing this book was revisiting my vinyl and CD collection, which I rarely do these days. It proved to be a pleasurable and nostalgic voyage of rediscovery. If you are in a similar situation due to the demands of everyday life, I hope this book inspires you to do the same.

Finally, while I've tried to keep my comments balanced and informative, time can play tricks on both judgement and memory. If you disagree (or agree) with anything I've written or spot any factual errors, then please feel free to contact me through the publisher.

Geoffrey Feakes, 31 May 2019

Introduction

2018 was a year marked by two significant events for the Moody Blues and their fans, one of sadness and one of celebration. In December 2017, it was announced that after years of campaigning by supporters (including a 2013 *Rolling Stone* magazine readers' poll) they would finally be inducted into the Rock & Roll Hall of Fame. The ceremony was scheduled for the 14 April 2018, and the 'classic' line-up were all expected to attend. Sadly, on 4 January 2018 with just four months to go, Ray Thomas, who co-founded the band with Mike Pinder in 1964, lost his battle with prostate cancer and passed away. The induction ceremony went ahead with Pinder, Justin Hayward, John Lodge and Graeme Edge joined by Ray's son Adam and former frontman Denny Laine. Although long overdue, it was a welcome acknowledgement of their longevity and achievements. Pinder said on his website 'The rock hall of fame people were wonderful' and Hayward admitted that he enjoyed it more than he expected. And if you visit the band's website, you can even buy the souvenir t-shirt.

According to the rules of eligibility, they could have been inducted as early as 1989. By that point, the Moody Blues had already earned their place in rock history as one of the most popular and influential bands of all time. John Lodge once wryly observed that the Moody Blues have always been people's third favourite group. Since they formed 55 years ago, hundreds of artists have risen to popularity only to fade away, few have endured like the Moodies. In their 1960s and '70s prime, not only were they consummate musicians, they boasted five songwriters and four lead singers which even the Beatles couldn't top. And if statistics are necessary, they've sold more than 70 million albums worldwide and have been awarded eighteen platinum and gold discs. The individual members have also received numerous awards, particularly for their songwriting achievements. While they've never been particularly fashionable as far as critics are concerned, thankfully they've never been accused of being a rich man's Barclay James Harvest! From *Days of Future Passed* in 1967 to *Seventh Sojourn* in 1972, they had an impressive run of seven classic albums before restyling themselves for the 1980s and beyond. They pioneered symphonic rock, striking a chord with music lovers on a global scale. That's not how it began, however.

They formed in Birmingham, a sprawling city in England's industrial heartland that would become associated with hard rock bands like Black Sabbath and Led Zeppelin. This was 1964 however, and the Moodies comprising Mike Pinder (keyboards, vocals), Ray Thomas (harmonica, flute, vocals), Denny Laine (guitar, vocals), Graeme Edge (drums) and Clint Warwick (bass, vocals) were part of the flourishing pop and R&B scene. They called themselves the M & B 5, hoping this would attract sponsorship from M & B (Mitchells and Butlers) breweries who owned many of the clubs and pubs where the local bands performed. While that never materialised, they had to be admired for their enterprising spirit. After a brief billing as the Moody Blues

Five, they eventually settled on the Moody Blues which reflected their twelve-bar blues-based sound and Pinder's interest in music's ability to create different moods.

Following their live debut in Birmingham in May 1964, they were noticed by managers Tony Secunda and Alex Murray who secured them a regular spot at the Marquee Club in London. They also arranged a recording deal with Decca Records. While the Beatles were monopolising the charts on both sides of the Atlantic, the Moodies had their own flush of fame with 'Go Now' which reached the top of the UK singles chart in January 1965. Later that same year it helped propel their debut LP *The Magnificent Moodies* to the upper reaches of the album chart. Subsequent singles fell mostly on deaf ears and following the departure of first Warwick and then Laine in 1966 the band splintered despite a second album in the works.

The Moody Blues 'Mark Two' surfaced in late 1966 with two new members and a new direction. Justin Hayward (guitar, vocals) and John Lodge (bass, vocals) would be crucial in shaping the band's sound (and international success) into the 21st Century. From the late '60s to the early '70s they embraced psychedelic pop, symphonic rock, prog and folk-rock. Producer Tony Clarke played a significant part in ensuring their polished sound remained at the forefront of recording technology. In 1969 they became one of the first bands to successfully launch their own label, Threshold Records.

Despite their success (or perhaps because of it) in 1974 they decided to take time out, although it was widely reported that they had disbanded. A flurry of offshoot activities followed including a compilation, solo albums and the successful Hayward and Lodge *Blue Jays* partnership and 1975 hit single 'Blue Guitar'. In 1977 the self-explanatory double LP *Caught Live + 5* was released, and the Moodies regrouped. The resulting 1978 album *Octave* sold well, spawning more hit singles, but Pinder was reluctant to tour and departed following the recording. His surprise replacement was Swiss keyboard virtuoso Patrick Moraz fresh from Yes. Also around this time, Hayward appeared on *Jeff Wayne's Musical Version of The War of the Worlds*, which is still wowing audiences to this day.

They continued to record throughout the 1980s with four successful albums and several singles including five significant Stateside hits. In 1985 the band received the prestigious Ivor Novello Award for 'Outstanding Contribution to Music'. In the 1990s, studio albums became more sporadic with diminishing degrees of commercial success. Touring continued throughout this period and they often performed with a full orchestra, something they had not done in their earlier years. Moraz departed acrimoniously in 1991, replaced by touring musician Bias Boshell backed by second keyboardist Paul Bliss. Gordon Marshall fulfilled a similar role as a second drummer to Graeme Edge. Founding member Ray Thomas retired at the end of 2002 due to ill health, replaced for tours by the classically trained Norda Mullen.

The last studio album, *December* was released in 2003. Although they could no longer rely on the general record-buying public, a loyal fan base ensured sold out concerts. Touring continued unabated throughout the noughties and studio albums were replaced by live releases, reissues and numerous compilations. In 2004 they attracted the attention of several renowned American country artists who covered their songs under the inspired title *Moody Bluegrass*. For touring duties, they enlisted Julie Ragins on keyboards and sax in 2006, Alan Hewitt took over as principal keyboardist in 2010 and Billy Ashbaugh as second drummer in 2016. A performance from the 2017 tour to celebrate the 50th anniversary of *Days of Future Passed* was recorded and released in 2018. Justin Hayward and John Lodge regularly feature Moodies songs in their solo sets and have shows booked for 2019 and 2020. Together with Graeme Edge, as the core members, they are keeping the music of the Moody Blues alive which so far has bridged six decades and several generations. Long may they continue.

The Key Players

The Moody Blues family tree is a relatively small one, especially compared with many of their contemporaries. Although the original line-up lasted for less than three years, since 1967 they have remained remarkably stable with just three (albeit significant) changes. I've summarised the dates, personnel changes and line-ups as follows:

1964 – 1966: Mark One: Mike Pinder, Ray Thomas, Denny Laine, Graeme Edge, Clint Warwick

1966: Clint Warwick leaves, replaced by Rod Clark

1966: Rod Clark leaves, replaced by John Lodge

1966: Denny Laine leaves, replaced by Justin Hayward

1966 – 1978: Mark Two: Mike Pinder, Ray Thomas, Justin Hayward, John Lodge, Graeme Edge

1978: Mike Pinder leaves, replaced by Patrick Moraz

1978 – 1991: Mark Three: Justin Hayward, John Lodge, Ray Thomas, Graeme Edge, Patrick Moraz

1991: Patrick Moraz leaves, reducing the band to a quartet

1991 – 2002: Mark Four: Justin Hayward, John Lodge, Ray Thomas, Graeme Edge

2002: Ray Thomas retires, reducing the band to a trio

2002 – present: Mark Five: Justin Hayward, John Lodge, Graeme Edge

In this section, I've included full-time band members only. Numerous other musicians, including Bias Boshell, Paul Bliss, Gordon Marshall, Norda Mullen and Alan Hewitt have performed and recorded with the band, but they never became fully fledged members. I've also omitted bass player Rod Clark who for a few short months in 1966 following the departure of Clint Warwick was a temporary replacement before the arrival of John Lodge. I have however included producer Tony Clarke who from 1967 to 1978 was the band's unofficial sixth member.

Mike Pinder (born: 27 December 1941)

1964 – 1978. Vocals, piano, Mellotron, keyboards

For fans of a certain age, Moody Blues founder Mike Pinder remains probably the most distinguished member. In a band that has always eschewed guitar histrionics, his keyboards were a prominent feature throughout his fourteen-year tenure. During the Denny Laine period, his distinctive piano playing was the lead instrument on many of the songs, most notably the 1965 hit single 'Go Now'. During the Moodies 'Mark Two' period, the symphonic sounds of the Mellotron and his enigmatic compositional style were chiefly responsible for the band's prog-rock tag in the late '60s and early '70s.

Like the other original members, he played in several groups that were part of the short-lived 'Brumbeat' scene which included over 250 bands at its peak. He was keyboardist with El Riot and the Rebels, formed by Ray Thomas (vocals) and John Lodge (bass). After a stint in Germany with the Krew Cats, he returned to Birmingham, and took a job with Streetly Electronics where he was introduced to the Mellotron.

In the spring of 1964, he and Thomas formed the Moody Blues with Denny Laine (guitar, vocals), Graeme Edge (drums) and Clint Warwick (bass). Under the management of Tony Secunda and Alex Murray, they secured a recording contract with Decca Records. In the summer of 1965, they released the debut album *The Magnificent Moodies* containing mostly cover versions. It sold well in the UK but did not represent their songwriting potential. In 1965 and 1966, Pinder co-wrote with Laine several superb but mostly ignored singles.

The acquisition of a Mellotron Mark II, that was sitting unused in a social club at a Dunlop tyre factory, was a major turning point. The instrument would play a key role on *Days of Future Passed* in 1967 and subsequent Moodies 'Mark Two' albums. As well as singing his own compositions, his rich baritone made him a natural for narrating Edge's poems which provided a unifying introduction to many of the band's albums.

Ray Thomas (born: 29 December 1941, died: 4 January 2018)
1964 – 2002. Vocals, harmonica, flute

Ray Thomas was born in Stourport-on-Severn, south-west of Birmingham just two days after Pinder and he later joined the Birmingham Youth Choir. It was his penchant for soul and blues however that led him to the Saints & Sinners who later morphed into El Riot and the Rebels. He sang lead vocals and played harmonica in the band, which also featured John Lodge and later Mike Pinder. He and Pinder joined the Krew Cats in 1963 where he was again the vocalist and Pinder the organist. Like the Beatles before them, the Krew Cats trod the boards at the Top Ten Club in Hamburg, Germany before returning disillusioned and penniless to the UK.

In 1964, Thomas and Pinder formed the appropriately named R&B group the Moody Blues. The band's remit was to perform soul and blues covers with the occasional original song written by Pinder and Denny Laine. With the gifted singer Laine in the band, Thomas sang lead on only a couple of songs although his voice was an integral part of the band's distinctive harmonies. In addition to harmonica and tambourine, he taught himself to play the flute to give himself an extra musical 'voice' within the band.

His talents as a songwriter would come to fruition in 1967 in the band's second phase. The whimsical 'Another Morning' and the psychedelic 'Twilight Time' on *Days of Future Passed* set the tone and his combination of quirkiness and charm would be a welcome feature on later albums. His flute playing was an integral part of the band's sound and when combined with Pinder's Mellotron added substance to their symphonic aspirations. With the possible exception of Jethro Tull's Ian Anderson, he was the best-known exponent of the instrument in rock. Until his retirement at the end of 2002, his charm and wit made him a natural spokesperson for the band during live performances.

Denny Laine (born: 29 October 1944)
1964 – 1966. Vocals, guitars, harmonica

During his time with the Moody Blues, which amounted to less than three years, Denny Laine was undeniably the face and voice of the band. Not only did he possess a rich, soulful voice, but his versatility as a singer allowed him to mimic almost every popular style of the 1950s and '60s, including, rock and roll, soul, pop and R&B. This made him a natural for singing other artists' songs, although ironically it was their reputation as a cover band that would be the undoing of the Moodies 'Mark One'.

Like the other band members, Laine was born and raised in Birmingham and was soon fronting his own band, Denny Laine and The Diplomats. They were one of the top bands on the circuit. In early 1964 after abandoning the Diplomats, he was approached by Ray Thomas and Mike Pinder to join the M & B 5, who soon changed their name to the Moody Blues. From May onwards they constantly gigged throughout 1964, appearing regularly at the legendary Marquee Club in London, with the Yardbirds and Manfred Mann amongst others.

The first single released in September 1964 demonstrated Laine's vocal abilities to the full, but it would be the second single 'Go Now' that would propel his voice and the band to the top of the UK chart in early 1965. Although he remained with the band for one album, *The Magnificent Moodies*, and half a dozen underrated singles, which he mostly co-wrote with Pinder, he could see the writing on the wall and departed at the beginning of October 1966. Ironically the song 'Boulevard de la Madeleine' released that same month contained his best guitar work with the band.

Graeme Edge (born: 30 March 1941)
1964 – Present. Drums, percussion

Graeme Edge has the distinction of being the oldest surviving member and the only founding member still with the band. Until 1964 he was a member of another Birmingham based band, Gerry Levene and the Avengers, who also boasted Roy Wood amongst their ranks. Ironically, the band's arch-rivals on the club circuit were Denny Laine and The Diplomats whose leader would later become Edge's bandmate. He effectively jumped ship to join the Moody Blues following an invitation from Ray Thomas and Mike Pinder.

Although Edge didn't write any songs during the first three years, that would change with the arrival of the Moodies 'Mark Two'. The 1967 *Days of Future Passed* album opens and closes with two of his poems, both recited by Pinder. His spoken verse poetry would become a distinctive feature of future albums, often providing the opening track. As his writing became more ambitious, he progressed onto fully fledged songs sung by the other band members.

Although not a flamboyant drummer, he is a highly respected musician providing a rock-steady pulse that drives the music. In the early '70s, he pioneered electronic drums (resembling a keyboard) which he played on the

1971 *Every Good Boy Deserves Favour* album. Like many drummers in their later years, in 1991 aged 50, he succumbed to the pressure of constant playing. For live work, Gordon Marshall was recruited as a second drummer, replaced by Billy Ashbaugh in 2016. While Edge is not a singer or frontman in the mould of fellow drummer Phil Collins, during the band's concerts, he relishes the opportunity to come stage front and engage with the audience.

Clint Warwick (real name Albert Eccles) (born: 25 June 1940, died: 15 May 2004)

1964 – 1966. Bass guitar, vocals

Another Birmingham boy, in the late 1950s Clint Warwick joined Danny King and the Dukes who played the local circuit of pubs and clubs. Like the other band members, it was his passion for R&B that persuaded him to accept Mike Pinder and Ray Thomas' invitation to join the Moody Blues in 1964. In addition to playing bass and his natural good looks, he sang harmonies and his distinctive falsetto pre-empted his replacement, John Lodge. On the 1965 album *The Magnificent Moodies* he also shares lead vocals with Denny Laine on the song 'I've Got a Dream'. In addition to the album, he played on all the Moodies 'Mark One' singles, even though the final two were released following his departure in the summer of 1966.

Disillusioned by the constant grind of touring (the band performed throughout '64, '65 and '66 with scarcely a break) and a wife and two small children at home, he retired from music altogether and returned to his trade as a carpenter in Birmingham. Sadly in 2004, at the age of 63, he passed away while working on a proposed second solo album.

Justin Hayward (born: 14 October 1946)

1966 – Present. Vocals, electric and acoustic guitars

Justin Hayward spent his formative years in Swindon town, 75 miles due south of Birmingham. In 1963, he acquired his signature cherry red Gibson ES-335 guitar and never looked back. In 1965, he joined The Wilde Three, fronted by Marty Wilde and his wife Joyce, and made his first TV appearance that year. Against Wilde's advice, he signed a publishing deal with Lonnie Donegan which he later said was the biggest professional mistake of his career. As a result, the copyright of his 1965 to 1973 songs would be owned by Donegan's Tyler Music. He recorded two singles under Donegan's management. Although Wilde had become a friend and mentor, after eighteen months he decided it was time to move on.

Mike Pinder met Hayward in August 1966 through Eric Burdon of The Animals and was suitably impressed by the record 'London Is Behind Me' he played him. As a result, in November Hayward was hired as a replacement for Denny Laine, a tough act to follow. His smooth, seemingly effortless vocal style was the polar opposite of Laine's soulful tones and he proved to be an equally accomplished guitar player.

Following a brief spell in Belgium and France, the band returned to the UK where they were still playing their now dated R&B repertoire. Hayward, in particular, would be the catalyst in turning their fortunes around. Following two singles, and the intervention of Decca Records, the 1967 album *Days of Future Passed* signalled a brighter future for the band. 'Nights in White Satin' in particular would be the forerunner of a succession of excellent album tracks and several hit singles that would establish Hayward as the band's most recognisable voice and prolific songwriter.

John Lodge (born: 20 July 1945)

1966 – Present. Vocals, bass guitar

Joining the band in late 1966 around the same time as Justin Hayward, John Lodge was a natural replacement for Clint Warwick (and Rod Clark). For one thing, he was a native of Birmingham (with a distinct 'Brummie' accent) and secondly his high falsetto was ideal for the vocal harmonies favoured by the band.

Lodge's passage to the Moodies was a smooth one. After leaving school, he enrolled in Aston College of Technology and had a spell as bassist with the pre-Moodies group El Riot and the Rebels. The band included his friend Ray Thomas on vocals and later Mike Pinder on keyboards. He returned to college and also formed a band called the Carpetbaggers. After completing his engineering course, he was invited to join the Moodies as a permanent replacement for Warwick.

He contributed two songs to the Moodies 'Mark Two' debut album *Days of Future Passed,* but it would be 'Ride My See-Saw' from the second album, *In Search of the Lost Chord*, that would signpost his future. Not only would it become a concert favourite that closed their shows, but it also established him as the writer and singer of some of their most popular songs. 1972, in particular, was a good year for Lodge with two hits, 'Isn't Life Strange' and 'I'm Just a Singer (In a Rock and Roll Band)', lifted from the *Seventh Sojourn* album. This, combined with his impeccable bass playing and boyish good looks (which he shares with Hayward), made him an undeniable asset for the Moody Blues. Together with Hayward and Graeme Edge, he keeps the flame burning.

Patrick Moraz (born: 24 June 1948)

1978 – 1991. Keyboards

When I read in the 1978 music press that Patrick Moraz had replaced Mike Pinder in the Moody Blues, I must admit I was sceptical. Having seen him with Yes several times, I was familiar with his virtuoso, often jazzy style and I couldn't see how it would fit into the more integrated, song-based style of the Moodies. I would be proved wrong, however. He was hired in July 1978 as a touring musician and became a full-time member in 1980 for the recording of the *Long Distance Voyager* album.

A classically trained native of Switzerland, he came to the UK in the 1960s to expand his musical horizons. His route to the Moodies was via proto-prog band Mainhorse, Refugee (essentially The Nice without Keith Emerson) and Yes. During his time with the Moodies he performed on five studio albums, but it was on stage where his prestigious keyboard talents would really make their mark. With just one co-songwriting credit to show for his thirteen years with the band, he found an outlet for his compositional talents with several solo albums during the same period. He also recorded two albums with ex-Yes drummer Bill Bruford, toured with noted jazz musicians and wrote several film scores in between his commitments with the Moodies.

Tony Clarke (born: 21 August 1941, died: 4 January 2010)
1967 – 1978. Producer

From their 1967 debut single 'Fly Me High' to the 1978 album *Octave*, Tony Clarke produced all the Moody Blues 'Mark Two' records. He worked almost exclusively for the band and on the inner sleeve of the *On the Threshold of a Dream* album his photo appears with equal prominence alongside the individual band members. He also helped to establish their own label, Threshold Records, in 1969 and the Threshold recording studio in the mid-'70s.

He began working with Decca Records as a session musician and moved into production in 1964. He produced several singles as well as writing songs for the label's artists. He was teamed with the Moodies in 1966 to help turnaround their flagging record sales. In 1967 he was assigned the *Days of Future Passed* project and the rest, as they say, is history. During his twelve year association with the band, his innovative techniques assisted by engineer Derek Varnals put them at the forefront of recording technology. He was also instrumental in getting the band back together for the *Octave* album, although he found the subsequent recording too stressful. Later producers for the band, including Pip Williams and Tony Visconti, as good as they were, had a lot to live up to.

The Magnificent Moodies (1965)

Personnel:
Denny Laine: guitars, harmonica, vocals
Mike Pinder: piano, organ, vocals
Ray Thomas: percussion, flute, harmonica, vocals
Graeme Edge: Drums, percussion, vocals
Clint Warwick: bass guitar, vocals
Additional personnel: Elaine Caswell: percussion
Produced by: Denny Cordell, Alex Murray ('Go Now')
Recorded: October 1964 – March 1965
UK and USA release date: July 1965
Highest chart places: UK: 5, USA: Did not chart
Running time: 34:23

This is where it began, although there are few debut albums in the history of rock less indicative of a band's later output than this one. Released in glorious mono, even the naive bravado of the title is firmly rooted in the swinging '60s. It reached number five in the UK album chart, not bad for a debut release, although the inclusion of the number one hit single 'Go Now' from January that year was clearly a contributing factor. Despite being retitled *Go Now – The Moody Blues #1* for the North American market, sales Stateside were disappointing. Of the twelve songs on the album, only four are original compositions, co-written by Mike Pinder and Denny Laine, and conspicuously all relegated to side two. Like many groups at the time, including the Rolling Stones and Manfred Mann, the Moodies were recycling obscure American R&B songs that would have been unfamiliar to a mainstream audience. As was typical for many UK acts in the '60s (including the Beatles), the album was altered for the US market with four songs replaced and a different running order. With the inclusion of the excellent singles 'I Don't Want to Go on Without You' and 'From the Bottom of My Heart', the American version is in my view the better of the two.

Despite a valiant effort from the band, and Laine and Pinder, in particular, other 1965 albums including the Beatles' *Help!* and *Rubber Soul*, the Who's *My Generation,* and the Rolling Stones' *Out of Our Heads* left *The Magnificent Moodies* in the shade. A string of singles followed in the wake of 'Go Now', but none cracked the top twenty either side of the Atlantic. The first two singles were reissued as a four-track EP in May 1965. The later singles written by Laine and Pinder would better demonstrate the band's potential, more so than the album. The advances from Decca, however, would leave them financially indebted to the record company.

They gigged constantly throughout the UK and parts of Europe in 1965 supporting the likes of Chuck Berry and the Rolling Stones. They played at the filmed annual *NME* Poll Winners Concert in April (performing a storming 'Hey! Bo Diddley') and made several TV and radio appearances in the UK and in France where they were especially popular. A proposed summer tour of the

USA with the Kinks was abandoned when the necessary visas had not been obtained. They did manage the trip in the latter half of December however, where they appeared on American TV. Having been dropped by Tony Secunda in favour of another Birmingham band, the Move, Beatles manager Brian Epstein signed the Moody Blues in September, and they supported the Fab Four on their final UK tour in early December.

All this work did little to halt their dwindling fortunes, however. In July 1966 the constant grind of touring with little reward got the better of Clint Warwick who quit the band and the music business altogether. For a short spell, Rod Clark was his replacement, and he did some live and session work with the Moodies before joining the Rockin' Berries (another Birmingham band). The biggest blow came In October 1966 when Laine departed, seeking fame and fortune as a solo artist and in the 1970s, with Paul McCartney and Wings. That same month, Epstein announced that he was no longer representing the band.

The Magnificent Moodies has been reissued in various formats over the years with the definitive being Esoteric Recordings' 2014 50th Anniversary two CD remastered edition. It boasts 29 previously unreleased tracks including nine from the sessions for the aborted second album. It provides an insight into what might have been if Laine had stayed with the band. The sequence of songs below is the same as the original UK album release. The additional songs on the North American version are included in the 'Related tracks' section along with the non-album singles and bonus tracks on later reissues.

Album Cover

In many ways, this is just as iconic as the later album covers. As was typical of mid-'60s record sleeves, the front cover is a photo of the group posing in an outdoor location, in this case on a jetty smartly dressed in suits and ties. There is no room for the band name with the title *The Magnificent Moodies* in bold graphics dominating the cover. On the back of the original UK LP sleeve is an introduction from Scottish pop-folk artist Donovan, who was big news in 1965. The USA release features a different cover photo of the band by a windmill within a dark blue frame with the title *Go Now – The Moody Blues #1* at the top.

'I'll Go Crazy' (James Brown)

The first of eight covers on the album, this plays fast and loose with the 1960 original with more of a rock and roll feel. Denny Laine's bluesy drawl and occasional screams echo not only James Brown but also the Beatles' 1963 take on 'Twist and Shout'. Instrumentally, its Mike Pinder's boogie-woogie piano that stands out.

'Something You Got' (Chris Kenner)

A blues song, it's taken at a slightly more pedestrian pace than the 1961 original with soulful harmonies supporting Laine's emotive vocal. His guitar dominates with a piercing solo backed by a touch of flute from Ray Thomas.

It's difficult to imagine that this has also been covered (in varying styles) by Fairport Convention, Bruce Springsteen and Jimi Hendrix.

'Go Now' (Larry Banks, Milton Bennett)
Produced by co-manager Alex Murray, this was the band's first and (to date) last number one single in the UK. It's one of the seminal torch songs of the 1960s thanks to Laine's impassioned vocal, the superb harmonies and Pinder's infectious descending piano chords. As I recall, whenever it came on the radio in its heyday, it often prompted spontaneous outbreaks of 'air piano' from all but the most cynical listener. It's boosted by Pinder's bluesy piano solo around the two-minute mark with Edge, Warwick and Laine locking together for the watertight rhythm. Murray directed a three-minute film to accompany the song which was one of the earliest examples of a promotional video. Filmed in sepia, the combined headshots of the band singing in unison with only their faces illuminated predates Queen's 'Bohemian Rhapsody' by more than ten years.

'Go Now' is the best song on the album by some distance and overshadowed the 1964 original sung by Larry Banks' wife, American soul diva Bessie Banks. Her version was one of many records that were sent to the band by a DJ in America who was friendly with their management. Laine later said that he chose the song because it suited his voice and the prominent piano would suit Pinder. In 2015, Thomas recalled that the band were rehearsing at the Marquee in London one afternoon and during the night they went into the part finished studio at the back of the club and recorded the song. Although it would be dropped by the band in 1967 (neither Hayward nor Thomas felt comfortable singing it), Laine performed the song many times in later years as the mega-selling 1976 live album *Wings over America* testifies.

'Can't Nobody Love You' (James Mitchell)
Harmonica, acoustic guitar and piano provide a sensitive backing to this slow blues ballad where Laine's delivery echoes Elvis Presley. It's a worthy, if less soulful, successor to the 1964 original as performed by Solomon Burke. Coincidently, the Zombies covered this song on their debut album *Begin Here* which was also released in 1965.

'I Don't Mind' (James Brown)
Someone in the band clearly liked James Brown, Pinder perhaps, as he provides lead vocals here. Barely recognisable compared with his later singing, his impassioned delivery is not a million miles from Laine's with bags of echo and soulful falsetto backing. A slow blues ballad, the original was an R&B hit for Brown in 1961.

'I've Got a Dream' (Jeff Barry, Ellie Greenwich)
From the co-writers of 'River Deep – Mountain High' and 'I Can Hear Music' amongst many other hits, this jaunty, mid-tempo pop meets gospel song is not

in the same league. Laine and Warwick harmonise delightfully, however, and Thomas adds some nice flute fills, an instrument he adopted to give himself more of a presence within the band. The Moodies 'Mark Two' also performed this song with Justin Hayward and John Lodge taking on Laine and Warwick's vocal parts. They played it live for French TV in July 1968, and it is included on the 2018 *In Search of the Lost Chord* box set.

'Let Me Go' (Denny Laine, Mike Pinder)
Opening side two of the original vinyl release, it's the first original song from the Laine and Pinder writing partnership. With Laine wearing his heart on his sleeve, it's a memorable piano-led ballad reminiscent of the 1963 Burt Bacharach and Hal David song 'Anyone Who Had a Heart'. The unison piano and flute playing is elegant and tastefully done, embellished by discreet but lush harmonies. It boasts a strong choral hook resulting in one of the album's best offerings.

'Stop' (Denny Laine, Mike Pinder)
Another original composition although the staccato instrumental hook owes a good deal to 'Can't Get Used to Losing You' written by Jerome Pomus and Mort Shuman. That song was a major hit in both the UK and USA for American crooner Andy Williams in 1963. Some nice acoustic guitar, piano and a catchy chorus elevate Laine and Pinder's melody above the ordinary. It was released as a single in 1966 and made it into the lower regions of the top 100 in both Canada and the USA.

'Thank You Baby' (Denny Laine, Mike Pinder)
This is another decent song from Laine and Pinder. The harmonies are reminiscent of early Four Seasons, especially Warwick's falsetto (a very passable Frankie Valli). Laine's lead, on the other hand, is informed by the Merseybeat tone of Gerry Marsden and John Lennon with a soulful shot of Ray Charles. The lively piano and rhythm playing is joyful, upbeat and very danceable, reflecting the title and chorus.

'It Ain't Necessarily So' (George Gershwin, Ira Gershwin)
Taken from the 1935 opera *Porgy and Bess*, this Gershwin standard features Ray Thomas on lead vocals, crooning in distinctive style over Pinder's walking piano phrase. The sparse arrangement allows Graeme Edge's tasteful drum fills to cut through.

'True Story' (Denny Laine, Mike Pinder)
Clocking in at well under two minutes, this is an almost throwaway song and Laine and Pinder's weakest on the album. The lead guitar sound and Bo Diddley style shuffle rhythm are clearly influenced by the Rolling Stones' version of 'Not Fade Away', a big hit the previous year. As usual, it's Laine's upfront and soulful singing that overcomes any shortcomings in the song.

'Bye Bye Bird' (Sonny Boy Williamson II, Willie Dixon)
The final song on the original vinyl album. It's a vehicle for Laine's raucous harmonica soloing, rock and roll vocal inflexions and stutter that channels both Elvis Presley and Jerry Lee Lewis. Released outside the UK as a single A-side in December 1965, it reached number three in France. Bizarrely, it was resurrected in 1968 by the Moodies 'Mark Two' with Thomas and Pinder providing harmonica and vocals respectively. It can be seen and heard on the 2018 *In Search of the Lost Chord* boxset as well as the video from the French TV show *Ce Soir On Danse* recorded in July 1968. Thomas and Pinder, in particular, are having a ball.

Related Tracks:
'You Better Move On' (Arthur Alexander)
This was recorded in July 1964 at Olympic Studios, London and, until 2006, went unreleased. The band's management had secured a recording contract with Decca Records who famously turned down the Beatles two years before. Not wanting to repeat that mistake, any group that dressed sharp and could sing in harmony were fair game. It's a stylish cover that should have had a place on the album. Laine's prominent Gerry Marsden like drawl (with a touch of echo) adds a Merseybeat vibe, superbly supported by the Motown inflected rhythm and the combined walking guitar and piano lines. It was covered by both the Hollies and the Rolling Stones that same year, but this is the better version. It's included on the 2014 edition of *The Magnificent Moodies*.

'23rd Psalm' (Traditional)
The band's take on 'The Lord is my Shepherd', this song is almost embarrassing. The opening section is sung pretty straight by Thomas in a 1950's slow ballad style. Then Laine takes over for a raucous, gospel meets rock and roll second half complete with hand claps and harmonica. Recorded in the same sessions as 'You Better Move On', this remained unreleased until the 2014 edition of *The Magnificent Moodies*. In a 2014 interview, Thomas claimed that neither he, Laine or Pinder could remember recording this track, and it's quite obvious why they would prefer to forget it.

'Steal Your Heart Away' (Robert Parker)
The band's very first single, released in September 1964. Written by R&B guitarist Bobby Parker, it's an angst-ridden rock and roll ballad with staccato riffs in the style of Elvis Presley's 'Heartbreak Hotel' and a terrifically soulful vocal from Laine. Joe Bonamassa also covered this song in 2010 and Parker has influenced legions of guitarists including Jimmy Page and Ritchie Blackmore. Like the following single 'Go Now', this was produced by Alex Murray but failed to chart in any country. It did, however, earn them their first TV appearance on the ITV pop music show *Ready Steady Go!*

'Lose Your Money (But Don't Lose Your Mind)' (Denny Laine, Mike Pinder)
The flipside of 'Steal Your Heart Away' and the first Laine and Pinder song to be released. It's a loose and jaunty two-minute affair with harmonica (the songs best aspect) driving the beat and providing the solo. Like 'True Story' on the album, it's indebted to the Rolling Stones with Laine attempting his best Mick Jagger drawl (although sounding curiously like Bob Dylan instead).

'It's Easy Child' (Sue Sandler, Kay Bennett, Gene Redd)
Released in November 1964, this was the UK B-side of the number one single 'Go Now'. It also appeared on the North American album version *Go Now -- The Moody Blues #1*. It's a mid-tempo, R&B ballad with another fine vocal from Laine. Pinder provides some superb honky-tonk piano soloing while Edge and Warwick for their part maintain a rock-steady rhythm.

'I Don't Want to Go On Without You' (Bert Berns, Jerry Wexler)
The third single, released in February 1965. A slow soulful ballad, Laine's vocal and Pinder's piano ring just the right level of emotion with engaging, close harmony backing. Originally recorded by the Drifters, this is one of the band's best covers, although Dusty Springfield's slower, more measured performance is generally regarded to be the definitive version. It reached number 33 in the UK chart, a disappointment given the recent success of 'Go Now'. It also appeared on *Go Now -- The Moody Blues #1*.

'Time Is on My Side' (Norman Mead, Jimmy Norman)
The B-side of 'I Don't Want to Go On Without You'. A song made famous by the Rolling Stones in 1964, the Moodies put their own spin on it. It's a decent version for the most part with lovely, soulful harmonies and rhythmic piano. But oh dear, it all falls apart in the mid-section where Laine's shambolic guitar playing and Big Bopper-style spoken posturing get the better of him.

'From the Bottom of My Heart (I Love You)' (Denny Laine, Mike Pinder)
The fourth single, released in May 1965 and the first A-side written by Laine and Pinder. A measured, minor-key ballad, it's one of their best songs ever. Laine's heartfelt lead is supported by sumptuous harmonies, acoustic guitar, piano and flute. His melodious screams at the end must have surely influenced Ian Gillan's iconic performance on Deep Purple's 'Child in Time'. It did better than the previous single reaching number 22 in the UK, although it should have been higher. It only just cracked the top 100 in America.

'And My Baby's Gone' (Denny Laine, Mike Pinder)
The B-side of 'From the Bottom of My Heart'. With its jaunty piano and handclap rhythm, this is a lively, feelgood tune with some nice weeping guitar

embellishments. Both this song and the A-side would appear on *Go Now -- The Moody Blues #1* released two months later.

'Everyday' (Denny Laine, Mike Pinder)
The fifth single, released in October 1965. At well under two minutes, they don't come much shorter than this. The vocal harmonies are lush, thanks to Denny Cordell's sprightly production, and it boasts a catchy chorus. A real surprise then that it didn't climb any higher than 44 in the UK chart, and even more surprising it didn't even brush the American charts. Perhaps it was due to a lack of airplay; as a music-loving eleven-year-old, I don't recall hearing any of these songs (with the exception of 'Go Now') on the radio at the time. Following an unbroken run, it would be another five months before the next single appeared.

'You Don't (All the Time)' (Denny Laine, Mike Pinder)
The B-side of 'Everyday'. It's another jolly, piano-led tune with massed harmonies and lively flute fills from Ray Thomas. The middle-eight is particularly memorable, something the Moodies 'Mark Two' would perfect in later years.

'Boulevard de la Madeleine' (Denny Laine, Mike Pinder)
The seventh single, released in October 1966 (the songs on the sixth single 'Stop' and 'Bye Bye Bird' released in March 1966 had been lifted from the album). With its evocative Parisian set storyline, it boasts their richest arrangement so far with classical guitar, accordion sounds, piano and Edge's militaristic drum pattern. It's a brave attempt to try something more ambitious (and a nod towards the Moodies 'Mark Two'), but it's perhaps not surprising that it failed to breach the charts. Laine had already left the band before the song's release. The title lent itself to a Dutch only compilation released in 1968 that also included the first two Hayward and Lodge era singles.

'This Is My House (But Nobody Calls)' (Denny Laine, Mike Pinder)
The flip side of the 'Boulevard de la Madeleine' single and they couldn't be more different. Two versions of this song were recorded in April and September 1966. It was intended for the proposed second album, aborted with the departure of Warwick and Laine. With twangy guitar, a chirpy lead vocal, plinky-plonk piano and mock howling backing voices, this is an unabashed throwback to the early '60s beat sound.

'People Gotta Go' (Denny Laine, Mike Pinder)
Until the 2006 reissue of *The Magnificent Moodies*, this track was a hard to find song that originally appeared on the French EP version of 'Boulevard de la

Madeleine'. It's a slow-burning song with a blues feel and a real grower. Laine sings staccato style with a simple but infectious rhythm while the harmonies are as impeccable as ever. Although two and a half minutes is average for a song from the period, it seems to fade all too soon.

'Life's Not Life' (Denny Laine, Mike Pinder)
The eighth single, released in January 1967. It's a song of lost love and the final gasp from the Moodies 'Mark One'. Hayward and Lodge had joined the band by this point, and the song was recorded with Laine earlier the previous year. It's a soulful, mid-tempo ballad evocative of 1960s Four Seasons with rich harmonies, prominent piano, flute and a ridiculously catchy chorus. Even though it fell mostly on deaf ears, it's a fine song to close the band's first phase.

'He Can Win' (Denny Laine, Mike Pinder)
The B-side of 'Life's Not Life'. The band may have hailed from Birmingham, but they could ape the Merseybeat sound with the best of them. It could very easily be a Gerry and the Pacemakers song with Laine's stirring lead vocal backed by unison guitar and piano and the now familiar sweet harmonies. In a fairer world, this could have been a hit in its own right.

'Sad Song' (Denny Laine, Mike Pinder)
Listed as 'The 1966 Denny Cordell Sessions', this is the first of the concluding tracks on Esoteric Recordings' 2014 50th Anniversary two CD remastered edition of *The Magnificent Moodies*. These tracks were all recorded for the aborted second album. Until 2014, they remained unreleased, although a version of 'This Is My House (But Nobody Calls)' was the B-side of the 'Boulevard de la Madeleine' single.

'How Can We Hang On to a Dream?' (Tim Hardin)
The band recorded two versions of this classic song, the latest in July 1966. It's a first-rate, mid-tempo cover of Hardin's slow ballad (released the same year) with Pinder's descending piano hook echoing 'Go Now'.

'Jago & Jilly' (Denny Laine, Mike Pinder)
A curious, upbeat pop offering with jangly, country and western style guitar and high harmonies that sounds nothing like the Moodies. Recorded in August 1966, it has demo written all over it, but the infectious chorus is a real earworm.

'We're Broken' (Denny Laine, Mike Pinder)
A solid pop-rocker with lush harmonies that combine Gerry and the Pacemakers with the Who. Pinder's rhythmic piano playing is stunning, complemented by an uncharacteristically heavy guitar riff from Laine. Recorded in August 1966.

'I Really Haven't Got the Time' (Mike Pinder)

This is the original September 1966 recording. It was re-recorded by the Moodies 'Mark Two' and released as the B-side to their debut 1967 single 'Fly Me High'. It's a brash, piano-led rock and roll salvo with a breathless lead vocal from Pinder. Although the later version has a little more finesse, there's no denying the energy and commitment here. There's superb TV footage (in glorious black and white) of this song on the internet with Rod Clark harmonising with Thomas.

'Red Wine' (Denny Laine, Mike Pinder)

Not to be confused with the Neil Diamond standard 'Red Red Wine', this is another song from the 1966 summer sessions produced by Denny Cordell for the aborted second album. Most of these songs including this one featured in the band's setlist at the time with Rod Clark on bass and backing vocals. Until their release in 2014, it was widely believed that these recordings were lost.

Days of Future Passed (1967)
Personnel:
Mike Pinder: Mellotron, piano, tambura, gong, vocals
Ray Thomas: flutes, percussion, piano, vocals
Justin Hayward: acoustic & electric guitars, piano, sitar, vocals
John Lodge: bass, vocals
Graeme Edge: drums, percussion, vocals
The London Festival Orchestra
Peter Knight: conductor, arranger
Produced by: Michael Dacre-Barclay, Tony Clarke
Engineered by: Derek Varnals
Recorded at: Decca Studios, London, May – November 1967
UK and USA release date: November 1967
Highest chart places: UK: 27, USA: 3 (1972)
Running time: 41:34

In November 1966 when Justin Hayward and John Lodge joined the band, the musical climate was rapidly changing. Still saddled with their reputation as an R&B cover band on the club circuit, their fee had dropped from £70 to £25 a night. With dwindling bookings, it was time to ditch the matching blue suits and take a new direction. If they needed any persuasion, following a cabaret performance in Stockton-on-Tees in the North East of England, an outraged punter told them exactly what he thought of them, and it wasn't complimentary. Hayward stated in a 2017 interview for *Rolling Stone* magazine that he had to sing 'Go Now' and was 'absolutely lousy at rhythm and blues'. This gave him the impetus to write his own songs. The first two singles released in 1967 didn't trouble the charts but they were at least original songs that demonstrated the band's potential. They had no desire at this point to record anyone else's music, but the record company had other ideas, and it certainly wasn't rock and roll.

If the previous album had almost been airbrushed out of the band's history (Genesis' debut suffered a similar fate), *Days of Future Passed* is for many (including the band themselves) the spiritual beginning of the Moody Blues. It also lays claim (as do several other landmark releases from 1967) to be the first, true progressive rock album. It certainly has the hallmarks: a concept with connected songs, cosmic lyrics and a symphonic grandeur rare in a rock-pop record of the time. The concept, intended as a stage show, is a day in the life of an ordinary person and cleverly links individual songs from all the band members. It could have turned out very differently, however.

The story goes that, in order to settle their financial debt to Decca Records, the band were approached to record a version of Dvořák's popular *New World Symphony*, complete with orchestra. The band and arranger-conductor Peter Knight, had other ideas, however. As Justin Hayward put it to the *Classic Rock Society* magazine in 2013: 'The original plan was for Peter Knight to do the real

Dvořák stuff in between our rock Dvořák bits, and I just knew we'd be crap at that.' As a result, they recorded a cycle of original songs linked by instrumental interludes performed by a full orchestra, 'a fusion of pop composition and classical writing', as the sleeve notes would have it.

Peter Knight's input cannot be overstated, his orchestral sections enhance the songs, and for this album, he was an unofficial sixth member. The London Festival Orchestra was not a full-time ensemble, but a pickup collection of musicians assembled for the recording. For the songs themselves, it's Mike Pinder's Mellotron that convincingly provides the orchestral sounds. The band and orchestra recorded separately under the watchful eye of staff producer Tony Clarke and engineer Derek Varnals in Studio One at Decca Studios, West Hampstead, North London. Over the next three years, it would become a second home for the band.

After recording each song, a rough mix was passed to Knight, who arranged the overture, orchestral links and finale. These parts, performed by the orchestra, were recorded on the final day of the sessions. In a 2014 interview for digitaltrends.com, Hayward who remixed the album in 2006 said, 'I was stunned with the quality of all of those early mixes, *Days of Future Passed* particularly.' It was released on the subsidiary label Deram, to showcase the new 'Deramic Sound System' (a derivative of 'Deram' and 'dynamic') developed by Michael Dacre-Barclay. Mono was still common in 1967 while stereo would often compress instruments into the left or right channel. DSS was designed to give a more natural, spacious spread of sound.

Against the odds, the attendant single 'Nights in White Satin' entered the UK top twenty and the album, while not peaking highly, remained in the chart for two years. Several of the songs, however, would have to wait until the 2017 50th Anniversary tour before being performed live. The popularity of the album, and in particular 'Nights in White Satin', in the 1970s adds weight to the claim that *Days of Future Passed* was ahead of its time. Although many recognised the album for its originality, in 1990 Hayward told *Q* magazine, 'There was one record that influenced us very much which was called *The Zodiac* by a group called Cosmic Sounds. A fabulous record.' A psychedelic concept album, it was based on the signs of the Zodiac.

When the finished work was presented to Decca only Walt Maguire, head of London Records (Decca's outlet in America) immediately recognised its potential. If Decca didn't know quite what to make of *Days of Future Passed,* the music press was similarly perplexed. While several journals praised the album for its originality, most including UK music weekly *Melody Maker* (who would later champion the band) were unimpressed by the orchestrations and poetry. *Rolling Stone* magazine, which was launched almost the same day as the album, was especially critical, although fortunately, it did not reflect the tastes of American record buyers. UK DJ Alan Freeman was an early supporter as he would be for prog bands like Emerson, Lake & Palmer in the 1970s. Over half a century on, the album still holds together pretty well with Hayward's songs and the orchestrations proving to be particularly durable.

To discuss each song, I've used a 2017 track listing rather than the original which did not identify all the titles. There are confusing variations, however; '(Evening) Time to Get Away' for example, which wasn't listed on the original is listed on some reissues as 'Time to Get Away' and on others as 'Time to Get Away (Evening)'. It should also be noted that due to the deterioration of the original master tapes, later vinyl and CD stereo mixes (recreated by Varnals in 1978) differ from the original 1967 version. In some cases, backing vocals and instrumental parts are missing, and the orchestral links vary. The 1967 tapes were restored and released as part of the 2017 50th anniversary reissue of *Days of Future Passed*.

Album Cover

The album title is inspired, a juxtaposition of 'past' and 'future' tenses that predates the film title *Back to the Future* by two decades. Given the concept, 'A Day in the Life' would have also been a fitting title had it not already been used for the closing song on *Sgt. Pepper's Lonely Hearts Club Band* released earlier the same year. A single non-gatefold sleeve, the front cover design is an incongruous combination of bold typeface typical of classical records and David Anstey's surreal, psychedelic-pop artwork, evidence that Decca was unsure how to present the album. The lengthy credit below the title reads 'The Moody Blues with The London Festival Orchestra conducted by Peter Knight'. The 'Deramic Sound System' logo is prominent and, unusual for a front cover, the song titles are listed (on some editions the DSS logo and song titles are missing, Anstey's painting fills the cover, and the lettering style is different).

The bland rear cover includes a single black and white photo taken at a production meeting (no one's even facing the camera). Graeme Edge's poetry (recited by Mike Pinder on the album) is also included. A telling sign of the times, executive producer Hugh Mendl's sleeve notes refers to the band as 'the beat group', but more baffling the credits include 'All music composed: Redwave-Knight', which was removed for later CD reissues. Mendl proved to be a staunch supporter of the band and the album.

'The Day Begins' (Peter Knight)

This sweeping orchestral intro sets the tone of the album. It opens with the symbolic sound of a gong rising to a crescendo; close your eyes, and you can almost visualise the sun rising above the horizon. Although rightly credited to Knight with elements composed by him, it is in part an overture incorporating themes written by the band members. These include 'Dawn Is a Feeling', 'Another Morning', 'Forever Afternoon (Tuesday?)' and 'Nights in White Satin'. It's a beautiful arrangement with lush strings, stirring brass and playful woodwinds. It brings to mind the romantic style of vintage Hollywood composers Max Steiner and Alfred Newman as well as English classical composer Vaughan Williams. Like all good orchestral pieces, it never dates, and segues into...

'Morning Glory' (Graeme Edge)
Underscored by the orchestra, Pinder's deep, resonant voice is ideal for spoken verse, delivering Edge's evocative poem with gravitas and eloquence. Edge's poems would open the next three albums. He originally wrote the words for the band to set to a melody, but the lines were too wordy to sing. Rather than cut them down, producer Tony Clarke suggested that Edge speak them with an orchestral backing. Although Pinder would eventually recite the words, Edge became the band's resident poet. Following the lines 'Brave Helios, wake up your steeds, bring the warmth the countryside needs' the orchestra rises to the heavens for a majestic intro to...

'Dawn: Dawn Is a Feeling' (Mike Pinder)
The title is very apt, not only does the song fit the concept but it also heralds a new era for the band. Although Pinder would sing all his own songs on future albums, here he shares lead vocals with Hayward who makes his debut album appearance. It's an understated song with a slow waltz-like rhythm underpinning mournful Mellotron and piano. Compared with the more natural timbres of the orchestra, Pinder's Mellotron tape loops create a noticeably darker and denser sound. Hayward's verses are measured, almost dreamlike, contrasting with Pinder's surging mid-section (more a bridge than a chorus). It's a melancholic song despite the optimistic title and lyrics, a stylistic trait that would be echoed in many of Pinder's later compositions. Like all the linking sections, producer Clarke combines the orchestra and band for a few short bars to ensure a smooth transition into the next song. 'Dawn Is a Feeling' was the first song written for the planned stage show and inspired Hayward to write 'Nights in White Satin' to close the show.

'The Morning: Another Morning' (Ray Thomas)
A brief orchestral intro heralds a lively, martial rhythm complete with bugle calls. This is Thomas' first writing credit for the Moodies. Pinder and Hayward were the band's most accomplished writers at the time, and they encouraged the others to contribute songs. This was Thomas' response, and it's like nothing else on the album. It has a joyful spring in its step with a foot-tapping flute melody and playful lyrics that evoke happy memories of childhood. This whimsical style would be a feature of Thomas' later songs including 'Dr. Livingstone, I Presume' and 'Floating', but it's rarely more uplifting than this. The orchestra returns for an equally playful variation of the main theme. 'Another Morning' was the B-side of 'Tuesday Afternoon', the second single release from the album.

'Lunch Break: Peak Hour' (John Lodge)
Knight's lengthy, bustling orchestral intro is one of his most inventive. It references both 'Another Morning' and 'Dawn Is a Feeling' and evokes rush hour in the city with brass and woodwind stabs. This is Lodge's first song

contribution, and it really rocks in a Beatle-ish vein with a touch of the Who's aggression. The rhythm was inspired by a bumpy van ride on the way home from a gig one night. The close harmonies in the slow bridge are especially reminiscent of the Fab Four with a hint of the Bee Gees. Edge's accelerating drum pattern which builds to the instrumental section would resurface five years later for another Lodge song, 'I'm Just a Singer (In a Rock and Roll Band)'. Hayward's twangy guitar break is pure Hank Marvin and the Shadows while Pinder extracts some unusually shrill sounds from the Mellotron. 'Peak Hour' was another of the first songs written for the stage show. It would be one of the few songs on the album other than 'Tuesday Afternoon' and 'Nights in White Satin' to feature regularly in the band's setlist, where it would remain on and off until 1971. It was revived in 2009 and had another long run.

'The Afternoon': 'Forever Afternoon (Tuesday?)'
(Justin Hayward)

Better known as 'Tuesday Afternoon' following its (drastically edited) UK single release in January 1968, this is a bonafide classic. The single did particularly well in North America when it was released in July 1968, reaching number 24 in the USA and twelve in Canada. In addition to providing a memorable opening to side two of the original LP, it has the distinction of being Hayward's first song on a Moodies album. It was written, along with all his other songs from this period, on a big blonde twelve-string acoustic guitar that he found in early 1966 in the attic at Lonnie Donegan's house. He has often related the story whereby the song came to him after smoking a joint while sitting in a country park with his dog named 'Tuesday' on what just happened to be a beautiful Tuesday afternoon.

His talent for countermelody is in evidence, contrasting a lovely main song section with a breezy middle-eight that really swings when performed live. Hayward developed this style as a way of bringing different moods and tempo changes into a song which would also become a key ingredient of prog-rock in the 1970s and beyond. The song would be a firm concert favourite throughout the band's career where the opening Mellotron notes would be greeted with spontaneous applause. The orchestra returns for a soaring variation of Hayward's melody which links with…

'(Evening) Time to Get Away' (John Lodge)

The title sums up this song perfectly, it's the end of a working day, and it's time to escape. Lodge's plaintive vocal with rippling acoustic guitar and piano builds with swelling Mellotron strings to a catchy chorus. Following a lively instrumental break, Pinder's short piano motif echoes the intro to 'River Deep – Mountain High'. On the original recording, the bridge features full harmonies but for later mixes Lodge's falsetto is unaccompanied and very distinct. This is a curious hybrid of a song. The sublime opening verses and slow build are characteristic of Lodge's later work while the rudimentary chorus, although tuneful, is very mid-'60s (as is the sudden fade at the end). The full potential of Lodge's songwriting talents would not be realised until the next album.

'Evening': 'The Sunset' (Mike Pinder)
A lush orchestral interlude leads into an Indian style raga. It's clearly influenced by George Harrison, although Pinder's inflected vocal (with a little waver at the end of each line) is uncannily close to John Lennon. The words are not so much sung, as chanted. It's beautifully arranged, with swooning strings, flute, sitar, hand cymbals and vocal echo enhancing the song's hypnotic, dreamlike quality. It's mystical, psychedelic and very 1967. The songs Pinder wrote with Denny Laine the previous year seem like a million light-years away. Towards the end, the orchestra strings take over the Mellotron refrain with no discernible break in continuity. It was regularly performed on stage, but like 'Peak Hour' it was dropped in 1971 to make way for songs from *Every Good Boy Deserves Favour*. The performance on the *Live at the Isle of Wight Festival 1970* DVD is accompanied by images of the sun setting over the 600,000-strong crowd.

'Twilight Time' (Ray Thomas)
A brief orchestral reprise of 'Tuesday Afternoon' leads into another Eastern flavoured offering, this time courtesy of Thomas. While Pinder's lyrics are stark in their imagery, Thomas' words are colourful, almost poetic, with lines like 'An aerial display by the firefly brigade, dancing to tunes no one knew', painting visions of the fading light. It's also a more up-tempo song and a pure slice of psychedelic pop with echoes of 'Strawberry Fields Forever' and Tamla Motown. It was performed live in the '60s and was revived in the late '70s and early '80s for the *Octave* and *Long Distance Voyager* tours. With a chugging acoustic guitar rhythm and ethereal, multi-tracked vocals, it takes itself more seriously than 'Another Morning' on side one. The two songs together, however, demonstrate that as a songwriter, Thomas is already a force to be reckoned with. Strings and clarinets pick up the melody, segueing into the familiar orchestral strains of the final song.

'The Night': 'Nights in White Satin' (Justin Hayward)
This is one of the most enduring and defining songs of its time and would become synonymous with the band. It's also their most performed. As iconic sixties ballads go, it sits comfortably alongside 'God Only Knows', 'Eleanor Rigby' and 'The Sound of Silence', amongst others. As a single edit, it topped the charts in France and charted three separate times in the UK, peaking at number nine in 1972. Initially, London Records were reluctant to release the song in America as it wasn't considered radio-friendly and it stalled outside the top 100. The 1972 reissue however reached number two in the *Billboard* chart and number one in Canada. Globally, it has sold over five million copies.

In 2016, it was the subject of a documentary *The Story Behind Nights in White Satin* by producer/director David Minasian, who has also directed live DVDs for Hayward. In 2007, the song received an unusual honour when it inspired the theme park ride 'Nights in White Satin: The Trip' at the Hard Rock Park, Myrtle Beach, South Carolina. The ride was closed in 2009 when the park was taken over by new management.

Hayward's lyrics were influenced by three separate female encounters. Firstly, there was the girl who ended their relationship even though he was desperately in love. Then there was another girl whose contribution to the story was to give him a set of white satin sheets. Finally, he met Anne-Marie Guirron working in a nightclub, a beautiful model who he would marry in December 1970. The result is one of Hayward's finest songs. It was first recorded for a BBC radio session, a version which Hayward recalls as atmospheric, but unfortunately, the Beeb wiped the tape before the band could get hold of a copy. It has been covered dozens of times both vocally and instrumentally, but I've yet to hear a version that comes close to the original. Hayward's favourite version is the one released by American soul singer Bettye Lavette on her 2010 album *Interpretations: The British Rock Songbook*. The first time he heard her interpretation, which relates to her daughter, he was moved to tears.

Although the song is undoubtedly Hayward's, Pinder was responsible for the haunting Mellotron phrase that punctuates the verse lines and gives the song that extra lift. Otherwise, it's very much an ensemble performance. A restrained orchestral intro gives way to twelve-string acoustic guitar, a stately bass line and a simple but refined drum pattern. The verses are deliberately sparse to add substance to the sweeping chorus. The lead vocal is full of yearning passion, carried by surging Mellotron strings into the heart-rending chorus 'Yes I love you' with its ethereal backing voices. Reverb was added to heighten the effect. Following a lyrical flute solo, the final rousing chorus is augmented by the orchestra (for the only time on the album), building to...

'Late Lament' (Graeme Edge, Peter Knight)

The soaring orchestral finale, incorporating Edge's now famous prose. Crashing chords subside into low strings and woodwind for Pinder's impassioned delivery. The full might of the orchestra returns for the epic crescendo before closing as it began with the sound of a gong. This time it's a single, sustained beat (struck by Pinder, not Edge) which fades into the distance. Although 'Nights in White Satin' was a successful single without this section, for anyone familiar with the album version, it always sounded incomplete. 'Late Lament' was resurrected for the orchestral concerts of the 1990s, where coupled with 'The Dream' (another Edge composition) it provided a dramatic introduction. Around 2007, it was rearranged for the stage with 'Late Lament' preceding 'Nights in White Satin', rather than the other way round.

Related Tracks:

'Fly Me High' (Justin Hayward)
Recorded in March 1967 and released in May, six months before *Days of Future Passed*, this single A-side was the first Moodies record to feature Hayward and Lodge. Musically, it's a far cry from the album, but it's a cracking song nonetheless. Hayward's twelve-string acoustic guitar picking is supported by pounding piano, a snappy bassline, tambourine and hand claps. This was Tony Clarke's first production assignment with the band, and the engineer was Gus Dudgeon, who would go on to produce Elton John amongst others. Despite failing to crack the charts in any region, it received radio play and would be performed live in 1967 and 1968.

Like all the non-album studio recordings from this period, it would resurface on the 1987 compilation *Prelude* and as a bonus track on CD reissues of *Days of Future Passed*.

'I Really Haven't Got the Time' (Mike Pinder)
This song is the B-side to 'Fly Me High', again recorded in March 1967. Like many of the band's singles in the '60s, it's a Mike Pinder song supporting Hayward's A-side. Fiery boogie-woogie piano dominates with Pinder making the most of his camp lead vocal with superb doo-wop harmonies from the rest of the band. It pre-empts the rock and roll meets glam-rock sound of acts like Mud, Showaddywaddy and the Rubettes who proliferated the UK singles chart in the 1970s. This song was intended for the Moodies 'Mark One' aborted second album, and their version can be found on the 2014 50th Anniversary edition of *The Magnificent Moodies*.

'Don't Let Me Be Misunderstood' (Bennie Benjamin, Gloria Caldwell, Sol Marcus)
Although this is not a studio recording, I thought it was worth including here, demonstrating that even with Hayward and Lodge in the band, they were not averse to the occasional cover. It was also recorded on my thirteenth birthday, 9 May 1967, for a BBC radio session. A song made famous by the Animals two years earlier, this is a worthy version with Hayward's voice and strummed rhythm guitar to the fore. The choral harmonies are decent but would be perfected in later recordings. This was a bonus track on CD reissues of *Days of Future Passed*, and the 2007 compilation *Live at the BBC 1967 – 1970*.

'Love and Beauty' (Mike Pinder)
This second Moodies 'Mark Two' single is a rare thing, a Pinder written A-side. Although upright piano dominates, released two months before *Days of Future Passed*, it has the distinction of being the first Moody Blues song to feature Mellotron. Pinder contrasts introspective verses (not too dissimilar to Abba) with a catchy, anthemic chorus and Lodge's bass is nicely upfront. Like

the previous single, it completely bypassed the record-buying public. This song, along with 'Fly Me High' and 'Cities' can also be found on the 1994 compilation boxset *Time Traveller*.

'Leave This Man Alone' (Justin Hayward)
Soaring close harmonies and upfront acoustic guitar unashamedly channel both mid-period Beatles and the Hollies. Clarke's bright, radio-friendly production mixes everything to the fore with Lodge's warm bass riff and Edge's clattering drums jostling for attention. This was the B-side to 'Love and Beauty'; both were recorded in July 1967 and released in September 1967.

'Cities' (Justin Hayward)
Recorded in July 1967, this was the non-album B-side to 'Nights in White Satin'. It's an engaging two and a half minutes that would have sat comfortably on *Days of Future Passed*. Hayward's measured lead vocal and the tight choral harmonies are backed by a sparse arrangement with drums and bass occupying the left stereo channel and harpsichord the right. The middle-eight is especially reminiscent of the Beatles' 1964 ballad 'If I Fell'.

Despite the single reaching a modest nineteenth position in the UK chart when it was released in November 1967, 'Nights in White Satin' had a longevity that lasted well into the 1970s. It was regularly played on the radio and in my late teens I remember it being a jukebox favourite, especially in pubs and bars popular with students.

'Please Think About It' (Mike Pinder)
A laid-back ballad with a waltz-like rhythm and, rare for Pinder, it's a straightforward love song. No Mellotron embellishments, just superb piano, drums and bass accompaniment with the now familiar wordless backing vocals soaring skywards. Although recorded in June 1967, this song together with 'Long Summer Days' would not be officially released until ten years later, on the fourth, studio side of the double LP *Caught Live + 5*.

'Long Summer Days' (Justin Hayward)
Recorded in May 1967, another mellow piano driven song, and the title says it all. With its lush and inventive harmonies and countermelodies in the style of 'Good Vibrations' (an international hit the previous year), the Beach Boys influences are ripe. Hayward even manages to sound vaguely like Brian Wilson during the verses. Despite the title, it wouldn't have suited the mood of *Days of Future Passed*, but it would have most certainly made a fine single.

In Search of the Lost Chord (1968)

Personnel:
Justin Hayward: 12-string guitar, acoustic guitar, electric guitar, sitar, tabla, piano, Mellotron, bass guitar, harpsichord, percussion, vocals
Mike Pinder: Mellotrons, piano, harpsichord, cello, acoustic guitar, bass guitar, autoharp, tambura, vocals
John Lodge: bass guitar, cello, tambourine, snare drum, acoustic guitar, vocals
Ray Thomas: C flute, alto flute, soprano saxophone, vocals, oboe, French horn, tambourine
Graeme Edge: drums, timpani, tambourine, percussion, tabla, piano, vocals
Produced by: Tony Clarke
Engineered by: Derek Varnals
Recorded at: Decca Studios, London, January – June 1968
UK and USA release date: July 1968
Highest chart places: UK: 5, USA: 23
Running time: 42:07

In 1968, there was political unrest on a global scale with demonstrations in America over the war in Vietnam and protests in Czechoslovakia over reforms and Russia's invasion (in July, the month before the invasion, the Moodies had been in Prague filming for TV). Young people were making their voices heard, and this same demographic would dictate the future of popular music. The previous year, album sales outstripped single sales for the first time and the commercial success of *Sgt. Pepper's Lonely Hearts Club Band*, in particular, gave record companies the confidence to support unprecedented artistic freedom. In this musical climate, the Moody Blues 'Mark Two' reconvened at Decca Studios for their all-important second album. Justin Hayward recalled recently that the recording was generally a happy, relaxed experience and when the album reached the upper regions of the UK chart, they knew they had a future. Essentially, they had turned the group around and established themselves as a successful albums band where hit singles were a bonus rather than a necessity. With everyone pulling in the same direction, they had a stable line-up that would remain intact for the next ten years. They toured America for the first time from October to December 1968, appearing with the likes of Ten Years After, John Mayall, Cream and Jeff Beck. It was an important and successful step, and over the ensuing years, America would become a second home for the band. In 1974, one member would move there permanently.

If Hayward favoured his Gibson ES-335 electric guitar and 1955 Martin D28 acoustic, John Lodge's instrument of choice was a Fender Precision Sunburst bass he acquired when he was just sixteen years old. Even in the 1970s when he used an Alembic bass on tour, the Fender was also played. Mike Pinder's bulky Mellotron Mark II had been obtained second-hand in 1967, which he customised. He removed the rhythm and effects tapes and replaced them with lead tapes which effectively doubled the orchestral sounds. It was so heavy, it took all of them to carry it into each gig, and in the early days when they travelled by transit, they took turns in sleeping on it. Around that time Pinder introduced the instrument to the Beatles who famously used it on 'Strawberry Fields Forever'. Ray Thomas for his part was a self-taught flute player and the Alto and 'C' flutes gave him the range he desired. He also developed a high, shrill sound for live performances to compete with the guitars and Mellotron. Graeme Edge's kit would vary over the years, generally favouring Ludwig drums. In the early '70s, he would pioneer electronic drums and in the late '70s incorporate Syndrums for live performance.

Although the group dynamic was a little blurred by the orchestral trappings on the previous album, here the formula that would see them through the next five albums is fully established. Each member contributes an average of two songs and generally sings lead on their own compositions. Edge's spoken verse is the exception, narrated by Pinder for the most part although here, it's Edge's voice that opens the album. Although each member has their own distinct and identifiable style, the songs complement each other, and the album flows smoothly.

Like *Days of Future Passed,* there is a concept of sorts, although the subject is much broader and more philosophical with exploration and discovery being just two of the themes. This album is generally perceived to be a natural successor to *Sgt Pepper*, more so than its predecessor. Certain band members, including Hayward, were indulging in hallucinogenic substances at the time. It influenced at least one song, Thomas' psychedelic anthem 'Legend of a Mind' dedicated to LSD advocator and psychologist Timothy Leary. No less than 33 instruments were played, including several of Indian and southeast European origin such as sitar, tabla and tambura. Pinder's Mellotron orchestrations are supplemented with traditional classical instruments including oboe, cello and timpani alongside Thomas' now familiar flutes. The intention was to emulate the lush orchestrations of the last album using overdubs. In the sleeve notes, Tony Clarke describes the band as 'the smallest symphony orchestra in the world'.

It was one of the first recordings on 8-track multi-track tape. Clarke is credited as the sole producer, a role he would fulfil until the end of the 1970s. The unofficial sixth member, he was pivotal in shaping the band's sound, and their working relationship was comparable to that of George Martin and the Beatles. There is a good deal of sonic experimentation on the album, for which engineer Derek Varnals should also take credit. Although there is no direct connection between each song as there was on *Days of Future Passed*, Clarke utilises crossfading (as he would on later albums) to link the tracks and give a sense of continuity.

The rock press were divided, and *Rolling Stone* magazine lambasted what they considered to be the more pretentious elements. Like many of the band's albums from this era, it has generally been treated kinder in more contemporary reviews. In November 2018, to mark its 50th Anniversary, it received a deluxe five-disc treatment. The three CDs and two DVDs include various mixes of the album, BBC sessions, bonus tracks and TV appearances plus a 76-page book. Well worth having if you're prepared to splash out.

Album Cover

The band's first gatefold sleeve (there was also a non-gatefold version) and the first featuring the artwork of Phil Travers. An ex-London Art College student and Decca Records employee, he was introduced to the band via their manager. Taking his inspiration from the music, over six albums (nine including solo projects) his fantastical images would provide a visual metaphor for the Moodies, in much the same way Roger Dean's creations would do for Yes. A unique aspect of this cover is that the band name and the album title are fully integrated into the artwork rather than given separate lettering. The focal point on the front cover is an ascending figure with the band name forming a blazing headdress. The image came to Travers while in the studio listening to the playback and everything else, he said, fell into place. The dark imagery of the skull and foetus represent death and birth respectively, with the album title rising ghost-like above. In stark contrast, the rear cover is typical of its time with a photo collage showing the band members individually and as a group. In keeping with the concept, the inner cover lists the band as 'Members of the Expedition', and on the opposite side, there is the image of the 'Yantra', a mystical diagram used in the Shri Vidya school of Hindu Tantra.

'Departure' (Graeme Edge)

Like *Days of Future Passed*, Edge has two poems on the album and to open, he delivers his own spoken words. A cascade of strummed notes from what sounds like an autoharp and a single, crashing chord provides the introduction. Lasting just 45 seconds, a piercing electronic drone increases in pitch as Edge's voice becomes increasingly more frantic. A manic (and processed) burst of laughter leads into the familiar strains of...

'Ride My See-Saw' (John Lodge)

One of Lodge's most enduring songs and probably his best known, despite later successes. With its breathless energy, it cried out to be performed live and quickly became the band's encore song and concert closer, a position it retains to this day. The song is essentially about the ups and downs of life, learning from experience and moving forward. It's off the starting blocks so fast; it feels like we're joining it mid-song. When performed live as the encore, however, it features a lengthy drum and keyboard intro while the rest of the band troop back onto the stage until Lodge counts in the song proper. The clipped harmonies throughout, courtesy of Lodge, Hayward, Thomas and Pinder, render the verses and chorus almost indistinguishable. This gives the song an added urgency while the wordless 'ah ah ah ah' repetition in the bridge would become a Moodies trademark. The whole thing is driven by Hayward's purposeful guitar riff and the solid rhythm section of Lodge and Edge. Hayward's lead guitar is far more evident on this album compared with the last, and here his soloing has a reverb-heavy, blues edge. He's playing a 1965 Fender Telecaster rather than his customary Gibson ES-335.

In October 1968, it became the second song on the album to be released as a single. Although it barely breached the top 50 in the UK and reached only 61 on the American *Billboard* chart, it entered the top twenty in both the Netherlands and France. Unsurprisingly, during Lodge's '10,000 Light Years' solo tours, which began in 2016, 'Ride My See-Saw' is the rousing set closer.

'Dr. Livingstone, I Presume' (Ray Thomas)
Another jaunty tune from Thomas and a natural successor to 'Another Morning' on *Days of Future Passed*. Lyrically, it's a child-friendly, three-minute history lesson. The basic four/four rhythm, wavering Mellotron and channel hopping guitar fills are very much of its time. The song's lyrical muse and singalong chorus are derivative of 'All You Need Is Love' and 'Yellow Submarine' (if this had been a Beatles song it would have probably been sung by Ringo Starr). That said, the rapid-fire verses are uniquely Thomas', while the deliberately ragged fade is a nod towards the Kinks. For me, Lodge's articulate bass lines are the song's best feature. There's a great video of this song from the UK TV programme *Colour Me Pop* in September 1968 which demonstrates the suits and ties had not been abandoned altogether. It had a regular place in the band's setlist until 1971, and it was also the B-side of the 'Voices in the Sky' single.

'House of Four Doors' (John Lodge)
One of the album's most ambitious offerings, it's in four distinct parts, each separated by the symbolic sound of a door opening. It links different styles of music, pre-empting 'Procession' on *Every Good Boy Deserves Favour*. The first part features a lovely chorus in the close harmony style of the Hollies and the second a delicate flute theme. The third is in the classical baroque style with harpsichord and cello, and the final part boasts Mellotron, piano and crashing cymbals in a bombastic prog style. Pinder is all over this track, providing much of the layered instrumentation while Edge's fills are reminiscent of the drum pattern on the Beatles song 'A Day in the Life'. It's all very proto-prog, and the individual sections are superb, but the song's concept, like the doors themselves, now seems very creaky. That said, at a little over four minutes, it's very lean compared with the epic indulgences by bands in the 1970s. The last door opens to reveal...

'Legend of a Mind' (Ray Thomas)
At six and a half minutes, this is one of the band's longest songs as Thomas takes the listener on a mind-expanding trip. The band worked on the ambitious arrangement very early on in the recording sessions. Beautiful

acoustic guitar and Mellotron underpin dreamy, psychedelic vocal imagery with plenty of echo on the chorus. The middle-eight is especially effective with Lodge's wordless backing providing a perfect foil for Edge's lively drumming and Thomas' lead vocal. The best part is the instrumental mid-section with mournful Mellotron, acoustic guitar and a rare improvised flute solo from Thomas that pans from left to right and back again. It builds dramatically to the final reverb-laden chorus. It's an exceptional arrangement for its time with superb ensemble performances. The call and response chorus 'Timothy Leary's dead, no, no he's outside looking in' certainly added to the LSD guru's fame and mystique, especially in the UK where he was little known outside the hippy culture. When they performed the song at Stoney Brook University, New York state in November 1969, Leary joined them on stage.

After 'Ride My See-Saw', this is the album's (and Thomas') best-known song. It was regularly played live until his retirement in 2002 where along with 'Nights in White Satin' and 'Question' it closed the main part of the set. In the 1980s with Patrick Moraz in the band, it featured an extended flute and keyboard duet which became a regular showpiece. This was continued into the 1990s with Bias Boshell on keys and can be heard on the 2003 deluxe edition of *A Night at Red Rocks with the Colorado Symphony Orchestra*. There is also an entertaining (albeit abridged) version on the video recording of the French TV show *Ce Soir On Danse* that coincided with the release of the album.

'House of Four Doors (Part 2)' (John Lodge)
Eerie Mellotron, a chugging guitar riff and a brief reprise of the chorus from part one closes side one of the original album in melodic style.

'Voices in the Sky' (Justin Hayward)
Side two opens with Hayward's first writing credit on the album. It's a beautiful, understated song with heartfelt vocals and daydreamy lyrics that reference idyllic scenes of birds singing, children playing and lying awake listening to the sea. The chorus is a delight, as is the instrumentation with restrained bass, lilting flute, acoustic guitar and a hint of Mellotron. Released as a single in June 1968, it preceded the album by four weeks and charted at a respectable number 27 in the UK. It was performed by the band during the 1968 tour and would periodically resurface in later years. Hayward would occasionally play an acoustic version in his later solo concerts. One of the most recent was 'On the Blue Cruise' in February 2019 backed by Mike Dawes (acoustic guitar), Julie Ragins (keyboards, vocals) and classically trained Karmen Gould (flute). At the grand old age of 72, Hayward is in superb voice and Karmen's flute playing is gorgeous.

'The Best Way to Travel' (Mike Pinder)
Opening with Pinder's own frantic acoustic guitar, this is another psychedelic tinged offering that wears its Beatles and early Pink Floyd influences on its

sleeve. That said, the simulated sound of a vehicle passing by predates similar effects on both Floyd's *The Dark Side of the Moon* and Kraftwerk's *Autobahn* by several years. The panning effect and use of reverb were devised by Pinder, Clarke and Varnals to demonstrate the capabilities of Decca's 20-channel state of the art recording console. The chorus 'Thinking is the best way to travel' (with backing from Hayward) makes clear the message in the title. For me, however, it lacks Pinder's usual consistency, sounding more like a few random ideas strung together. He's in fine vocal form, however, as he is throughout the album. At a little over three minutes, the song fades before fully delivering on its initial promise. This song was also in the 1968 setlist, although its spell as a stage song was short-lived.

'Visions of Paradise' (Justin Hayward, Ray Thomas)
A descending flute line announces the first Hayward and Thomas composition on record, a partnership that would feature on the next two albums. A beautiful flute melody, acoustic rhythm guitar and sitar underpin Hayward's vocal which sounds both distant and heavenly. Mostly acoustic, it's a slice of blissed out psychedelia that lives up to its title and is one of the most underrated songs in the Moody Blues canon. Clearly, the aim was to create a song free from the busy arrangements of some of the other songs on the album. Mellotron, however, makes an appearance for the surging middle-eight. CD reissues of the album include an instrumental version as a bonus track, which works beautifully. In the absence of vocals, the sitar is more prominent, demonstrating Hayward's proficiency on the instrument.

'The Actor' (Justin Hayward)
Continuing the mood of the previous song, this is another delightful flute and acoustic guitar arrangement. It's a typically bittersweet ballad from Hayward with homespun, downbeat lyrics like 'It's such a rainy afternoon, no point in going anywhere'. The heartrending chorus 'Oh, oh, darling, you're all I'll ever see' with Mellotron and ethereal backing chants brings to mind 'Nights in White Satin'. Bass and drums remain respectfully restrained throughout. This is another song that Hayward wrote very late one night after returning home from a gig. The band resurrected it in the 1990s, and it was part of Hayward's solo set from that same decade onwards. It can be seen and heard on the 1998 CD and video *Live in San Juan Capistrano*. Since the turn of the millennium, It has also made the occasional appearance in the band's shows where it's always welcomed by fans of a certain age.

'The Word' (Graeme Edge)
Pinder's deep, resonant tones recite Edge's poetry unaccompanied. When it was remixed for the 1974 *This Is The Moody Blues* compilation, the instrumental 'Beyond' from *To Our Children's Children's Children* was incorporated, albeit very low in the mix. It resolves the search alluded to in the

album title with the closing lines 'To name the chord is important to some, so they give it a word, and the word is Om', serving as an introduction to the final song...

'Om' (Mike Pinder)

After the mind-expanding travels of 'Legend of a Mind' and 'The Best Way to Travel', the band come to the conclusion that Om is where the heart (or rather art) is. Influenced by Indian raga and Eastern mysticism; flute, sitar and tabla hand drums provide the backdrop while the title is the single word chorus. The mood, especially Lodge's mournful cello, is very similar to the haunting instrumental 'Silent Sorrow in Empty Boats' on Genesis' 1974 album *The Lamb Lies Down on Broadway*. It makes full use of its six minutes and pre-empts the popularity of world music in the 1980s. While the instrumental mid-section that gets progressively faster is similar to George Harrison's 'Within You Without You' on *Sgt. Pepper*, both are influenced by traditional Indian dance music. The brooding Mellotron and stunning choral chants at the end, however, are pure Moody Blues. This is not just a song, it's an experiment in sound. The production is stunning with Pinder and Thomas' voices panning from left to right for the call and response verses and full-blooded harmonies occupying the centre. Unsurprisingly, like several songs on the album, the complex arrangement and overdubs didn't lend itself to live performances.

Related Tracks:

'A Simple Game' (Mike Pinder)

Wasted as the B-side to the 'Ride My See-Saw' single, this is one of Pinder's catchiest tunes with inspired lead guitar from Hayward. With its anthemic choral hook, no wonder it was a big hit for the Four Tops, peaking at number three in the UK in October 1971. The original made its album debut on the band's first compilation *This Is The Moody Blues* in 1974. An alternate mix with Hayward replacing Pinder on lead vocals is available as a bonus track on the CD reissue of *In Search of the Lost Chord*. Tony Clarke also produced the Four Tops version and he and Hayward (under the pseudonym Gurron) co-wrote the B-side. 'You Stole My Love' is a lively combination of soulful vocals and guitar driven rock arranged by Arthur Greenslade. Pinder would later receive an Ivor Novello Award for 'A Simple Game'.

'Gimme a Little Somethin'' (John Lodge)

A catchy pop song with Hayward singing lead joined by Lodge's unmistakable falsetto for the foot-tapping chorus. Despite the lovely wordless harmonies in the bridge, it's not hard to see why it didn't make the album, but it would have made a cracking single. Although recorded in 1968 this song, along with 'King and Queen' and 'What Am I Doing Here?' made its first official appearance in 1977 on the fourth (studio) side of the double album *Caught Live + 5*.

'King and Queen' (Justin Hayward)
A near four-minute ballad with haunting, almost dreamlike verses building to a typically Hayward surging chorus. The counterpoint Beach Boys-style harmonies are superb as is Pinder's expansive orchestrations. Like all the non-album studio tracks from this period, it would resurface on the 1987 compilation *Prelude* and as a bonus track on CD reissues of *In Search of the Lost Chord*.

'What Am I Doing Here?' (Justin Hayward)
A beautiful, lilting ballad with swaying Mellotron strings, piano, a distinctive bass line and a stylish drum pattern. The stunning choral harmonies are worth the price of admission alone. It's a crying shame that these songs remained mostly unheard for nine years before finding their way onto the *Caught Live + 5* album.

'A Beautiful Dream' (John Lodge)
This is a rather shaky live performance from the ORTF French TV show *Ce Soir On Danse* recorded in July 1968. Following the flute intro, it has an early Pink Floyd psychedelic vibe with Lodge's falsetto supported by Hayward and Thomas' more subdued tones. Edge runs rampant over his kit while the young French audience demonstrates that you can dance to almost anything if you put your mind and body into it. It's captured for posterity on DVD as part of 2018's *In Search of the Lost Chord* 50th Anniversary five-disc box set.

On the Threshold of a Dream (1969)

Personnel:
Justin Hayward: vocals, acoustic guitar, electric guitar, twelve-string acoustic guitar, cello, Mellotron on 'Never Comes the Day'
John Lodge: vocals, bass, cello, double bass
Ray Thomas: vocals, harmonica, flute, tambourine, oboe, piccolo
Graeme Edge: drums, percussion, vocals, EMS VCS 3
Mike Pinder: vocals, Mellotron, Hammond organ, piano, cello
Produced by: Tony Clarke
Engineered by: Derek Varnals
Recorded at: Decca Studios, London, January – February 1969
UK release date: April 1969, USA release date: May 1969
Highest chart places: UK: 1, USA: 20
Running time: 36:59

This 1969 masterpiece is arguably their best album of the 1960s and first UK number one, demonstrating that artistic ambition and commercial success could go hand in hand. It remained at the top for two weeks and in the charts for an impressive 70 weeks. It also scraped into the *Billboard* top twenty, their highest USA chart placing so far. Although the attendant single 'Never Comes the Day' failed to spark the public's imagination, the Moody Blues were now fully established as a successful albums band. There's no conspicuous attempt at a hit single here. Recording once again began in January, a work ethic that clearly suited the band (perhaps it was the Christmas break that stimulated creativity). On this occasion, however, because they didn't have to work around concert dates, the sessions were completed fairly quickly. You would hardly know it from the results, however, particularly considering the number of overdubs evident in the songs.

All in their twenties, the band were still young and ambitious, and despite developing family ties, they lived for their music. This is evident in the songs which compared with many of their contemporaries sound mature and sophisticated. The individual personalities often come across in the songs; even without reading the writing credit, it's not difficult to identify the originator of each song. Although the songs are all distinctive in their own way, they complement and balance each other. It is, without doubt, one of their most polished sounding albums with a clarity unmatched by almost anything else around at the time. Unsurprisingly, it's another concept, and as the title alludes, dreams provide the subject. The title also gave the name to their record label 'Threshold', formed later that same year, and this would be the last release on the Deram label.

The psychedelic tendencies of *Days of Future Passed* and *In Search of the Lost Chord* are almost (but not quite) behind them. Again, the song contributions from each band member are fairly even, and the material is mostly excellent even though there are no obvious 'classics' in the mould of 'Nights in White Satin' or 'Ride My See-Saw'. Given the quality of his songs on the last album, John Lodge's offerings are a tad disappointing, although for my money Mike Pinder excels. His richly orchestrated suite that concludes the album is particularly impressive and would receive due recognition as one of his most accomplished works. Although the Mellotron would soon become synonymous with acts like King Crimson, Genesis and Yes, no one could tease an authentic sound out of the instrument quite like Pinder. Having previously worked for Streetly Electronics, the UK company that manufactured the Mellotron, he had the technical know-how to tame this notoriously unreliable beast, in the studio and on tour.

In the first half of 1969, they played dates in the UK and mainland Europe as well as recording several BBC radio sessions and TV appearances. On tour, they shared the bill with anyone and everyone including The Nice, Fairport Convention, the Hollies, Pink Floyd, Gladys Knight and the Pips, Pentangle and the Everly Brothers.

In 2007, *Classic Rock* magazine placed *On the Threshold of a Dream* at a respectable number nine in their 'Top 30 Prog Rock Albums', eclipsed only by prog heavyweights Pink Floyd, Jethro Tull, ELP, Yes and Genesis. Most significantly, it was one of only four albums from the 1960s in the list, which says a great deal about the band's pioneering spirit. They had strong competition in 1969 however from King Crimson's debut *In the Court of the Crimson King* which is often cited as the first true progressive rock album and also features Mellotron prominently. In an interview on the BBC Radio Two *Steve Wright in the Afternoon* show in May 2018, Hayward stated 'I never considered the Moody Blues a prog rock band'.

Album Cover

A distinctive aspect of Phil Travers' work is that each album brings a different design style and lettering. He eschews the consistency that characterises Roger Dean's artwork for example and never produced a definitive logo in the same way that Dean did for Yes. Unlike the previous album, his artwork covers both sides of the gatefold sleeve. For me, however, it's not one of his most eye-catching. A strange, robotic creature with mechanical tentacles is holding a wizened branch (on the front cover) and a rose (on the rear cover) against a murky blue background. Closer inspection reveals images inspired by the lyrics to 'Are You Sitting Comfortably?' and 'The Dream', including Merlin, a white eagle, galleons and Camelot.

On the inside cover, there's a full-size photo of the group looking very dapper (few bands dressed as smartly as the Moodies in the '60s) in a rain-soaked park. Opposite are six smaller photos, one of each band member (the sixth of course being Tony Clarke looking conspicuous in his plain brown suit and tie). Most impressively, inside the sleeve, there's a twelve-page album-size booklet rather than the customary single insert sheet.

'In the Beginning' (Graeme Edge)

An atmospheric intro of ambient, synthesised sounds and a surging wave of Mellotron that wouldn't have sounded out of place on the soundtrack to Stanley Kubrick's sci-fi epic *2001: A Space Odyssey*, released the previous year. A self-doubting narrator (spoken by Hayward) quotes French philosopher René Descartes before being confronted by a computerised voice (a manic sounding Edge) representing the establishment. It concludes with calming words of wisdom from the man's inner self (Pinder naturally). This is Edge's most ambitious and (at just over two minutes) longest opening salvo so far. The 'Full Version' bonus track on the 2008 CD is over a minute longer but doesn't improve on the original.

'Lovely to See You' (Justin Hayward)

This is a breezy, upbeat opener from Hayward. It boasts his most assertive guitar playing thus far with a melodic tone (and a hint of distortion) that would become his signature, as would the Gibson ES-335. It boasts a memorable chorus with a hint of echo and close harmony backing from Pinder. Like many of Hayward's songs, the lyrical premise is a simple one which made him a natural for writing first person ballads. Here he re-acquaints himself with an absent (female?) friend.

When played live, it rocks harder than the studio version thanks to Hayward's meaty guitar work. It could have been a forgotten gem, but from the beginning of the 1990s, it was given a new lease of life and regularly featured in the setlist. It often followed the overture, but for me, it never sat comfortably with the orchestral backing during this period. Between 2003 and 2009 the chorus greeting made it a natural concert opener and it also has the distinction of providing the title for the 2005 album *Lovely to See You: Live*.

'Dear Diary' (Ray Thomas)

The title says it all with Thomas' introspective (and slightly processed) half sung, have spoken delivery relating an uneventful day in the life of a lonely person. The mostly acoustic combination of flute, piano, guitar and a suitably lazy, walking rhythm are perfect for the song's poignant tone. Thomas' deadpan delivery towards the end where he reads from the diary is just perfect. The contrast between this and a track like 'The Voyage' on side two couldn't be more acute. As none of Thomas' songs were ever chosen as singles, this would become a staple of compilation albums to represent his contribution to the band. The 'Alternate Vocal Mix' version on the 2008 CD remaster adds a wordless vocal backing to the flute solo at the midway point.

In 2001, 'Dear Diary' received the unlikely attention of rapper Masta Ace who took the title for his own song which unashamedly sampled the original. There is also a fun version on the 2011 album *Moody Bluegrass TWO... Much Love* which plays fast and loose with the original lyrics and features Thomas on flute and Pinder on Mellotron.

'Send Me No Wine' (John Lodge)

Two back-to-back songs from Lodge, and to be honest, the first is not one of his best. The singalong chorus has not dated well despite the combined vocal might of Lodge, Hayward, Thomas and Pinder. Even the Mellotron has a languid, cabaret feel. Still, at a little under two and a half minutes, it doesn't outstay its welcome. Like 'Dear Diary', a cover of this song features on the *Moody Bluegrass TWO... Much Love* tribute album where its jaunty style suited the country treatment. Lodge provides the lead vocals amongst a company of seasoned Nashville artists playing banjo, fiddle, mandolin and dobro.

'To Share Our Love' (John Lodge)

This track is better, a mid-tempo rocker with Hayward's gutsy guitar fills standing out. The intricate, counterpoint harmonies during the chorus are superb, and unusually for a Lodge song, it features a lead vocal from Pinder. The band was blessed with four strong singers which they put to good use on all their albums, including this one. This is the kind of song Lodge excels at and adds weight to his growing reputation as the band's resident rock and roller. It also sounds like a self-conscious attempt to emulate 'Ride My See-Saw' from the previous album. That's probably why it didn't make it into the live setlist where the latter song had already become firmly established.

'So Deep Within You' (Mike Pinder)

Pinder again, this time providing lead vocals on his own song to close side one. It's another lively tune with both guitar and flute vying for attention. The chorus is decent although it's the staccato flute, drums and guitar bridge following each chorus that leaves its mark. The 'Extended Version' bonus track on the 2008 CD features a low-key instrumental intro but otherwise, they are identical.

This song was the B-side to the album's only single 'Never Comes the Day'. Like Pinder's 'A Simple Game' (which coincidentally was the B-side on the last single 'Ride My See-Saw'), 'So Deep Within You' was covered by the Four Tops. Their version was again produced by Tony Clarke and arranged by Arthur Greenslade, although as a single it failed to match the success of 'A Simple Game'. It's a good version however with typically gutsy vocals, fuzzed guitar and brass stabs.

'Never Comes the Day' (Justin Hayward)

To open side two, Hayward's delicate acoustic guitar and bittersweet vocal. He's supported by tight, wordless harmonies and surging Mellotron strings that build to the chorus which, given the plaintive verses, is surprisingly uplifting. Pinder plays the Mellotron M-300, which was smaller and lighter than his cumbersome Mark II model, for the first time here. The song is about love, delicate relationships, insecurity and the feeling when love is slipping away. This was another of Hayward's songs where he was expressing his own inner emotions and insecurities.

The promo video for this song is a delight with Hayward and Lodge on guitar and bass with the other three standing behind looking slightly awkward (especially Pinder) providing the hand-clapping rhythm. When this song was released as a single three weeks before the album it was ruthlessly edited, losing a full two minutes. Although it did nothing in the UK, it scraped into the Canadian and USA top 100 charts at number 74 and 91 respectively. It was better received live, however, remaining in the band's setlist until 1971 when like several others it was dropped to make way for songs from *Every Good Boy Deserves Favour*. It made a welcome stage comeback during the '90s and also the noughties with Hayward playing acoustic guitar and Thomas' stage replacement Norda Mullen playing harmonica.

'Lazy Day' (Ray Thomas)

In contrast to 'Dear Diary', a typically warm and light-hearted diversion from Thomas that makes no attempt to disguise its Beatles influences. The wordless choral harmonies are memorable, some of the best on the album, while harmonica (not flute for a change) provides the delightful instrumental break. File in the same category as the Kinks' 'Sunny Afternoon', Queen's 'Lazing on a Sunday Afternoon' and 10cc's 'Lazy Ways'. Although it was never a live song, 'Lazy Day' featured in a French TV show filmed at La Taverne de l'Olympia, Paris in April 1970. Released on DVD in 2004 as *The Lost Performance – Live in Paris '70*, the band dutifully mime to the studio version with Pinder making a playful attempt to encourage the French audience to join in.

'Are You Sitting Comfortably?' (Justin Hayward, Ray Thomas)

Hayward and Thomas complement each other so well, and this is another of their gentle acoustic songs that I never tire of hearing. Discreet percussion, rhythmic acoustic guitar and tasteful flute interludes underscore the evocative lyrics that reference the Arthurian legend of Camelot, Guinevere and Merlin.

Like 'Lazy Day', it was filmed at La Taverne de l'Olympia, Paris in 1970, although Hayward's singing and Thomas' flute are recorded live this time. Up until the band's hiatus in 1974, this song, together with 'The Dream', 'Have You Heard (Part 1)', 'The Voyage' and 'Have You Heard (Part 2)' would form a fifteen-minute sequence that regularly closed the main section of their shows. The same sequence would form the bulk of a *David Symonds BBC Radio One Concert* recording at the BBC Paris Theatre on 17 December 1969. This appears on the bonus disc of the 2006 'Deluxe Edition' of *To Our Children's Children's Children*. In the concerts of the noughties following Thomas' retirement, Norda Mullen's extended flute solo would give the song an extra dimension.

'The Dream' (Graeme Edge)

In a similar manner to 'The Word' on the last album, Edge's poetry reveals the significance of the album title and concept. Pinder again provides the eloquent narration and the final line 'Live hand-in-hand and together we'll stand on the threshold of a dream' is a perfect introduction to his own three-part suite. This was revived for the orchestral concerts of the 1990s where together with 'Late Lament' it provided the prologue with Edge reciting his own words.

'Have You Heard (Part 1)' (Mike Pinder)
And so to Pinder's album finale, commonly referred to as the 'Have You Heard' suite. Although listed as three separate tracks, it plays as one seamless eight-minute piece, a testimony to Tony Clarke's editing skills. It's arguably Pinder's finest and most fully realised contribution to a Moody Blues album. This haunting song with strummed acoustic guitar, cello and flute-like Mellotron provide the opening although lyrically it's almost a continuation of 'The Dream'. To underline Pinder's warm, heartfelt vocal, Edge resurrects the 'Day in the Life' style drum pattern from the song 'House of Four Doors' on the previous album.

'The Voyage' (Mike Pinder)
A precursor to later prog epics by the likes of Yes, Genesis and Italian band PFM, this four-minute instrumental marvel is, as many have observed, a nod towards 'Also Sprach Zarathustra'. Like many music and film fans during the late '60s, Pinder would certainly have been inspired by the mind-expanding *2001: A Space Odyssey* where Richard Strauss' tone poem was co-opted by Stanley Kubrick to open and close the film. Discerning ears will also recognise a similarity to the sweeping *Lawrence of Arabia* theme from 1962 by French film composer Maurice (father of Jean Michel) Jarre. With Mellotron strings and flute plus timpani at the heart of the piece (and a total absence of lead guitar), it is grandiose and symphonic one moment and all crashing chords the next. Following a hint of Hammond organ, flute spirals in and out, and to close, Pinder counters with a rhythmic piano solo.

'The Voyage' was originally recorded as a standalone instrumental. The 'Original Take' is included as a bonus track on the 2008 CD remaster, and without the edits at the beginning and end, it is marginally longer. For its time, 'The Voyage' was unprecedented; even during the progressive 1970s, very few bands would allow a member the same artistic freedom that Pinder enjoys here.

'Have You Heard (Part 2)' (Mike Pinder)
Brooding cello leads into the plaintiff closing song which memorably reprises part one before playing out with eerie electronic sounds, bringing the album full circle. 'Have You Heard' was originally recorded as one continuous, four-minute song. The 'Original Take' can be found as a bonus track on the 2008 CD remaster, but without 'The Voyage' interlude, it's nowhere near as effective.

Related Tracks:
None. One single 'Never Comes the Day' b/w 'So Deep Within You'. Both songs were album tracks.

Although it contains no new or previously unreleased songs, the 2008 remastered CD has a generous nine bonus tracks including different versions of five songs and BBC radio sessions. As they've generally been superseded by more expansive (and expensive) boxsets, all the core seven album re-releases from 2006 and 2008 can be picked up at a very modest price at the time of writing.

To Our Children's Children's Children (1969)
Personnel:
Justin Hayward: vocals, electric guitar, acoustic guitar, sitar
John Lodge: vocals, bass guitar, harp, acoustic guitar
Ray Thomas: vocals, flute, tambourine, bass flute, oboe
Graeme Edge: drums, percussion
Mike Pinder: vocals, Mellotron, piano, EMS VCS 3, Hammond organ, acoustic guitar, celesta, double bass
Produced by: Tony Clarke
Engineered by: Derek Varnals, Adrian Martins, Robin Thompson
Recorded at: Decca Studios, London, May – September 1969
UK and USA release date: November 1969
Highest chart places: UK: 2, USA: 14
Running time: 40:15

The Moodies were clearly on a roll in 1969 with this, the second album recorded and released that year. Earlier that spring, they all bought houses in Cobham, a picturesque village located in the stockbroker heart of Surrey, south west of London. This attracted unfavourable comments from the press; apparently, it was acceptable for the Beatles and the Rolling Stones to exhibit their wealth but not the Moody Blues. With the blessing of Decca chairman Sir Edward Lewis, they established their own record company 'Threshold', based in the heart of Cobham, and this was the first release under that label. It allowed them to have greater control over their releases, the master tapes and the artwork. None of the acts they signed, however, including Trapeze, Tymon, Providence and Nicky James, became big names and they later came to the conclusion that they were more comfortable (and successful) as musicians than businessmen.

To Our Children's Children's Children was a worthy successor and followed the last album into the upper reaches of the UK chart, although it just missed out on the top spot. Again, it was their highest USA chart placing so far. The Moody Blues were not the only ones having a memorable year, however. On 21 July 1969, Apollo eleven astronaut Neil Armstrong became the first person to set foot on the Moon. At the time of writing this book (Spring 2019), the 50th anniversary is fast approaching. It was a momentous occasion that captivated the entire world (or at least those with a TV set). I can still remember staying up all night, eyes glued to the screen even though I had school the next day. Tony Clarke was similarly enthralled and inspired, and he convinced the band to adopt space travel and exploration as the theme for this album. In 1971, when the Apollo fifteen mission was launched, the astronauts had onboard twelve cassette tapes of various music which included *On the Threshold of a Dream* and *To Our Children's Children's Children*.

Like all the band's albums from this period, it has a well thought out structure with a beginning, middle and an end, rather like a good film or novel. Each track flows seamlessly into the next and again there is a fairly even balance of writing contributions. While no one song stands head and shoulders above the rest, that's the album's strength rather than its weakness. Every track, with perhaps one minor exception, is memorable and they continue the trend set by the last two albums of dividing two of the songs into two parts. Graeme Edge, Ray Thomas and Mike Pinder adhere closely to the space theme while Justin Hayward and John Lodge adopt a more personal worldview in their songs. Loneliness and the passing of time (recurring themes for the band) form the basis of several songs. With his name attached to four songs, Hayward's songwriting is spread more thinly than almost any other album. Like the last album, multiple overdubs are used to create a lush sound, but the layering of instruments made it difficult to recreate the songs live. As a result, only one song, 'Gypsy', was initially played on stage with any regularity and it quickly became one of their most popular.

After the initial flush of success, sales of the album remained slow (due to the absence of a hit single) but steady. Hayward's 'Watching and Waiting' was released as a single three weeks before the album but failed to make an impression in any region. In August and November 1969 they returned to America playing support to homegrown acts like Steppenwolf, Jefferson Airplane and Canned Heat, as well as Humble Pie. They were invited to play the opening day at the legendary Woodstock festival on 15 August but they cancelled and returned to Europe instead. At the end of August, the band made their first appearance at the annual Isle of Wight Festival. To round off a busy year, on the 12 December 1969 they performed at the Royal Albert Hall in London, although it would be more than seven years before the resulting live album surfaced. Despite their musical development, the band's name still caused confusion for many UK rock fans. Bizarrely, in the *NME* magazine readers poll for 1969, they were voted third in the 'British Blues Group' category (behind Fleetwood Mac and the Rolling Stones).

Album Cover

The cover is another gatefold sleeve where Phil Travers' artwork wraps around the front and back. Two, almost full-size hands (the artists?) are shown drawing a hunting scene on a brightly lit cave wall in the style of prehistoric man. The inside cover is one of his best, depicting the band inside a cave sitting around a campfire with all the comforts of contemporary life close by (although by today's standards the computer looks like something out of the ark). The band were photographed separately and combined with Travers' artwork. At the bottom, the distinctive 'Threshold' flying head logo makes its first appearance. The insert sheet features monochrome images of the band's faces overlaid with the lyrics. Graeme Edge is noticeably wearing spectacles for the first time on an album photo. A portion of the inner sleeve artwork was used as the cover for the 'Watching and Waiting' single in certain regions.

'Higher and Higher' (Graeme Edge)
The fourth successive album with an opening composition from Edge, but this time it's a full band arrangement with Pinder singing as well as reciting the words. A rocket launch is simulated with crashing chords, swirling electronic effects and ethereal chants. Like 'In the Beginning' and 'The Voyage' on the last album it draws inspiration from the *2001: A Space Odyssey* soundtrack, notably the dissonant tones of Hungarian-Austrian composer György Ligeti. Hayward adds some blistering guitar fills backed by a busy and loose shuffle rhythm from Edge. Since 2003, it has been an almost permanent fixture in the band's setlist, giving the always-genial drummer the opportunity to come out from behind his kit and banter with the audience. The title was also co-opted for a 2005 Moodies tribute album featuring a host of prog-related artists, as well as an American fanzine magazine, although the latter is no longer in print.

'Eyes of a Child, Part 1' (John Lodge)
After his disappointing contributions to the last album, this is a minor classic from Lodge. Like 'House of Four Doors' on *In Search of the Lost Chord*, it's divided into two parts separated by a Ray Thomas song. The swirling harp that opens and continues throughout the song (played by Lodge himself) creates a magical atmosphere, joined by mournful oboe and acoustic guitar. Add an infectious chorus, and you have a beautiful, and perhaps underrated song. The lyrical premise is quite simple; Lodge is inviting the listener to look at the world through the eyes of a child and appreciate all its wonders. The slow build during the verses and surging transposition to the chorus is one of Lodge's trademark qualities and would be a feature of later songs, especially 'One More Time to Live' on *Every Good Boy Deserves Favour*.

'Floating' (Ray Thomas)
Assuming the role of an awestruck astronaut floating in space, this is a typically jaunty and catchy tune from Thomas. With a feel-good factor, it follows in the footsteps of his previous creations 'Another Morning' and 'Dr. Livingstone, I Presume'. It has a wistful innocence that only he could conjure up and sing. The arrangement is lean and crisp with tinkling bell-like percussion, acoustic guitar and an irresistible bass line. With its child-friendly lyrics, it sits perfectly between Lodge's two-part 'Eyes of a Child' and also strikes a chord with the album title. If this doesn't put a smile on your face and get your foot tapping, nothing will.

'Eyes of a Child, Part 2' (John Lodge)
Surprisingly, given the title, this is not a reprise of 'Eyes of a Child, Part 1'. The only element the two tracks have in common (apart from the title) is the lyrics in the chorus. Otherwise, it's an energetic, but still very melodic rocker, that rushes into view and then fades all too quickly. A terrific song with superb wordless harmonies but at a little under a minute and a half, it's way too short. Since the advent of home computers and the internet in the 1980s, the song's

opening line "I'm gonna sit and watch the web" has taken on a whole new meaning.

'I Never Thought I'd Live to Be a Hundred' (Justin Hayward)
And speaking of short, this is an introspective, solo acoustic ballad from Hayward clocking in at just over one minute. It contains just five lines of words and no chorus as such, but it conveys Hayward's message perfectly, that time is infinite. The even shorter second part 'I Never Thought I'd Live to Be a Million' is on side two and, like this song, it's also the fifth track. The premature ending gives the song an added sense of sadness and loneliness.

'Beyond' (Graeme Edge)
Following in the footsteps of 'The Voyage' from *On the Threshold of a Dream*, this is another rare instrumental. It's a lively Mellotron driven piece with a slight, but still-memorable melody that pans from the left stereo channel to the right. The two slow sections with brooding electronic effects are not convincingly integrated, however. Each section simply fades in and out again, giving the piece a rather disjointed feel. That said, it predates the ambient sounds of Icelandic art-rockers Sigur Rós by 25 years. For the 1974 compilation album *This Is The Moody Blues*, part of this track was mixed into 'The Word' (another Edge composition) from *In Search of the Lost Chord* to provide a backing to Pinder's narration.

'Out and In' (Mike Pinder, John Lodge)
To close side one, a rare songwriting pairing of the keyboardist and bassist, although it sounds very much like a Pinder song with his lead vocal and prominent Mellotron strings. That's perhaps why on the 1997 CD reissue, Lodge's name was removed and only Pinder is credited. Typically, he takes a spiritual viewpoint and is 'Gazing past the planets'. The Melly has rarely sounded sweeter and sharper, cutting through like a knife through butter. It contrasts with Hayward's trebly lead guitar, and Pinder makes good use of the pitch control to create a descending effect similar to 'The Voyage'. 'Out and In' backed the single 'Watching and Waiting' making it Pinder's third successive B-side. This song, along with 'Watching and Waiting', 'Higher and Higher' and 'Eternity Road' featured briefly in the setlist of the 1973/1974 world tour just prior to the band's extended mid-'70s sabbatical.

'Gypsy (Of a Strange and Distant Time)' (Justin Hayward)
'Gypsy' provides a rousing, proto-prog opening to side two. It features tremolo lead guitar (underpinned by acoustic), lush Mellotron strings, flute and the now familiar chant-like wordless harmonies. The words are lean and delivered at a rapid pace. Although Hayward's guitar technique is less flamboyant than many of his contemporaries, his playing is always inventive, combining melody and rhythm and never indulgent. As a stage song, 'Gypsy' has staying

power. Until 1972 it would open each show before returning to the setlist from 1978 to 1984. It occasionally featured in the orchestral concerts of the 1990s and resurfaced again in 2009 where it has remained a regular fixture. It was performed for *David Symonds BBC Radio One Concert* at the BBC Paris Theatre on 17 December 1969. The recording is included on the bonus disc of the 2006 'Deluxe Edition' of *To Our Children's Children's Children*. Both the 2006 and 2008 CD remasters of this album include as bonus tracks alternate versions of 'Gypsy', 'Candle of Life' and 'Sun Is Still Shining'. These are roughly half a minute longer with extended playouts. The early fade on the album versions was to allow each song to segue into the next.

'Eternity Road' (Ray Thomas)

This track is a more conventional offering from Thomas, with his reverb-drenched contemplations on space travel and the vastness of the universe. The opening words 'Hark, listen, here he comes' are based on memories of his infancy in World War Two Britain. They were spoken by his grandmother and neighbours as they sheltered from the air raids. It's nicely orchestrated, with swaying Mellotron strings from Pinder, busy percussion from Edge, a twangy double-tracked guitar break from Hayward and a subtle, tip-toeing bass riff from Lodge. It plays out with a spontaneous burst of flute from the man himself. At just under four and a half minutes it's the album's longest track by a whisker. Instrumentally, it's more complex than meets the eye and the riff under the line 'Searching to find a peace of mind' is very similar to 'Lovely to See You' on the previous album. Seldom performed during the '70s, it was a surprise addition to the orchestral concerts of the 1990s, but it worked well with fine acoustic guitar playing from Hayward.

'Candle of Life' (John Lodge)

This song has a beautiful arrangement with piano and Mellotron to the fore, Hayward singing the verses and combining with Lodge for the chorus. Pinder's rhythmic piano bridge is superb; an instrument I wish he played more regularly although the same could be said for many rock pianists. It's ironic that Lodge chose to give the sublime verses to Hayward as they are more memorable than the chorus. When the band performed the song for the French TV cameras at La Taverne de L'Olympia in April 1970, they are clearly miming to the album track. This show was released on DVD in 2004 as *The Lost Performance – Live in Paris '70*. 'Candle of Life' would not receive a proper live airing until September 2016 during Lodge's first ever solo tour. A recording is included on the 2017 *Live from Birmingham: The 10,000 Light Years Tour* DVD/CD box set. This studio recording would resurface as the B-side of the 'Question' single released in April 1970.

'Sun Is Still Shining' (Mike Pinder)

By now, Moody Blues fans had come to expect the unexpected from Pinder, and this is no exception. It's a rhythmic song that settles into a hypnotic groove and never strays. He forgoes the traditional verse-chorus format but does take in a middle-eight around the halfway mark. The see-sawing strings, transcendental sitar, chugging acoustic guitar and chant-like vocals are a return to the psychedelic muse of his earlier meditations on *Days of Future Passed* and *In Search of the Lost Chord*. While remaining true to the theme of space and the universe, the lyrics are steeped in his usual mystical flights of fancy 'See with your mind, leave your body behind'. Although this is less elaborate than some of his other songs, it burrows deep into the subconscious and stays there.

'I Never Thought I'd Live to Be a Million' (Justin Hayward)
At well under a minute, this is easily Hayward's shortest song despite the title being one of his longest. It's the conclusion to 'I Never Thought I'd Live to Be a Hundred' on side one. It has the same vocal melody, although the guitar playing is more intricate. A rare, if very brief opportunity to hear a solo acoustic guitar song on a Moodies album.

'Watching and Waiting' (Justin Hayward, Ray Thomas)
This song is another beautiful ballad from Hayward and Thomas, in which, typically, the guitarist provides the lead vocal, and it's one of his most moving. Mellotron ebbs and flows, accompanied by gentle acoustic guitar, piano and tasteful drum fills. Flute, however, is conspicuously low-key. An understated song, it was not obvious material for a single and unsurprisingly when it was released in that format in October 1969, it didn't trouble the charts in any country. The band had high hopes for the single, however, and in a 2014 interview, Hayward said that 'It was soft, it was quiet' when played on the radio, blaming the mastering and disc transfer. The 2006 'Deluxe Edition' of *To Our Children's Children's Children* would be remastered by Hayward himself and Alberto Parodi at Logical Box Studios, Genova, Italy. In later years, Hayward would revive this song for his solo tours, and he has performed it as recently as 2018. It's also included on the *Live in San Juan Capistrano* CD and DVD, recorded in 1998, and the *Live In Concert at the Capitol Theatre* DVD recorded in 2015.

Related Tracks:
None. One single, 'Watching and Waiting' b/w 'Out and In'. Both songs were album tracks.

A Question of Balance (1970)

Personnel:
Justin Hayward: vocals, acoustic & electric guitars, mandolin
John Lodge: vocals, bass
Ray Thomas: vocals, flute, tambourine
Graeme Edge: drums, percussion, whispered vocal on 'Don't You Feel Small'
Mike Pinder: vocals, Mellotron, Moog synthesizer, piano, maracas, acoustic guitar
Produced by: Tony Clarke
Engineered by: Derek Varnals, Adrian Martins, Robin Thompson
Recorded at: Decca Studios, London, January – June 1970
UK and USA release date: August 1970
Highest chart places: UK: 1, USA: 3
Running time: 38:41

For their fifth album, the band made a conscious attempt to eschew the multi-layered instrumentation of the previous albums and record songs that could be played on stage more easily. It certainly worked for the record-buying public and remains a firm favourite amongst fans. It was their second UK number one, where it remained for three weeks. Although that honour still eluded them in the USA, it was their first top five record in the *Billboard* chart. It also reached the top ten in Canada, Australia and several European countries. The pre-emptive single 'Question' is one of their best-selling ever, reaching number two in the UK where it lingered in the chart for nearly three months. It was the band's highest UK chart placing since 'Go Now' from five years earlier. Mike Pinder's 'Melancholy Man' was a rare number one in France that same year. Also in 1970, sales for the previous four albums all reached gold status. Unsurprisingly, the 'straightforward rock and roll' (their words not mine) struck a chord with the rock press, especially *Rolling Stone* magazine. In January, UK music weekly *Melody Maker* tipped them to be the group of the '70s.

The album title links the opening and closing songs, Justin Hayward's 'Question' and 'The Balance' written by Graeme Edge and Ray Thomas. Hayward's song is a rallying cry against hate, war and greed (in the opening and closing sections) and a yearning for love and fulfilment (in the slower, mid-section). Edge and Thomas' song, on the other hand, is a spiritual journey to awakening and enlightenment. 'Question' would become a permanent fixture in the band's setlist alongside 'Nights in White Satin' and 'Ride My See-Saw' where it would usually close the main part of the show. In March and April, the band took time out from the recording sessions to tour America and were also filmed for French TV at La Taverne de l'Olympia in Paris.

While the sound has been stripped back somewhat, Mellotron is once again to the fore, and although it's not exactly unplugged, acoustic guitar is prominent throughout. Reflecting the album title, there is once again a fairly even balance of songs from each band member. In addition to 'Question' and

'Melancholy Man', Thomas' 'And the Tide Rushes In' stands out while the rest are mostly good rather than essential. Edge's contributions are an attempt to combine his poetry with a more formal songwriting style. For me, John Lodge's songs are the least effective, although that would change on the next two albums. Despite the individual writing credits, the songs were thrashed out in the studio, ideas passed around, and each song developed into what had now become, after three years, the Moody Blues sound.

The band had become a very polished and successful headlining act and performed at two festivals that summer. At the end of June, after completing the album, they played the Bath Festival of Blues & Progressive Music which also featured Led Zeppelin, Pink Floyd and Frank Zappa, amongst many others (festival line-ups were so good in those days). Just three weeks after the album's release they made their second appearance at the annual Isle of Wight Festival. They gave one of the finest performances of the weekend, despite stiff competition from the likes of Free, Jethro Tull and Jimi Hendrix (sadly, the legendary guitarist died less than three weeks later). The recording *Live at the Isle of Wight Festival 1970* is available on CD, DVD and Blu-ray and aired on satellite TV in the UK. When Hayward remixed the recording for 5.1 surround sound in 2007, he noted that even as early as 1970 the live arrangements were departing from the studio versions. In December, they made their third of three visits to America that year taking with them Threshold Records signing Trapeze as their support band.

Album Cover

This is one of Phil Travers' most colourful designs and the most intricate. The gatefold sleeve opens vertically rather than horizontally. On the back of the original, there is a tuck-in flap which has to be released to open the gatefold. The busy design depicts a seemingly tranquil day at the beach dwarfed by a stormy night-time sky full of unrelated images inspired by the band's lyrics. On the back, the drawing of the man pointing a revolver was based on a real person, and so true was the likeness that the design was changed with a pith helmet added to conceal his identity. Given that it was altered to avoid litigation, the CD edition bizarrely reverted back to the original design. The inner sleeve has the usual individual and band photos, but this time it's a montage effect where each photo merges into the next. Like the outer sleeve, the double-sized lyric sheet opens out vertically.

'Question' (Justin Hayward)

Without question (if you excuse the pun), this is one of the band's most popular and durable songs. A perennial live favourite, it quickly became the song of choice to close the main part of the set. It struck a chord with the audience's concerns over the ongoing war in Vietnam, especially in the colleges of America where the band performed. Recorded several months before the rest of the songs on the album, it's a combination of two half-completed compositions. It was put together by Hayward the night before the recording, and it's not hard to spot the joins. Opening with Pinder's Mellotron stabs, the first section is a heady rush, driven by Hayward's frantic acoustic strumming, Lodge's intense bass line and Edge's thundering drum fills. The melancholic middle section is virtually a song unto itself with Hayward's heartfelt verses and soaring chorus against a simple twelve-string acoustic guitar and strings backing. The transition to the third section is superb, reprising the crashing Mellotron chords and ethereal, wordless harmonies before rushing headlong to the final fade with Edge's drumming going into overdrive. Hayward later said that it was 'Recorded live, with no overdubbing or double-tracking, just a bit of echo'. When performed on stage in the '70s and early '80s, playing acoustic guitar wasn't a practical option, so Hayward used his 1965 Fender Telecaster instead.

Nudging the six-minute mark, this is one of the band's longer songs, although 'Melancholy Man' on side two just shades it for distance. The edited single released in April 1970 (over three months before the album) fades before the final verses but still retains the song's impact. Reaching number two in the UK chart, it took the full might of the 1970 England World Cup Squad and their novelty hit 'Back Home' to keep it off the top spot. The 1989 *Greatest Hits* compilation includes a new 'symphonic' version of 'Question' (which Hayward later regretted) with the band augmented by the London Symphony Orchestra. The LSO version also appears on the 2014 box set *The Polydor Years: 1986-1992*.

'How Is It (We Are Here)' (Mike Pinder)
Although this song features Pinder's familiar symphonic Mellotron swells, it's also a showcase for his recently acquired Moog synthesizer. The latter weaves in and out, making siren-like calls, unrestrained by the lightweight rhythmic backing. The catchy chorus is a bonus, although it remains perhaps one of Pinder's most unassuming and most often forgotten songs. Despite the title, the subject is less about the meaning of life and more about the ecological concerns for the planet's future. A very spiritual person, the line 'Descending from the apes as scientist-priests all think' is Pinder's gentle sideswipe at the theory of evolution. In an album full of short songs, this clocks in at well under three minutes.

'And the Tide Rushes In' (Ray Thomas)
A typically restrained but sincere ballad from Thomas. It's a song fondly remembered by fans of a certain age and a personal favourite of the author. The lyrics were written following an argument with his former wife and reflect on their inability to communicate: 'You keep looking for someone to tell your troubles to, I'll sit down and lend an ear yet I'll hear nothing new'. Although the other band members would mirror their personal experiences in their writing, Thomas was perhaps the most open, which gives songs like this an

added poignancy. The melancholic lyrics aside, it's perfect listening for a lazy sunny afternoon (the album did originally appear in the height of summer, after all). Hayward's acoustic and mandolin picking is both delicate and dexterous matched by Pinder's dreamy Mellotron swells during the chorus. The rhythm playing is suitably discreet.

'Don't You Feel Small' (Graeme Edge)
At just two minutes and 40 seconds, this is a song for the full band rather than a spoken verse poem from Edge. The close, four-part harmonies in the verses are stunning, although Edge's obtrusive whisper which is high in the mix does negate their impact somewhat. His explosive drumming during the instrumental bridge is most welcome, however. Thomas' improvised flute soloing is superb, as is the exotic, world music percussion. Unusually, it has a middle-eight but no chorus with a variation of the line 'Bet you'll feel small, it happens to us all' sung at the end of each verse. Although this is credited solely to Edge and the words are undoubtedly all his, he would later acknowledge the significant input of the other band members in creating his songs.

'Tortoise and the Hare' (John Lodge)
With its relentless shuffle groove, this certainly swings, driven by chugging acoustic guitar, a foot-stomping rhythm, Mellotron fills and a pulsating bass line. The snap vocals and double-tracked choral harmonies playoff each other convincingly and Hayward lets loose with a bluesy guitar break at the halfway mark. Lodge's falsetto harmonies during the chorus are not his strongest, however. It's not one of the band's most ambitious or indeed memorable efforts, but it was included in the *A Question of Balance,* and *Every Good Boy Deserves Favour* tours to no doubt demonstrate that they could rock with the best of them. It certainly rocked harder and with more conviction when played live, as the performance on the *Live at the Isle of Wight Festival 1970* DVD testifies.

'It's Up to You' (Justin Hayward)
To open side two of the original vinyl album, a foot-tapping, mid-tempo ballad from Hayward. It has a loose, jangly guitar feel combining rhythmic acoustic with engaging lead fills. The distinct, American country-rock vibe anticipates the sound of the Eagles in the 1970s. Although not one of his most enduring offerings, the choral hook is suitably upbeat and as always in a Hayward song, the vocal bridge is especially memorable. In the lyrics, Hayward is trying to persuade a reluctant partner to commit to love. During his solo tours in the 1990s, Hayward performed this song solo on acoustic guitar, and it is included on the 1998 DVD *Live in San Juan Capistrano*.

'Minstrel's Song' (John Lodge)
For me, this is the albums weakest link. It begins promisingly enough with a

slow-burning, almost folky acoustic guitar, bass and drum shuffle. The close harmonies throughout are an absolute delight but the sing-along chorus, with lines like 'Everywhere love is all around', is cloyingly twee. The deliberately disjointed coda owes a clear debt to the Beatles' 'All You Need is Love' and 'Hey Jude'. Given that the Fab Four would be no more by the end of the year this could easily be a tribute of sorts. Like Lodge's other song on the album, 'Tortoise and the Hare', it made its way into the setlist for the 1970 Isle of Wight Festival appearance, but its days as a stage song were numbered.

'Dawning Is the Day' (Justin Hayward)
Hayward's third song contribution is another thoughtful acoustic guitar ballad. Edge's tasteful drum pattern is a further variation on the 'Day in the Life' fill previously used on 'House of Four Doors' and 'Have You Heard'. The rousing middle-eight stands out with a lustrous backdrop of flute, Mellotron strings and crashing piano chords. The closing section is particularly effective with the repeated line 'Listen, we think we have found you', supported by Mediterranean-flavoured acoustic guitar and mandolin. Hayward's lyrics are a simple but joyous celebration of life; wake up, put your troubles behind and appreciate the world around you. This is another song Hayward would resurrect for his later solo concerts, and he played it as recently as February 2019 unplugged 'On The Blue Cruise'.

'Melancholy Man' (Mike Pinder)
At five minutes and 45 seconds, this is the albums longest track by a whisker (topping 'Question' by two seconds). It's one of Pinder's best-known songs and the title sums up the mood perfectly. His voice is to the fore and never has he sounded more vulnerable with mournful choral backing from the rest of the band. It features stark acoustic guitar, drums and bass for the most part with haunting Moog synth effects. The counterpoint harmonies towards the end are just sublime. It's not surprising that this song was so popular in France, the country that gave us Edith Piaf and Charles Aznavour. It would remain in the band's setlist until the 1974 hiatus and would have almost certainly had a much longer life if Pinder hadn't departed in 1978. The song's performance at the 1970 Isle of Wight Festival is especially powerful with raw emotion in Pinder's impassioned singing while a typically buoyant Thomas looks on.

'The Balance' (Graeme Edge, Ray Thomas)
This song is a rare effort from the writing team of Edge and Thomas, although as usual Pinder narrates the spoken verses. Compared with 'Don't You Feel Small' it's a very wordy, spiritual song with lines like 'And he thought of those he hurt, for he was not a cruel man' taking on biblical proportions. Subtle acoustic guitar and hushed Mellotron underscore Pinder's dignified tones until the band, led by Lodge's wordless falsetto, break the calm with a stirring choral hook. Hayward adds soaring lead guitar embellishments and both the song and

the album, close on a note of blissful optimism. This song would return to the band's setlist for the *Octave* and *Long Distance Voyager* tours in the late '70s and early '80s.

Related Tracks:

'Mike's Number One' (Mike Pinder)
This is a leftover from the *A Question of Balance* sessions and it clearly never got beyond the working title stage. It was previously unreleased until it turned up as a bonus track on the 2006 CD remaster. It's a song with an optimistic message although the trippy chorus 'There's gonna be a happening, will you go?' does date it somewhat. With swaying Mellotron against a backdrop of piano, acoustic guitar and rhythm section, it's a solid enough song, although it's not hard to see why it never made the original album.

Also on the 2006 (and 2008) remasters are 'Alternate' and 'Original Mix' versions of 'Question', 'Minstrel's Song', 'It's Up to You', 'Don't You Feel Small' and 'Dawning Is the Day', which are all slightly longer than the album versions.

Every Good Boy Deserves Favour (1971)
Personnel:
Justin Hayward: vocals, acoustic guitar, electric guitar, sitar
John Lodge: vocals, bass, cello
Ray Thomas: vocals, flute, tambourine, oboe, woodwinds, harmonica
Graeme Edge: electric and acoustic drums, percussion, vocals
Mike Pinder: vocals, Mellotron, harpsichord, Hammond organ, piano, keyboards, Moog synthesizer
Produced by: Tony Clarke
Engineered by: Derek Varnals
Recorded at: Wessex Sound Studios, London, November 1970 – March 1971
UK and USA release date: July 1971
Highest chart places: UK: 1, USA: 2
Running time: 40:05

This is a quintessential Moody Blues album, and quite possibly the author's favourite. It was the first Moodies album that I bought on its initial release, so I'm probably biased. The significance of the title will be known to all budding musicians and links directly to the opening track, 'Procession'. Everything falls into place here, and the songwriting, arrangements and performances are of an exceptionally high standard. They had matured as musicians, especially Justin Hayward, John Lodge and Graeme Edge who play with more skill and confidence. It also marked the debut of Edge's electronic drum kit. Compared with *A Question of Balance* it's a more expansive work, recalling the ambitious arrangements of earlier albums. The sound is more contemporary, however; the 1960s and psychedelia are well and truly behind them ('Procession' being the possible exception). It also has a progressive edge, totally in keeping with 1971. Given the technology at their disposal, they were producing the best possible sound in the studio and through intense rehearsals, they were able to deliver the goods on stage.

It was their first recording away from Decca Studios, relocating just a few miles across North London to the Victorian surrounds of Wessex Studios in Highbury New Park. The sessions were interrupted by a December tour of the USA. Tony Clarke and Derek Varnals remained in control, resulting in probably their best recorded and sonically rich offering to date. It certainly impressed record buyers who placed it at number one and two respectively in the UK and USA album charts. It was also warmly greeted in most other regions. Even the normally indifferent *Rolling Stone* magazine was reasonably impressed. The companion single 'The Story in Your Eyes' also impressed several nationalities, especially Canada (reaching number seven), but it wasn't deemed suitable for the UK market. The UK singles chart was pretty dire in 1971 with novelty records like 'Grandad' by Clive Dunn and 'Chirpy Chirpy Cheep Cheep' by Middle of the Road dominating. Even the album's single week spell at number one was bookended by compilations of recent hit singles performed by anonymous session artists.

That same summer, they expanded the Threshold Records empire by opening a record shop on the ground floor of the three-storey headquarters located in Cobham, Surrey. The notes in the 1971 tour programme paint an idyllic scenario whereby it was possible for fans to drop into the shop and meet the band members. When it came to recording, however, it was still necessary for the band to make the busy commute across London to the studios located on the other side of the city. More Threshold record shops were opened in the South of England during the 1970s, totalling twelve at one point. By 1990, they had all closed due to stiff competition with only the original Cobham store remaining. That eventually closed its doors in February 2011.

During the subsequent world tour 'Our Guessing Game', 'After You Came', 'One More Time to Live' and 'The Story in Your Eyes' from the album featured in the setlist alongside established favourites 'Tuesday Afternoon', 'Nights in White Satin' and 'Ride My See-Saw'. I was due to catch them at the De Montfort Hall, Leicester in November 1971, but Lodge came down with the flu, and the concert was postponed to 27 February the following year. The support act that evening was a band called Hotlegs whose paths would cross with Hayward's again three years later after they changed their name to 10cc.

Album Cover

A wonderful piece of art from Phil Travers, which I'm sure attracted many record buyers. The front cover has shades of *The Lord of the Rings* with a wizard-like character dressed in robes and a long grey beard. He's holding a glowing crystal while the wide-eyed 'good boy' of the title looks on in wonderment. Open out the gatefold sleeve, however, and the rear cover tells a different, more sombre story. Standing in the shadows behind the man are two boys, one holding out a toy bear and the other a flower. The distinctive lettering for the band's name was reused for the 1974 compilation *This Is The Moody Blues* and the 1971-1974 tour programmes in certain regions. It was also adapted for the covers of some later compilation albums and tour programmes.

The painting spread across the inner cover is based on the opening track with a procession of musicians and dancers through the ages led by Graeme Edge no less. As was now typical, there are no details of who played what other than the line 'All instruments played by the Moody Blues'. The insert sheet is a little bland, with the lyrics on one side and a dark and grainy stage photo occupying the other. In addition to the now familiar 'Threshold' logo, the individual songs (with the exception of Justin Hayward's) are credited to 'Threshold Music'.

'Procession' (Graeme Edge, Justin Hayward, John Lodge, Mike Pinder, Ray Thomas)

If anyone could write a song that condensed the history of music into less than five minutes, then it would be the Moody Blues. Understandably it's a truncated history, and although original, they could have only got away with it in the experimental musical climate of the early '70s. It also has the distinction of being the only Moodies song attributed to all five members, although to my ears it sounds like an Edge and Pinder creation. The best way to describe it is to break it down into its separate components:

> It begins with spacey Moog synth effects which seem to simulate the sound of a flying saucer landing (suggestions of Erich von Däniken and Arthur C. Clarke if I'm not mistaken).
> The sounds of wind, thunder and rain accompany the chanted words 'Desolation' and 'Creation'.
> Pinder plays the ascending scale E-G-B-D-F on piano, which pans from the left stereo channel to the right.
> Tribal drums ('Communication') and Neanderthal grunts develop into a coherent chant.
> Early Eastern civilisation is represented by sitar, high flute and tabla drums, and medieval Western civilisation by low flute, piano and harpsichord.
> Celestial Hammond organ is joined by majestic Mellotron strings and Hayward plays some rich guitar harmonics (predating the Brain May sound by two years) which segues into his own song...

'The Story in Your Eyes' (Justin Hayward)

The album kicks into gear with the first song proper, and they don't come much better than this. It's not hard or heavy but it rocks all the same. It has a driving urgency led by Hayward's barnstorming lead guitar, underpinned by acoustic, Mellotron, piano arpeggios and an inspired bass line. With Pinder pounding the piano keys for all he's worth, the coda is pure rock and roll. It also boasts Hayward's best guitar work thus far plus superb vocal gymnastics for one of his trickiest and speediest vocal arrangements. The song's protagonist seems to be looking to the future with both optimism 'From the ashes we can build another day' and concern 'The sunshine we've been waiting for will turn to rain'. Stunning stuff, and at under three minutes it's a supremely crafted exercise in economy.

The band has performed the song at virtually every concert, and from 1990 onwards it provided a rousing close to the first half of the set before the intermission. The 'Original Version', which is included as a bonus track on the CD remasters in the noughties, is half a minute longer but doesn't improve on the 1971 album version. It features a spoken intro and instead of the familiar fade around the three-minute mark, it has an extended coda with a deliberately light-hearted, loose finish.

'Our Guessing Game' (Ray Thomas)

After the drama of the opening couplet, Thomas' ballad opens with sweet piano and Mellotron strings as he ponders the truth and meaning of life. A change of pace for the stunning choral hook with intricate counterpoint harmonies. Hayward's melodic guitar harmonics are once more to the fore, superbly underscoring the chorus and the instrumental bridge. Edge's drum and cymbal sound is quite dry, so unless I'm very much mistaken, he's using his newly developed electronic kit here. When performed live, the harmonies, in particular on songs like this, would test the band's vocal abilities. The chorus is so strong on this song, it deserved to be single, or at least a B-side where it might have picked up some airplay. At a little over three and a half minutes, it's certainly radio-friendly.

'Emily's Song' (John Lodge)

This song is one of Lodge's most exquisite ballads, or should I say lullaby as it was written to celebrate the birth of his daughter. It's an intimate song, the kind normally found on a solo album, but its placing here is perfect. And who could not be moved by the opening verse 'Lovely to know the warmth your smile can bring to me, I want to tell you but the words you do not know'. The double-tracked harmonies are reminiscent of Crosby, Stills, Nash & Young while the rhythmic cello, chiming percussive effects and soothing Mellotron are a delight.

It was performed live for the first time during the 1975 *Blue Jays* tour and is included on the deluxe edition of the *Timeless Flight* box set. The band performed it for the first time in September 1992, as featured on the 2003 deluxe edition of *A Night at Red Rocks with the Colorado Symphony Orchestra*. Following the success of that performance, it was also played on the 1993 orchestral tour with both Lodge and Hayward playing acoustic guitars. The pure magic and intimacy of the original take some beating, however.

'After You Came' (Graeme Edge)

Following the precedent set by 'Don't You Feel Small' on the previous album, this is another song proper from Edge. With a monumental riff, it's also the band's hardest rocking song to date. Driven by energetic acoustic guitar, the combined might of the band's four singers perform both the stop-start verses and the explosive chorus. The counterpoint harmonies in the latter are ridiculously infectious, and there's even a brief bass solo from Lodge before playing out with Hayward's sterling lead guitar. The ending with Edge beating the skins with all his might is a riot, demonstrating that the Moodies certainly knew how to rock. A cracking way to close side one. They were by now in the habit of hopping between albums for single B-sides, and in April 1972 this would be paired with the A-side 'Isn't Life Strange' from *Seventh Sojourn*.

'One More Time to Live' (John Lodge)

It's not an easy choice with such a superb collection of songs, but for me, this is the album's crowning glory and no better way of launching side two. Led by Thomas' haunting flute theme, the gentle verses are backed by rippling acoustic guitar and piano. Mellotron slowly rises to the surface for the anthemic, and at the time, most original choral hook. During the chorus, Lodge sings a counter melody punctuated by a succession of chanted rhyming words with Pinder's voice to the fore. With words like 'Pollution', 'Revolution' and 'Starvation' it could be the ultimate protest song, but this is the Moody Blues, and the chorus concludes on a positive note with 'Communication', 'Compassion' and 'Solution'. It links nicely with the opening track 'Procession' and still has the power to send shivers down the spine. Despite successes like 'Ride My See-Saw' and 'I'm Just a Singer (In a Rock and Roll Band)', it remains, for me, Lodge's most powerful song.

The song featured in the band's setlist until the 1974 hiatus. It was also played extensively throughout the latter half of the noughties following Thomas' retirement, with Norda Mullen skilfully providing the flute and backing vocals. During live performances, Edge's extra drum fill at the start of the challenging one minute ten seconds chorus was presumably added to allow the singers to take a deep breath.

'Nice to Be Here' (Ray Thomas)
Following the introspective ballad 'Our Guessing Game' on side one, 'Nice to Be Here' displays the other, more playful side of Thomas' songwriting persona. The storytelling lyrics paint a scene of child-friendly wonder and innocence supported by a jaunty brew of flute, hand drums, acoustic guitar and Mellotron. Lodge's agile bass figure doubles the melody while Hayward's slide guitar embellishments have a country music feel that suits the mood perfectly. Edge's tasteful fills sound synthetically crisp, so I assume the electronic drums are once more in use. The lyrical imagery evokes William Roscoe's early Nineteenth Century poem 'The Butterfly Ball and the Grasshopper's Feast', and like several of Thomas' songs, it has the charm and wit of a classic Disney animated film.

'You Can Never Go Home' (Justin Hayward)
A masterclass in songwriting from Hayward that combines silky smooth verses with a soaring chorus and a memorable middle-eight. The bittersweet words are sung partly in the first person; he's not sure what he's searching for, but he knows he can never return to a past life. Once again, surging Mellotron strings signal the choral hook where the wordless harmonies are simply stunning. The evocative bridge includes the uplifting 'High above the forest lie the pastures of the sun', a line of which Jon Anderson might have been proud. Unusually, the song title appears in the last line of the verse rather than the chorus. In 2016, Hayward said that he never gave this song much attention until he met someone who became very emotional about it. He decided to try it in his solo concerts, and it resonated with the audience. He said it also helped put his own life into perspective.

'My Song' (Mike Pinder)

Fittingly, it's another Pinder mini-epic to close the album. Like 'Melancholy Man' it's a very personal song and instrumentally a return to the majesty of 'The Voyage'. Opening with mournful Mellotron and piano, Pinder's plaintive vocal has a spiritual resonance, but essentially it's a tribute to life. The instrumental sequence is jaw-dropping with a hushed flute melody that's achingly beautiful and superbly orchestrated. The grandiose Mellotron and guitar exchanges put many progressive rock songs around at the time to shame. Six minutes and twenty seconds of musical nirvana that flies by, it competes with 'One More Time to Live' as the album's most ambitious track.

Unsurprisingly given its complexity, in the subsequent tours it did not replace 'Have You Heard' or 'Melancholy Man', both of which had become staples of the band's repertoire. In Europe, this was the B-side of the August 1971 single 'The Story in Your Eyes', although curiously in America they went with 'Melancholy Man' from the previous album. Either way, it continues the tradition of a Pinder song providing the flipside to a Hayward or Lodge single.

Related Tracks:

'The Dreamer' (Justin Hayward, Ray Thomas)

This song was a bonus track on the remastered CD reissues of *Every Good Boy Deserves Favour* in 2007 and 2008, along with the 'Original Version' of 'The Story in Your Eyes'. It's a mid-tempo song with a chugging, looped riff and a lead vocal from Thomas. The arrangement is solid and uncluttered, built around acoustic guitar, bass and drums with minimal vocal backing from Hayward. The no-frills approach works and the song is compelling in its own way, but it would have clearly been out of place as an album track.

Seventh Sojourn (1972)

Personnel:
Justin Hayward: vocals, acoustic & electric guitars
John Lodge: vocals, bass, acoustic guitar
Ray Thomas: vocals, flute, tambourine, saxophone, oboe
Graeme Edge: drums, percussion, vocals
Mike Pinder: vocals, Mellotron, Chamberlin, piano, harmonium
Produced by: Tony Clarke
Engineered by: Derek Varnals and Tony Clarke ('Isn't Life Strange')
Recorded at: Decca Tollington Park Studios, London, January – September 1972
UK release date: October 1972, USA release date: November 1972
Highest chart places: UK: 5, USA: 1
Running time: 39:29

If they were to match the quality of *Every Good Boy Deserves Favour*, the band and producer would have to be at the top of their game. They responded with probably their most stylish recording so far, the aptly titled *Seventh Sojourn*. Things got off to a hesitant start, however. When they returned to the studio in the summer of 1972 after touring, the earlier recordings, with the exception of 'Isn't Life Strange' (which had already been released as a single), were discarded and they began afresh. It was the first album to be recorded on sixteen track, and Mike Pinder especially appreciated the polished sound. He was also responsible for the album title. A personal favourite, when I bought the LP back in 1972, I played side one several times before listening to side two. They handle protest songs and sweet ballads with equal conviction. Justin Hayward and John Lodge, in particular, surpass themselves as songwriters. The latter was responsible for two successful singles, 'Isn't Life Strange' and 'I'm Just a Singer (In a Rock and Roll Band)', both of which sold well in Europe and North America. The album itself surprisingly stalled at number five in the UK but in December it became their first chart-topping album in the USA where it stayed for five weeks. Typically, the review in *Rolling Stone* magazine was almost damning in its praise. In the videos from this year, the band are far more casually dressed, with shoulder length hair and Pinder, Edge and Thomas sporting beards, capturing the look of the early '70s.

They had stiff competition that year with ground-breaking albums from Yes (*Close to the Edge*), Jethro Tull (*Thick as a Brick*), Stevie Wonder (*Talking Book*), ELP (*Trilogy*), Wishbone Ash (*Argus*), Genesis (*Foxtrot*) and Focus (*Focus 3*), which all struck a chord with record buyers (including the author). Although several of their contemporaries were recording side-long pieces, the Moodies songs generally averaged around five minutes each. They never once breached the ten-minute barrier, although the music was no less expansive for that.

Both 'Nights in White Satin' and *Days of Future Passed* were re-released in 1972, and during November and December, they had two albums in the American *Billboard* top twenty. 'Nights in White Satin' outsold both 'Isn't

Life Strange' and 'I'm Just a Singer (In a Rock and Roll Band)'. Also in 1972, producer Tony Clarke and engineer Derek Varnals mixed quadraphonic versions of the core seven albums *Days of Future Passed* to *Seventh Sojourn*. This was in anticipation of the format succeeding stereo in the home entertainment market, but that failed to happen. Decca, however, had the foresight to keep the quadraphonic masters and these were utilised for the 5.1 surround sound mixes issued on SACD in 2006 and 2007. In a 2014 interview for digitaltrends.com, Hayward who was involved with the remixes said, 'It really was Tony and Derek who did it, and I'm so glad they did, the quad version in such beautiful quality because it saved me a lot of time and pain.'

The *Seventh Sojourn* sessions saw another change of studio, although they remained in North London. The recording was not an altogether happy experience, however. There were tensions within the band, and Graeme Edge was going through a painful divorce. It would be five years before the band recorded another album. Call it creative tension if you will, but given the circumstances, the results are far better than one would expect and their most polished sounding album to date. To my ears, no UK band were making better-produced records.

That same year, Marlon Brando was chewing the scenery in his Oscar-winning role as *The Godfather*, but Mike Pinder was the undisputed godfather of the Mellotron. He had very strong competition in 1972, however, from the likes of Tony Banks (Genesis) and Rick Wakeman (Yes). In addition to the Mellotron Mark II and M-300, on this album, he plays the Chamberlin. It wasn't exactly the new keyboard in town, predating the Mellotron by a decade, but he chose it for its reliability. He achieves a symphonic sound unmatched by any other rock keyboardist in the 1970s.

With the success of this album, the band embarked on a lengthy world tour with extensive dates in America. Due to surmounting pressures and living in each other's pockets for the past seven years, after completing the tour in February 1974 the band decided to take a break from the annual treadmill of recording and touring. A compilation album, solo projects and a surprise live album would keep the flame burning over the ensuing three years.

Album Cover

An unusually bleak gatefold cover from Phil Travers with strange, weathered rock formations and no obvious focal point. The band name and album title are surprisingly faint. The brownish hues are carried over to the inner sleeve with some very lifelike headshot drawings of the five band members. Again, the credits read 'All instruments played by the Moody Blues'. The insert sheet is more colourful with the lyrics on one side and 25 photos of the band members on the other. Note Graeme Edge's keyboard-like electronic drum kit.

This was Travers' last cover for the band, although his artwork would grace later solo projects from Justin Hayward & John Lodge (1975) and Ray Thomas (1975 and 1976).

'Lost in a Lost World' (Mike Pinder)

For the first (and only) time, a Pinder song opens a Moody Blues album. Lyrically he doesn't beat around the bush; it's an indictment of revolutions and nationalistic disputes that inflict suffering on the innocent. Edge's simple but incisive drum pattern drives the song aided by Lodge's articulate bass motif and Hayward's rhythmic guitar embellishments. The verses are compelling, and the chorus with its counterpoint harmonies really draws the listener in. Appropriately, Pinder's haunting strings during the instrumental bridge forgo the usual lush timbres for a more ominous but still engrossing sound. This is even more apparent on the fully worked 'Instrumental Demo' that appeared as a bonus track on remastered CD reissues of *Seventh Sojourn* in the noughties.

'New Horizons' (Justin Hayward)

I fell in love with this song the first time I heard it. It's one of Hayward's most moving statements, full of beauty and emotion with unambiguous lines like 'I've got love enough for three'. The song was written as a way of coping with the recent death of his father and is therefore especially poignant for Hayward. Similar to 'You Can Never Go Home' on the last album, it features many of his trademark qualities including the song title in the last line of the verse rather than the chorus and a gorgeous middle-eight. The melodic guitar break in the instrumental bridge sums the song up beautifully, and the sustained Mellotron note seems to go on forever. Hayward plays a Martin D-35 twelve-string on this song and Edge's drum fills are superb.

This song was performed on the 1975 *Blue Jays* tour and regularly by the band during the 1980s. In the 1990s, it readily lent itself to an orchestral arrangement and is included on the 2003 deluxe edition of *A Night at Red Rocks with the Colorado Symphony Orchestra* as well as the original video.

'For My Lady' (Ray Thomas)

An uncomplicated, uncluttered and blissfully romantic song from Thomas. It was written shortly after his divorce and finds him yearning for a true love: 'Oh, I'd give my life so lightly for my gentle lady'. It's supremely elegant with a gossamer layering of flutes, strings, acoustic guitar and minimal vocal backing. The vocal bridge is heavenly, and percussion and bass are respectfully hushed throughout. The song's untainted emotion is a perfect example of an artist wearing his heart on his sleeve. As a single B-side, it was a calming respite to the A-side 'I'm Just a Singer (In a Rock and Roll Band)'.

'For My Lady' could have been performed live with Pinder playing the flute parts on the Mellotron while Thomas sang. However, it wasn't until the orchestral concert at the Red Rocks Amphitheatre in September 1992 that they felt they could do the song full justice. It's one of the highlights of the show with Thomas serenading from the heart and the orchestra woodwinds playing the countermelody. It would feature in subsequent orchestral shows up to Thomas' retirement in 2002.

'Isn't Life Strange' (John Lodge)

To close side one, another love song and one of their best known. Lodge wrote it one evening using an old harmonium he had in his house at the time. Pinder provides a very convincing string quartet sound on, if I'm not mistaken, the Chamberlin, with flute accompaniment from Thomas. To be honest, I always found the wavering effect on Lodge's voice at the end of each line in the verses an unnecessary distraction. Otherwise, they are a delight, a tranquil prelude to the wonderful choral harmonies that lead into the chorus. And it's one of Lodge's most memorable, no wonder the song was a hit worldwide. The edited single released in April 1972 reached number thirteen in the UK chart, helped by an appearance on the BBC TV show *Top of the Pops*.

Following a short linking section featuring just oboe, the song's second half is even better. The vocal waver has gone, Edge adds a drum roll to announce the choral hook and Hayward's soaring guitar during the lengthy coda is magnificent. The even longer eight-minute plus 'Original Version' on the CD reissues is well worth hearing. As well as an extended intro, Pinder's orchestral sequence is mesmerising, capturing the spirit of Pachelbel's 'Canon In D', upon which this song is reputedly based.

This song has been a constant feature in the band's setlist over the decades and received the full orchestral treatment on the 1993 release *A Night at Red Rocks with the Colorado Symphony Orchestra*. There is also a newly recorded version with the London Symphony Orchestra on the 1989 compilation *Greatest Hits*. The LSO version is also included on the 2014 box set *The Polydor Years: 1986-1992*.

'You and Me' (Justin Hayward, Graeme Edge)

Hayward's storming one-minute guitar intro launches side two in style, underpinned by a tight rhythm on a sea of strings. Although it's a song about needless suffering, the verses (sung by Hayward) and the chorus (Hayward, Lodge, Thomas and Pinder) in particular are exhilaratingly exuberant. As a show opener (which it never was) it would have been perfect, and one can only speculate on how it would have fared had it been released as a single. It did, however, make a live appearance during the 1975 *Blue Jays* tour. The double-tracked guitar harmonies that close the song are a real joy and a sign of Hayward's confidence as a player evident throughout the album. Even though compositionally it's a joint effort with guitar to the fore, Edge's rhythmic imprint is all over this song. The six and a half minute 'Backing Track' version on the 2007 and 2008 CD reissues is proof if needed that instrumentally it stands up in its own right.

'The Land of Make-Believe' (Justin Hayward)

This song is a simple message of love, peace and harmony with an added eco twist. Lyrical flute, acoustic guitar, chiming percussion and a prominent bass figure set the tone. Hayward's verses (with just a hint of echo) are gorgeous, and like the bird referenced in the lyrics, the chorus soars skywards. The double-tracked vocals in the later verses enhance the effect, and the electric guitar harmonics are beautiful. This is, without doubt, one of Hayward's most overlooked and undervalued songs, although it did feature briefly in the *Seventh Sojourn* tour and he would play an acoustic version in his later solo concerts.

'When You're a Free Man' (Mike Pinder)
One of Pinder's most intimate songs, and when you're talking about the man that wrote and sang 'Melancholy Man' and 'My Song', that's saying something. It's a relaxed song with light acoustic strumming, oboe and hypnotic strings. The lyrics echo the message of the previous track, this is a songwriter and musician clearly at peace with the world and himself. It also featured for a spell in the subsequent world tour. In addition to tasteful rhythm work from Lodge and Edge, it features some of Hayward's most classy guitar playing and the fluid solo around the halfway mark is no exception. He even adds a touch of distortion to close the song. It would have been a perfect song to end the album, but John Lodge has a message for the band's overzealous fans.

'I'm Just a Singer (In a Rock and Roll Band)' (John Lodge)
The Moody Blues are of course more than a rock and roll band and Lodge more than just a singer, but the message is clear. It's a riposte to their more fanatical fans who saw the band as gurus, reading all kinds of meanings into their lyrics. This song, followed by 'Nights in White Satin', 'Legend of a Mind' and 'Question' would close the main part of the band's shows for many years to come. It begins with Edge's drum solo which is off the starting blocks like an accelerating train with Lodge's propulsive bass riff joining the fray. All four singers combine to add weight to both the verses and the chorus which boasts a superb countermelody from Lodge. In the official video (which is a gas) Thomas is wielding a saxophone (which he doesn't play on the record) and the way Pinder pounds the keys, you would think they were still an R&B band. Hayward's guitar really rocks, and the ending is a barely controlled wall of cacophony. It was released as a single in January 1973, reaching a respectable twelfth position in the American *Billboard* chart and 36 in the UK. The single would be the last record from the band before their sabbatical.

Related Tracks:

'Island' (Justin Hayward)
Tentatively recorded for the 1973 follow-up album that never was, this is a haunting and neglected ballad. It surfaced as a bonus track on CD reissues of *Seventh Sojourn* in the noughties. During the verses, Pinder's strings have rarely sounded sweeter. They become more menacing in the lengthy instrumental coda that could easily pass as one of John Barry's orchestral

cues for a Bond movie. Even at four and a half minutes, the song sounds half finished, a telling indication that it was never fully developed. It's a pity there were no more gems like this hiding in the vaults. The 2007 and 2008 CDs also include alternate versions of 'Isn't Life Strange', 'You and Me' and 'Lost in a Lost World'.

After 50 years, the seminal *Days of Future Passed* makes a triumphant return to the stage. A superb live recording from Toronto in July 2017 was released in March 2018 in both audio and video formats. (*Eagle Rock*)

Left: The Moody Blues' changing musical styles is reflected in the album artwork of the 1960s. *The Magnificent Moodies* cover finds the band waiting at the jetty, but the boat had already departed as far as the R&B boom was concerned. *(Decca)*

Right: Should *Days of Future Passed* be aimed at rock fans or classical fans? The label couldn't decide, as reflected in the disparate elements of the cover artwork. *(Deram)*

Left: The psychedelic artwork, the first by artist Phil Travers, is only one clue as to the diverse musical content of *In Search of the Lost Chord*. The success of this album, in particular, indicated that the future was bright for the band. *(Deram)*

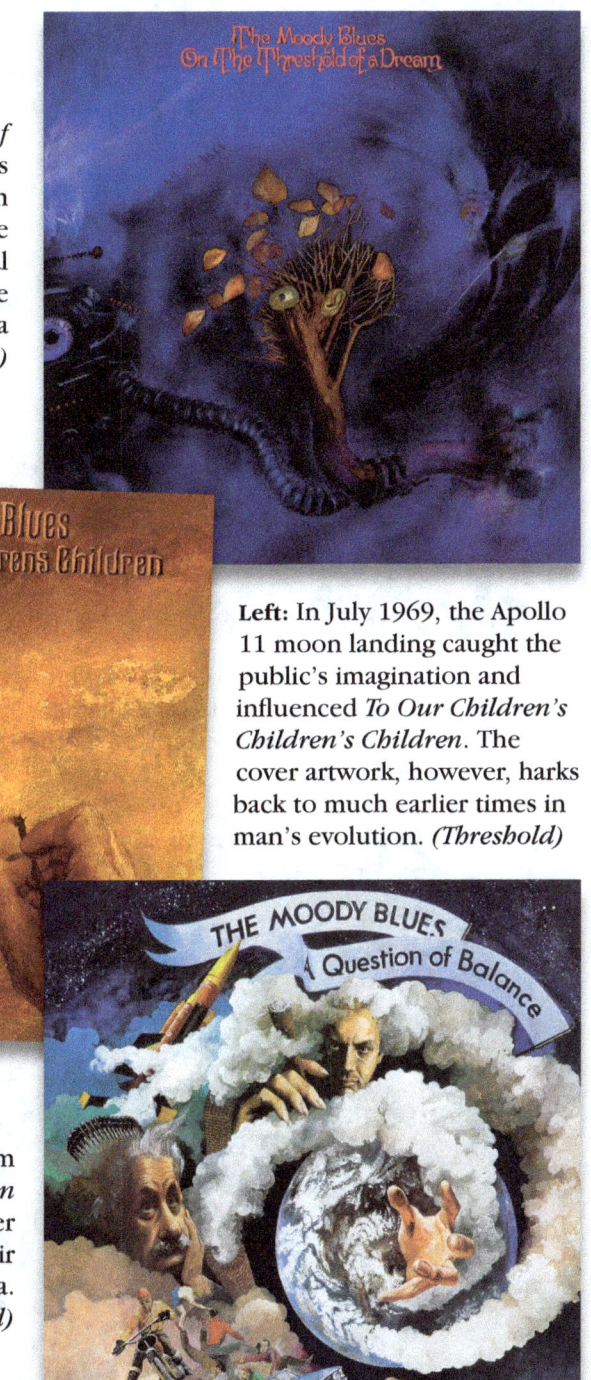

Right: *On the Threshold of a Dream* was the band's first UK number one album and the author's favourite from the 1960s. The original LP included a twelve-page booklet rather than a standard lyric sheet. *(Deram)*

Left: In July 1969, the Apollo 11 moon landing caught the public's imagination and influenced *To Our Children's Children's Children*. The cover artwork, however, harks back to much earlier times in man's evolution. *(Threshold)*

Right: This band's first album of the 1970s, *A Question of Balance* was another UK number one and their first top five in America. *(Threshold)*

Above: The Moodies mark one circa 1964 with Ray Thomas (centre) in particular, looking more apprehensive than 'magnificent'.
Below: The Moody Blues mark two in 1967. The 1920's style gangster outfits give little indication of the direction in which the band were heading.

Right: Justin Hayward singing 'Question' on the BBC TV programme *It's Lulu*, first aired on 29 August 1970. *(BBC)*

Left: John Lodge during the band's landmark performance at the Isle Of Wight Festival on 30 August 1970. *(Eagle Rock)*

Right: Mike Pinder and Ray Thomas from the official promotional video for 'I'm Just a Singer (In a Rock and Roll Band)' in 1972. *(Universal Records)*

Left: *Every Good Boy Deserves Favour* is quite possibly the author's favourite Moody Blues album. It also boasts Phil Travers' best cover artwork for the band. *(Threshold)*

Right: *Seventh Sojourn* was the last album before the five-year hiatus, and the bleak artwork was Travers' final cover for the band. Containing some of their best ballads, it's a quintessential Moody Blues album. *(Threshold)*

Left: Not strictly a Moody Blues album, *Blue Jays* was nonetheless a superb stopgap before the next album proper, which followed three years later. *(Threshold)*

Right: Undaunted by the onset of punk and new wave, 1978's *Octave* carried on from where the pre-hiatus albums left off. It was Mike Pinder's swansong with the band, and tellingly, he is hidden from view on the cover photo. *(Decca)*

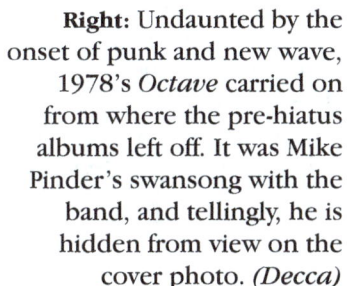

Left: It was the early 80s, and *Long Distance Voyager* reflected the musical styles of the time. Patrick Moraz takes over the keyboard reins for the first of five albums. *(Threshold)*

Right: Like the previous album, *The Present* utilised a borrowed piece of artwork for the cover and again incorporated the Voyager space probe. *(Threshold)*

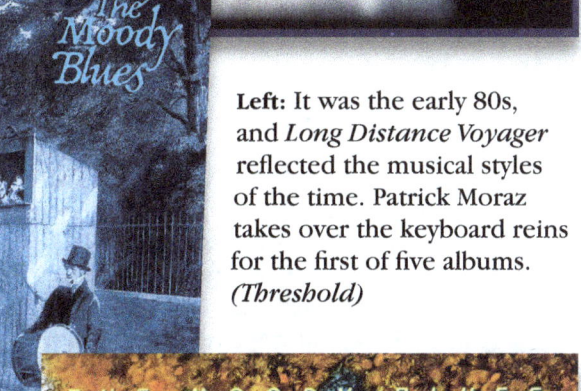

Left: The *Every Good Boy Deserves Favour* 1971-1972 UK tour programme. The front cover. Note the support band Hotlegs who would find fame and fortune later in the 1970s after changing their name to 10cc. *(Geoffrey Feakes)*

Right: The back cover of the *Every Good Boy Deserves Favour* 1971-1972 UK tour programme with the Moody Blues pictured in Cobham, Surrey. *(Geoffrey Feakes)*

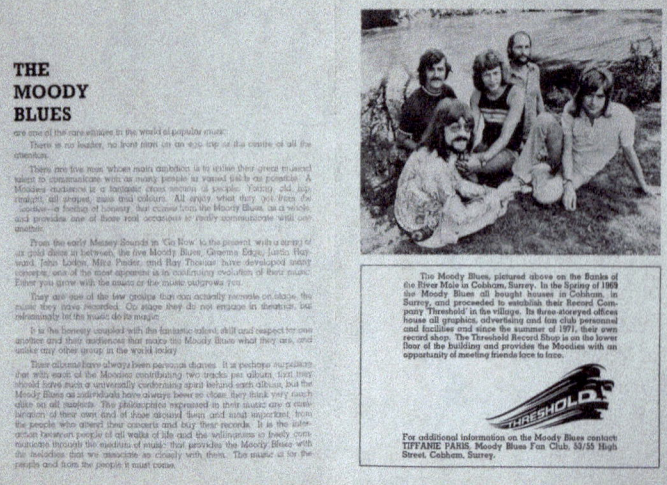

Left: The inner pages of the *Every Good Boy Deserves Favour* 1971-1972 UK tour programme, featuring the story of Threshold Records. *(Geoffrey Feakes)*

Right: The lacklustre cover artwork for the *Octave* UK tour programme was an advertisement for the 1979 compilation album *Out of This World*. *(Geoffrey Feakes)*

Below: Inner pages of the *Octave* UK tour programme with Patrick Moraz in the lineup. *(Geoffrey Feakes)*

Left: A reflective Justin Hayward from the 1988 promotional video for the 'No More Lies' single, filmed in glorious black and white *(Universal Records.*

Right: John Lodge in full voice from the 'No More Lies' video. *(Universal Records)*

Left: Hayward with Patrick Moraz in the background in the 'No More Lies' video. The tiny keyboard is a far cry from the large rig Moraz used on stage with both the Moody Blues and Yes. *(Universal Records)*

Above: The video for the 1988 single 'I Know You're Out There Somewhere' is probably the band's most entertaining. Although Ray Thomas appears playing tambourine, he never actually performed on the song. The video portrays a younger version of the Moody Blues with actor Ben Daniels (pictured far right) as Justin Hayward. *(Universal Records)*
Below Left: Patrick Moraz and Graeme Edge in the video looking a little lost and bewildered. *(Universal Records)*
Below Right: Hayward in front of a sign for the famous Marquee Club, where the Moody Blues first performed in London in 1964, towards the end of the 'I Know You're Out There Somewhere' video. *(Universal Records)*

Left: *The Other Side of Life* and the single 'Your Wildest Dreams' in particular captured the imagination of the MTV generation and brought a younger audience to the band. This was the third, and last studio album cover to feature images of the band members. *(Polydor)*

Right: Although *Sur la mer* included the hit single 'I Know You're Out There Somewhere', it was the first album since *The Magnificent Moodies* not to enter the American *Billboard* top 30. *(Polydor)*

Left: The first of two albums in the 1990s, *Keys of the Kingdom* was the last to include Patrick Moraz. His photo is absent from the rear cover, having been dismissed from the band during the recording sessions. *(Threshold)*

Right: The aptly titled *Strange Times* was the band's penultimate album. It was the last to feature founding member Ray Thomas who retired from the band three years later. *(Threshold / Universal)*

Left: The final studio album *December* was a seasonal offering that's rather better than the uninspired artwork would suggest. Following poor sales, It was repackaged in the UK with the compilation album *Ballads* *(Universal)*

Right: The band's first live album *Caught Live + 5* was a long time coming but it was generally worth the wait. The fish out of water cover artwork struck a chord with Yes fans. *(Decca)*

Above: Jusin Hayward (acoustic guitar and cravat) from a performance of 'Tuesday Afternoon' in Toronto during the 2017 *Days of Future Passed* 50th Anniversary tour. *(Eagle Rock)*

Below: Graeme Edge on drums during the Toronto concert on the 2017 *Days of Future Passed* 50th Anniversary tour. *(Eagle Rock)*

Above: John Lodge playing a Fender bass guitar during the Toronto concert on the 2017 *Days of Future Passed* 50th Anniversary tour. *(Eagle Rock)*
Below: The Moody Blues and the Toronto World Festival Orchestra in full swing during the Toronto concert on the 2017 *Days of Future Passed* 50th Anniversary tour. *(Eagle Rock)*

Left: An autographed publicity photo of the four piece line-up from the 1990's.

Below: The changing face and price of front row tickets in a single decade. £1 in 1972 for the *Every Good Boy Deserves Favour* tour and £6.50 in 1979 for the *Octave* tour. *(Geoffrey Feakes)*

Right: A souvenir pin badge from the *Octave* tour, which has survived longer than the T-shirt. *(Geoffrey Feakes)*

Justin Hayward & John Lodge – Blue Jays (1975)

Personnel:
Justin Hayward: guitar, vocals
John Lodge: bass, guitar, vocals
Jim Cockey: violin
Tim Tompkins: Cello
Tom Tompkins: viola
Kirk Duncan: piano
Graham Deakin: drums
Peter Knight: orchestra conductor
Produced by: Tony Clarke
Engineered by: Derek Varnals and Dave Baker
Recorded at: Threshold Studios, Decca, London, June – December 1974
UK and USA release date: March 1975
Highest chart places: UK: 4, USA: 16
Running time: 47:12

Although this is not strictly a Moody Blues album, I felt compelled to include it here. Without wishing to downplay the significance of the other solo projects from this period (which are discussed later in the book), it closely mirrors the sound, style and quality of the band recordings. Released roughly halfway through the band's sabbatical, it also conveniently bridges the five and a half year void between *Seventh Sojourn* and *Octave*. Justin Hayward originally planned to collaborate with Mike Pinder, but the keyboardist declined to be involved. As well as being a personal favourite of this author, its credentials are impeccable. Hayward and Lodge combine their vocal and songwriting talents for the first and only time outside the band. Had the band not opted to take time out after *Seventh Sojourn*, several of these songs could have ended up on the proposed follow-up. Tony Clarke and Derek Varnals are on production and engineering duties respectively, Phil Travers contributes some gorgeous artwork and to cap it all, a full-blown orchestra features on several tracks with Peter Knight returning from *Days of Future Passed* as conductor. The album title is a subtle play on words that references the band and Hayward and Lodge, whose Christian names both begin with 'J'. Unsurprisingly, during the UK tour to promote the album, they included several Moodies songs in the setlist.

It was recorded at the new state of the art Threshold Studios, which had recently been rebuilt from Decca's old Studio One under Clarke's direction. Decca chairman Sir Edward Lewis had gifted it to the band in appreciation of their record sales. *Blue Jays* was very popular on its release, almost matching the band's own record sales. Hayward's 'I Dreamed Last Night' did moderately well as a single in the USA and his song 'Blue Guitar', released six months after the album and credited to Hayward and Lodge, was added to CD reissues as a bonus track.

The album is an appealing balance between expansive, orchestral songs and delicate ballads. As well as individual compositions from Hayward and Lodge, it features two co-written songs for the first time. Although Hayward contributes five songs to Lodge's three, in terms of total playing time, they both average roughly the same and at 47 minutes long, they certainly couldn't have crammed another note on the original LP. Song titles like 'Remember Me (My Friend)', 'My Brother', 'You' and 'Saved by the Music' seem to emphasise a camaraderie and a common goal shared by the pair.

The deluxe edition of the 2013 *Timeless Flight* box set includes a disc dedicated to the UK *Blue Jays* tour recorded at Lancaster University in December 1975. Four *Blue Jays* songs are included plus 'Blue Guitar', the other eight are Moody Blues songs. It's not the full concert, however, as several *Blue Jays* songs performed in the first half of the set are missing. Compared with the mammoth trek that followed the *Seventh Sojourn* album, it was a modest two-month tour of medium size halls and universities with a backing band that included members of Trapeze.

Album Cover

This is a rare instance where Phil Travers includes group members in his cover artwork. Justin Hayward and John Lodge are depicted looking out from a ruined archway onto a picturesque hillside with a setting sun above. The gatefold rear cover continues the same scene. It's almost a mirror image of the front, but now it's a twilight sky with a bright moon, and the hillside has been replaced with jagged rocks. The inner sleeve is most striking with two full-size headshot photos of Hayward and Lodge with possibly the most coiffed hairstyles you'll likely to see gracing an album sleeve. A splendid four-page insert has shots of the individual musicians plus variations of the cover art on the outside and the lyrics on the inside.

'This Morning' (Justin Hayward)

A sedate opening with gently picked acoustic guitar, piano and skipping hi-hat gives way to soaring strings and sanguine guitar harmonies. Add a catchy chorus, and suddenly we are in Moody Blues territory. Strings, woodwind and Lodge's warm bass figure are discreetly integrated into the lengthy instrumental coda. Hayward's lucid guitar break is the icing on the cake, and the sustained violins at the end beautifully echo 'New Horizons' on *Seventh Sojourn*. A stripped-down version was performed on the subsequent tour.

'Remember Me (My Friend)' (Justin Hayward, John Lodge)

This song was the B-side to the 'I Dreamed Last Night' single released the following month. A heavenly introduction of strummed acoustic guitar and joint harmonies for both the slow-burning verses and the infectious chorus. Although it's the first song credited to the pair, it seems to owe more to Lodge's style of songwriting than Hayward's, especially the repetitive chorus.

That said, the latter contributes some beautifully controlled lead guitar. The almost acapella finale is divine. Contrary to the title, the line in the song is actually 'I am your friend, you must remember me'. The track was performed during the UK *Blue Jays* tour at the end of 1975.

'My Brother' (Justin Hayward)
This is a deceptively laid-back tune from Hayward. It has a clear message (to an absent keyboard player perhaps?) with lines like, 'So far that our voices are divided by an ocean' (Pinder had relocated to America in 1974). He's supported by sweet, Eagles-style harmonies, organ, searing guitar lines and Graham Deakin's agile drumming. Like the previous song, this featured in the set list of the subsequent *Blue Jays* tour.

'You' (John Lodge)
With its see-sawing strings and jaunty piano, instrumentally this has a distinct Country feel. Even Hayward's guitar playing has a Country twang and once again Deakin's drumming is superb. The upbeat chorus is undeniably catchy, but somehow Lodge sounds like he's trying just a little too hard to please. The instrumental outro, however, is sublime. They breathed new life into the song during the 1975 *Blue Jays* tour.

'Nights Winters Years' (Justin Hayward)
The album's highpoint in my view, this was clearly an attempt to recapture the majesty of Hayward's most famous song. It features a double-tracked vocal backed by a full orchestra and piano with a sweeping grandeur that evokes the combined might of 'Nights in White Satin' and 'Late Lament'. At a little over three and a half minutes, it never seemed quite long enough, which is perhaps why I always felt compelled to play it over again. A stunning way to end side one of the vinyl LP, although, in my opinion, it would have been more fitting as the album finale.

Two years later, Peter Knight would provide the orchestrations on the Carpenters' stunning version of 'Calling Occupants of Interplanetary Craft'.

'Saved by the Music' (John Lodge)
A barnstorming orchestral intro appropriately opens side two before subsiding into the piano-led verses with Lodge sounding typically melancholic. He's joined by Hayward for the foot-tapping chorus, which couldn't be more jubilant, with the strings riffing for all their worth, assisted by Kirk Duncan's lively piano. It's joyfully infectious, and Hayward's guitar break at the halfway mark is superb. The final chorus with vibrant harmonies and energetic flute playing concludes the song on a breathless note. In my opinion, this is Lodge's best contribution to the album. It has a similar sentiment to John Miles' song 'Music', a big hit in Europe the following year. It also proved to be a rousing show opener on the subsequent tour.

'I Dreamed Last Night' (Justin Hayward)
Another standout song and no wonder it was released as a single in April that year. It's a heart-wrenching love song with Hayward's emotive vocal backed by acoustic guitar and a sweeping orchestral arrangement. The strings and brass soar to new heights in a typically strong middle-eight and who can deny the power of lines like 'If there's a time and a place to begin love, it must be now'. Unlike the separate recording sessions for *Days of Future Passed*, Hayward performed this song with the orchestra for the recording. It was played, sans the orchestra, on the *Blue Jays* tour.

'Who Are You Now' (Justin Hayward)
If Hayward wanted to emulate the refined sound of Simon and Garfunkel, he couldn't get any closer than this. It's a delicate ballad with beautifully understated acoustic guitar and strings with exquisite lyrics like, 'Who are you now, first love of mine'. There's even a brooding cello solo at the midway point. At just two and a half minutes it's short, and most definitely sweet. Hayward would continue the quest for his first love in 1988 with 'I Know You're Out There Somewhere'. This song, along with 'New Horizons', and 'Emily's Song', provided a mellow start to the second half of the show during the *Blue Jays* tour.

'Maybe' (John Lodge)
If 'Nights Winters Years' on side one was Hayward's symphony for voice and orchestra, Lodge responds with his own mini-concerto. A regal orchestral intro echoes the classical baroque period, subsiding for Lodge's hushed verses with a backing of harp, celestial organ, woodwinds and strings. It builds slowly to the stately chorus with the orchestra in celebratory mood with jaunty strings and brass rising to the surging finale. One of the most unconventional songs in the Moody Blues canon, although stylistically it sits comfortably alongside 'Isn't Life Strange'.

'When You Wake Up' (Justin Hayward, John Lodge)
The final song on the album, it was also commandeered for the B-side of the 'Blue Guitar' single. It begins promisingly with Hayward's vocal joined by Lodge for the lovely stop-start verses with melodious lead guitar to the fore. The Moody Blues' trademark wordless harmonies have been mostly absent so far, but they are very much in evidence here, providing the choral hook. What the song lacks, however, is a memorable chorus, and with seemingly nowhere to go, it simply fades away. A somewhat disappointing ending to an otherwise superb album. This song also closed the main part of the set during the *Blue Jays* tour before the encore, 'Question'.

Related Tracks:

'Blue Guitar' (Justin Hayward)
Although credited to Hayward & Lodge, the latter is conspicuously absent from

this single released in September 1975. Hayward (guitar, lead vocals) is backed by the band 10cc, namely Lol Creme (guitar, vocals), Kevin Godley (drums, vocals), Graham Gouldman (bass, vocals) and Eric Stewart (keyboards, vocals). It was produced by the band at their famed Strawberry Studios in Stockport, Manchester. The label on the record also credits Tony Clarke as co-producer.

10cc released the hugely successful 'I'm Not in Love' earlier that same year, and clearly the intention was to have some of that magic rub off onto this song. Anyone misreading the title as 'Blues Guitar' will be in for a surprise. 'Blue Guitar' is a dreamy ballad with soaring strings and Hayward's voice strongly to the fore. Although the intro is clearly Hayward's Gibson ES-335, the trebly guitar soloing sounds more like 10cc, no doubt due to Eric Stewart's engineering.

Although America remained unconvinced, it reached a respectable eighth position in the UK singles chart. The picture sleeve features a blue version of the ES-335 against a painted sky with a cloud shaped like a guitar. Although uncredited, it looks very much like the work of Phil Travers. When the song was promoted on the 1975 ITV music show *Supersonic*, an amused Lodge is onstage with Hayward, miming acoustic guitar and backing vocals.

Octave (1978)

Personnel:
Justin Hayward: vocals, acoustic & electric guitars, keyboards
John Lodge: vocals, bass, keyboards
Ray Thomas: vocals, flute, harmonica, tambourine
Graeme Edge: drums, percussion, vocals
Mike Pinder: vocals, organ, synthesizer, Mellotron, piano, keyboards
Additional personnel:
Robert A. Martin: horns, saxophones
Dr. Terry James: conductor & string arranger
Jimmy Haskell: conductor & string arranger
Produced by: Tony Clarke
Engineered by: Gary Ladinsky, Chris Brunt, Richard Kaplan, Pete Carlson, Dennis Hanson
Recorded at: The Record Plant, Los Angeles; Indigo Ranch Recording Studios, Malibu, October 1977 – April 1978
UK and USA release date: June 1978
Highest chart places: UK: 6, USA: 13
Running time: 46:09

In July 1977, *Melody Maker* magazine ran the headline 'Moody Blues to re-form'. This was the band's long-awaited comeback studio album and their first in over five years. Although the *Caught Live + 5* album, released the previous year, had been reasonably successful, it was important that they re-establish themselves following the lengthy break. This was a changed musical environment in which disco and punk were the flavours of the day and *Saturday Night Fever* and *Grease* were sweeping all before them. Fortunately, the material is strong, if noticeably less lush, due in part to the lack of full participation by Mike Pinder, whose contribution is noticeably muted throughout. Following the solo albums, Pinder, in particular, found it difficult to make any meaningful contributions to the songs from the other band members. They, in turn, perceived this as a lack of enthusiasm and commitment on his part. As a result, strings, horns (and saxes) feature on a Moody Blues album for the first time since *Days of Future Passed*. Instrumentation apart, with one or two exceptions (Justin Hayward's 'Top Rank Suite' for example), everyone's songwriting is true to form, maintaining the tried and trusted format of *Seventh Sojourn* and *Every Good Boy Deserves Favour*. As usual, there are compositions from all band members, although, with four contributions, Hayward dominates.

The album is one of the more credible late 1970s releases from any of the old guard of bands that had come to prominence in the late '60s/early '70s. Tony Clarke is once more behind the studio desk, and he and the band travelled to California to record the album with no less than five engineers credited. This was, in part, a concession to accommodate Pinder who had relocated there in

1974. The recording was dogged with problems, including a fire at the Record Plant in Los Angeles, severe weather conditions after relocating to Pinder's 24-track Malibu studio and Clarke going through a personal crisis compounded by being far from home.

The album was well received by a loyal fanbase and sales were strong across many regions, including the UK and USA, eventually reaching platinum. Two singles, 'Steppin' in a Slide Zone' and 'Driftwood', reached the lower regions of the North American charts, although they failed to make an impression in the UK. In Canada, where the band remained especially popular, a big promotional campaign included the pressing of 40,000 blue vinyl copies. The response from the UK rock press was mixed, not helped by Decca's lavish garden party to launch the album, which was out of step with the times. In America, the album was mauled by *Rolling Stone* magazine.

In September the previous year, the band received a backhanded compliment of sorts when Barclay James Harvest included the song 'Poor Man's Moody Blues' on their 1977 album *Gone to Earth*. It was guitarist John Lees' response to a comment from a journalist who later admitted that he hadn't actually listened to the album he was reviewing. The song's resemblance to 'Nights in White Satin' is uncanny but apparently, Hayward was not best pleased. Earlier in their career, BJH performed 'Nights in White Satin' in their live set.

Octave was significant in that it marked the start of the next phase in the band's career. The previous eight albums (including *The Magnificent Moodies*) had been released over a period of eight years whereas the final eight, including this one, would be spread out over 25 years. This was typical for many bands during the 1980s and 1990s where a declining output of studio recordings would be supplemented by live albums, compilations, videos and later, DVDs.

It was, sadly, both Mike Pinder and Tony Clarke's swansong. The founding keyboardist was prepared to continue making records, but he was reluctant to return to the stage, deciding that family life was more important. With a tour of the USA and mainland Europe looming, he took his leave. Swiss keyboard virtuoso Patrick Moraz was recruited in July 1978 (although not announced by the press until September) as a touring replacement. He would also play on the next five albums in his thirteen-year tenure with the band. The *Octave* tour did not reach the UK until October 1979 where they played a handful of dates, the shows being the first concerts in their homeland in six years. In November 1979, I travelled down to London to witness a superb performance at the Wembley Arena.

Album Cover

This was the first without Phil Travers and a clear departure from his old school style of artwork. The design and art, which is credited to 'Kosh', is very much of its time with bold graphics and simple, but eye-catching, images. Taking its cue from Lodge's 'Steppin' in a Slide Zone' and Pinder's 'One Step into the Light', the band are shown walking through a doorway into a brightly lit environment on the front cover, only to emerge on the double spread inner cover. The album tracks are listed on the rear cover for the first time since *In Search of the Lost Chord*. The standard insert sheet has the lyrics and album credits on one side and the band logo from the front cover on the reverse.

'Steppin' in a Slide Zone' (John Lodge)

Following his two hit songs on *Seventh Sojourn*, appropriately it's another single from Lodge that opens the album. Released two weeks before the album, it slipped into the top 40 on the USA *Billboard* chart. It's cut from the same cloth as 'I'm Just a Singer (In a Rock and Roll Band)' updated for the late '70s and it was Lodge's response to new wave and punk rock. As opening statements go, they don't come much bolder than this. The eerie intro featuring the sound of a door closing and a car driving away followed by an ominous synth line and bluesy guitar is very Pink Floyd. From here on it's all Moody Blues with Edge's drum volley bringing the band in with all guns blazing. Lodge's chant-like verses are spliced with the euphoric chorus performed by all four singers. The rhythmic hand clapping bridge section is simple but effective. The Moodies are back, and they mean business.

Unsurprisingly, this song opened the shows on the subsequent American tour and would become an almost permanent fixture in the band's setlist. When performed with a full orchestra, it benefits from an extended, magisterial intro. This was carried over into the band only concerts in the noughties where flautist Norda Mullen really came into her own.

'Under Moonshine' (Ray Thomas)

And now for something completely different. This song is a typically elegant ballad from Thomas with prominent strings (yes strings, not Mellotron), flute, guitar and synth, lifted by Edge and Lodge's tasteful rhythm work. The extended coda is a delight with plucked strings and memorable guitar and synth exchanges from Hayward and Pinder to play out. This would have sat comfortably on either of Thomas' mid-'70s solo albums and may well have been a leftover from that period. The opening line is, to my knowledge, the only time he had difficulty pronouncing the sound 'r' in a song.

'Had to Fall in Love' (Justin Hayward)

This bittersweet ballad is Hayward wearing his heart on his sleeve as only he can. The way his voice drops at the end of each verse adds a touching sadness to the lyric. Thomas' sublime harmonica playing has a rare leading role, backed by a delicate acoustic guitar phrase, Lodge's walking bass line and Edge's discreet drumming. The haunting choral harmonies in the chorus and bridge are stunning. In the 2006 *Classic Artists: The Moody Blues* documentary, Pinder discusses one of Hayward's songs for the album which he says was 'A good song, but the guitar part was monotonous and went all the way through'.

As a result, he was unable to provide a Mellotron or piano part that would fit. He doesn't name the song, but given the repeated guitar line and absence of keyboards, I believe this is the one he was referring to. In his solo concerts, Hayward performs an acoustic version of this song to this day.

'I'll Be Level with You' (Graeme Edge)
This is a typically energetic rocker from Edge and a throwback to 'After You Came' on *Every Good Boy Deserves Favour*. Like that song, the lively verses and memorable chorus boast fluid, unison singing from the rest of the band with Hayward taking the lead in the middle-eight. The words are a plea for a world free from pain, hate and suffering. The staccato riff, fuzzed guitar, swirling synths and Hayward's expressive solo in the instrumental bridge are superb and very proggy, as is Pinder's stately keyboard outro. This song provided a triumphant start to the second half of the set during the subsequent *Octave* tour.

'Driftwood' (Justin Hayward)
To close side one, another song that looks to the past, most obviously 'New Horizons'. This features prominent saxophone, however, for the first time on a Moodies song, courtesy of Robert Martin. It's a haunting ballad tinged with sadness, and the sax, horns and keyboards are sublime with suitably elegant bass and cymbal work from Lodge and Edge respectively. Hayward's guitar bridge has a hint of distortion that suits the song's melancholic tone and the counterpoint vocals linking the verse and chorus are inspired. This song, along with 'Nights in White Satin' and 'I Know You're Out There Somewhere', remains one of Hayward's personal favourites.

'Driftwood' was released as a single four months after the album and although it stalled outside the top 50 it had a seven-week run on the American *Billboard* chart. The promotional video is worth catching, if only to see Thomas and Moraz miming the saxophone and keyboard parts. The song was regularly played in concert until the 1986 *The Other Side of Life* tour and was resurrected in the 2010s.

'Top Rank Suite' (Justin Hayward)
An unusually retro-sounding song from Hayward provides a lively opening to side two of the original album. It's driven by Martin's energetic saxophone, guitar, piano, a foot-tapping beat and Lodge's nimble bass figure. The swing sound, boogie-woogie rhythm, twangy guitar and vocal harmonies capture the spirit of '60s dance halls that would have been familiar to Hayward in his teens. To be truthful, it never sounded like a Moody Blues song to me, and one's tolerance of sax is tested to the full, but it's hard not to be swept away by its infectious charm. It was performed on the *Octave* world tour with a harder rock sound, extended guitar solo and Moraz filling in for the absent sax. It was played along with 'I'm Your Man' and 'The Day We Meet Again', but all three were dropped soon after.

'I'm Your Man' (Ray Thomas)
This is a more contemporary sounding song from Thomas, and as a result, it has not dated as well as his earlier ballads which have a timeless quality. The relaxed pace and gentle flute are certainly on familiar ground, but the staccato organ motif at the end of each verse and smooth jazz guitar licks give it a late '70s sheen. Although the closing lines 'I'm yours, I'm simply yours' take it dangerously close to MOR territory, Thomas' passionate vocal and the ascending strings (arranged and conducted by Terry James) give the song its lift. The *Live in Seattle 1979* version recorded on 25 May 1979 on the *Octave* tour surpasses the original with the band in top form and Moraz's majestic Mellotron orchestrations.

'Survival' (John Lodge)
The verses here are deceptively laid-back but richly arranged with muted strings, synth, acoustic guitar and bass. Evocative lines like 'Shadows of days hanging endless in time' are some of Lodge's best. The orchestra builds with spiralling strings for the triumphant one-word choral hook. The band Yes also had a song called 'Survival' that closed their 1969 debut album and the chorus here has a similar feel. Everything about this song is a delight, including Jimmy Haskell's lush orchestrations, Hayward's harmonious guitar fills and Pinder's commanding, trumpet-like synth line in the chorus. Special mention should go to Lodge for his playing throughout the album. While he's perhaps better known for his talents as a singer and songwriter, his bass playing is both tasteful and inventive. During the *Octave* tour, this featured in the second half of the set amongst the band's more familiar songs.

'One Step into the Light' (Mike Pinder)
This was a song left over from Pinder's 1976 solo album *The Promise* and a longer version than the one here would appear on the 1996 CD reissue of that album. The Mellotron is more prominent on Pinder's version, which alone makes it worth seeking out. Although he may not have realised it at the time of recording, this was Pinder's parting shot for the band. It features his familiar thoughtful vocal and gradual layering of instruments. The rich arrangement includes glorious guitar harmonics, swelling Mellotron, piano, discreet percussion and a superb bass line. It's a song with a spiritual message, although I can't help thinking that the hippy-Christian tone is a result of too much time in the California sun. And who but Mike Pinder could get away with the line 'There's one thing I can do, play my Mellotron for you'. Although this line is backed by an organ-like sound, it was produced by Pinder's Mellotron Mark V. A fitting song on which to bow out.

'The Day We Meet Again' (Justin Hayward)
This, along with Hayward's other songs on the album demonstrate that the quality of his material had not been exhausted by the *Blue Jays* and *Songwriter*

solo projects. Although it's a song about lost love, the title is a perfect eulogy for the departing Mike Pinder. With strummed acoustic guitar and an ascending organ hook, it builds slowly from humble beginnings taking in haunting choral harmonies and Hayward's plaintive lead vocal. The measured double-tracked guitar solo around the two-minute mark is one of his best. The finale with its stirring strings, counterpoint harmonies, ringing guitar and the dexterous rhythm work of Edge and Lodge is superb. With a final sustained organ note from Pinder, it's a suitably powerful way to end the album. When performed during the *Octave* and *Long Distance Voyager* tours, the emotion was cranked up even higher. It made a strong comeback in the noughties with Hayward playing the opening keyboard refrain, and it usually followed 'The Voice' as the second song in the set.

Related Tracks:
None. The two singles 'Steppin' in a Slide Zone' b/w 'I'll Be Level with You' and 'Driftwood' b/w 'I'm Your Man' were all album tracks.

Long Distance Voyager (1981)

Personnel:
Justin Hayward: guitars, vocals
John Lodge: bass, vocals
Ray Thomas: flutes, harmonicas, vocals
Graeme Edge: drums
Patrick Moraz: keyboards
Additional personnel:
B.J. Cole: pedal steel guitar on 'In My World'
The New World Philharmonic: string section
Pip Williams: string arrangements
Dave Symonds: spoken voice on 'Reflective Smile'
Produced by: Pip Williams
Engineered by: Greg Jackman
Recorded at: Threshold Studios and RAK Studios, London, February 1980 – April 1981
UK and USA release date: May 1981
Highest chart places: UK: 7, USA: 1
Running time: 46:32

The 1980s had arrived. New wave, synth-pop and the new romantics were enjoying a flush of popularity (albeit short-lived), and many bands from the 1970s were simplifying their style, disbanding or morphing into different line-ups. Despite all this, the Moody Blues could still command allegiance from record buyers, especially in North America where this album reached number one in July 1981 on both sides of the border. Although the band had inevitably been pigeonholed with the prog-rock fraternity in the 1970s, it was their innate ability to produce quality, radio-friendly songs that would see them through the 1980s. They had also engaged the services of rock entrepreneur Jerry Weintraub for their American management.

Three years had elapsed since the release of the last album, and the band had filled the void with a busy touring schedule. With worldwide sales from the previous albums in excess of twenty million, they were in a position financially to record and release albums on their own terms. The extended *Octave* tour had also been very lucrative, especially the sold out concerts in America where they seldom played to less than 10,000 people and often in excess of 20,000. Arenas had replaced the provincial halls and universities of the late '60s and early '70s.

Ex-Yes keyboardist Patrick Moraz had been hired in 1978 to replace Mike Pinder for touring purposes and became a full-time member for the recording of this album. Fortunately, with his arsenal of keyboards, when it came to performing the older songs, the Swiss virtuoso was an adept Mellotron player, as he had displayed so beautifully on the song 'Soon' from Yes' *Relayer* album. Compared with Pinder's modest setup, on stage Moraz was utilising no less than ten keyboards including the Mellotron Mark V. He certainly makes his mark on this album, although it's his synth playing that's most evident. Similar to *Octave*, a string section was also utilised to give specific songs an orchestral gloss.

A good deal of the album was recorded in 1980 which, touring-wise, was a quiet year for the band. The lag between the last album and the recording of this one was due in part to Moraz living in Brazil and working on solo projects. It was the only time the band recorded at Threshold Studios, although *Blue Jays* was also recorded there. Former session guitarist and Status Quo producer Pip Williams and renowned engineer Greg Jackman were brought onboard, and they brought a sharpness and clarity of sound totally in keeping with the 1980s. Adding his trademark pedal steel guitar to one song is top session man B.J. Cole who also played on Ray Thomas' 1975 solo album *From Mighty Oaks* and the Graeme Edge Band's 1977 album *Paradise Ballroom*.

There was no shortage of material, being their longest studio recording to date with a strong showing from Thomas to close the album. His three linked songs were often performed together during the subsequent 1980's tours. Typically, however, the two Stateside top twenty singles lifted from the album, 'Gemini Dream' and 'The Voice', are from the pens of Justin Hayward and John Lodge. As the first three songs on the album were released as singles, clearly it was front-loaded with the most commercial tracks. It's a different sounding Moody Blues in many ways, due in part to the input from Moraz and Williams. Although the overall style is more mainstream, several tracks rank alongside some of their best work.

Album Cover

Designed by Cream based on a concept by the band, the blue-tinged cover painting across both sides of the gatefold sleeve is from the Arts Union, Glasgow. The Voyager space probe which had completed its flyby of Saturn in November 1980 can be just made out at the top of the front cover. Its inclusion was to provide a connection with the album title and several of the songs. The artwork includes several hidden images. The inner cover gatefold spread includes the lyrics with extracts from the cover painting next to each song title.

'The Voice' (Justin Hayward)

This is sleek, 1980s pop-rock and no wonder it reached number one on the American mainstream rock radio chart launched just a few months before. Moraz's synths are everywhere, providing the atmospheric intro, the instrumental hook and the showy embellishments. There is also a warm and welcome colouring of keyboard strings throughout. In addition to modern keyboard technology, Moraz claims Moog and Mellotron were used on this song, although to my ears there is little evidence of the latter. The instrumental intro certainly bears his stamp, taken from a longer piece he had previously composed. The choral harmonies are sharp, and Hayward's guitar fills workmanlike with Lodge and Edge's solid rhythm driving the song at a brisk pace. As opening songs go, it has a freshness that must have given expectant fans a welcome sigh of relief. The lyric also has a positive message that looks to the future.

This was the first of many songs of the 1980s that Hayward demoed at home using acoustic guitar and a click track. When presented to the rest of the band, they would play their parts to the same click track. Like 'Question', the song title was an afterthought when Hayward couldn't think of anything else to call it. Occasionally played back to back with 'Gemini Dream' in the 1980s, this song has hardly been out of the band's setlist. Following the turn of the millennium, it would often open each show.

'Talking Out of Turn' (John Lodge)
At seven minutes plus, this is Lodge's longest song to date. In November 1981 it was the third song from the album to be released as a single (edited by three minutes), but it failed to shift the same units as its predecessors. Moraz again provides the ambient intro which sounds like his old band Yes, leading into Pip William's rich string arrangement. Synths provide a bubbling, rhythmic undercurrent with Lodge's fragile but expressive verses contrasting with the robustly infectious chorus. Hayward's Stratocaster guitar solos are almost histrionic by his standards, and in the final minute, the high violins playfully paraphrase the choral hook. Played throughout the 1980s, this song occasionally opened the second half of the show following the intermission. Since the 1990s, it has made the occasional and welcome stage appearance with Lodge playing acoustic guitar.

'Gemini Dream' (Justin Hayward, John Lodge)
I must confess when I first heard this song back in the 1980s I wondered what the band were thinking of, but I suppose I've become more tolerant in my old age. It's synth-pop (the bouncing rhythm and Human League-like synth hook) meets the Electric Light Orchestra (the exuberant verses, radio-friendly chorus and Jeff Lynne stylised harmonies). There's nothing wrong with the sources per se, but it remains a strange concoction that hasn't dated particularly well. Reflecting the input of the two writers, the song has two themes, the joys of being on the road and shared love.

As a single, it sold well in North America, especially Canada where it reached number one. Like 'The Voice' It was helped by regular airplay, but without the same support in the UK, it didn't go anywhere. Throughout the 1980s it proved to be a popular stage song and regularly opened the band's shows. When performed live, the tricky chorus tests Hayward and Lodge's vocal abilities to the full. Along with 'The Voice', it was one of a handful of '80s songs performed during *A Night at Red Rocks with the Colorado Symphony Orchestra* in September 1992, although it didn't appear on the original CD.

'In My World' (Justin Hayward)
From the ridiculous to the sublime, you could say. A typically thoughtful ballad from Hayward with his one-chord strummed acoustic guitar providing a solid foundation. It's enriched by B.J. Cole's dreamy steel guitar and Moraz's lyrical synth lines. Hayward's lead guitar harmonises beautifully with Cole and provides a sumptuous extended solo around the five-minute mark. The rising choral harmonies and layering of instruments and voices are a delight, as is Edge's bell-like percussion. Although probably the least known song, for me this is the highlight of side one. Not to be outdone by Lodge, at seven minutes and twenty seconds, it comfortably matches 'Talking Out of Turn' in length.

'Meanwhile' (Justin Hayward)
Opening side two of the vinyl LP, another Hayward song. It's a breezy acoustic guitar and electric piano-led tune that recalls Gerry Rafferty's 'Get It Right Next Time'. A song of lost love and resignation, the subject and lines like 'I let love slip right through my fingers' are at odds with the jaunty chorus. Drums and bass are simple but effective, and there's a neat little Stratocaster guitar bridge while synths underscore the chorus. Not one of Hayward's most convincing songs it has to be said but an agreeable four minutes nonetheless. Like '22,000 Days' it found its way into the setlist for the *Long Distance Voyager* tour but went no further. It was, however, resurrected for the 'Voyage 2011 Precious Cargo Tour'.

'22,000 Days' (Graeme Edge)
This song is Edge's sound advice to live life to the full, although 22,000 days (a little over 60 years) does seem a little pessimistic for an average life span. The Led Zeppelin influenced intro is superb with a chugging riff and Edge's John Bonham-like stomp topped with Hayward's edgy lead guitar. Lodge sings the verses, joined by Thomas and Hayward for the muscular, chant-like chorus. Vocals are panned to the extreme left and right for the middle-eight followed by a quirky 'harmonica' solo (which sounds suspiciously like a synth). Speaking of which, Moraz's fingerprints are all over the song with inventive keyboard fills throughout, including a welcome solo at the three and a half minute mark.

'Nervous' (John Lodge)
In complete contrast, a beautiful ballad from Lodge in sad, bittersweet mood. It's a song of unrequited love, 'Please explain to me why you're always out of reach' with rippling acoustic guitar and flutes for the verses and romantic strings for the ridiculously catchy chorus. Like many of Lodge's better songs, it boasts a striking counterpoint choral hook and a vibrant bass line. Had it been recorded in the '70s, I feel sure it would have been released as a single. Like 'Gemini Dream', it also has echoes of Jeff Lynne (a fellow 'Brummie') and ELO. This ties with 'In My World' as the album's best offering, in my opinion, capturing the band's classic sound. As well as being played on the subsequent

tour, the song was revived for more recent concerts featuring gorgeous flute playing from Norda Mullen.

'Painted Smile' (Ray Thomas)
If this was the new wave 1980s, someone forgot to tell Ray Thomas. Playing the part of the sad clown, his quaintly old-fashioned words and vocal delivery are accompanied by lyrical synth flourishes and superb, waltz-like piano. Lodge enters into the spirit with a noble bass figure and at the halfway mark, Moraz's swirling keys take us on a carousel ride. The pontifical backing vocals and swing chorus are deliberately tongue-in-cheek, and Edge flays his kit before segueing into....

'Reflective Smile' (Ray Thomas)
Thomas takes a leaf out of Edge's book by including a poem. In the absence of Mike Pinder who previously handled such duties, radio DJ and friend of the band Dave Symonds does the honours as narrator. Moraz's Wurlitzer-like organ provides the appropriate backing, and we are introduced to...

'Veteran Cosmic Rocker' (Ray Thomas)
The song title, of course, refers to the phrase used to describe Thomas by a New York journalist. Edge's storming drum intro and crashing chords set the tone, joined by Lodge's pulsating bass line and together with Moraz's rhythmic piano they ensure the pace never lets up. The anthemic chorus borders on the absurd (and intentionally so), offset by Hayward's hard rock guitar. The highpoint, however, is the instrumental mid-section with a shuffle rhythm overlaid with back to back harmonica and flute solos and an exhilarating Middle Eastern flavoured sequence. It's like nothing else in the band's repertoire and Thomas' most esoteric song since 'Legend of a Mind' back in 1968. When performed live throughout most of the 1980s it allowed Moraz to show-off his keytar talents and usually closed the first half of the band's set on a high.

Related Tracks:
None. The three singles 'Gemini Dream' b/w 'Painted Smile', 'The Voice' b/w '22,000 Days' and 'Talking Out of Turn' b/w 'Veteran Cosmic Rocker' were all album tracks.

The Present (1983)
Personnel:
Justin Hayward: guitars, vocals
John Lodge: bass, vocals
Ray Thomas: flutes, harmonicas, vocals
Graeme Edge: drums
Patrick Moraz: keyboards
Produced by: Pip Williams
Engineered by: Greg Jackman
Recorded at: Strawberry Studios South, Dorking, March 1982 – December 1982
UK release date: August 1983, USA release date: September 1983
Highest chart places: UK: 15, USA: 26
Running time: 41:47

Album number eleven from the band and they are still going strong. Again, Justin Hayward and John Lodge are responsible for the majority of the songs, although Ray Thomas brings things to a satisfying close with linked tracks as he did on the previous album. Graeme Edge makes his usual single song contribution (with Thomas on vocals). In a partnership that had begun with the *Blue Jays* album, Hayward and Lodge were developing into a regular songwriting team. If there's a concept here, then time and space (regular themes for the band) would fit the bill. The album title neatly links with the title of the 1967 album *Days of Future Passed*, adding 'Present' to the 'Future' and 'Past' tenses.

His second album with the band, Patrick Moraz was staking his claim as a legitimate member. He had already proven himself to be an asset on stage with a flamboyant presence, moving lively around his semi-circular (Rick Wakeman influenced) keyboard rig. Although he sprinkles his magic dust all over this album, his style is far removed from Mike Pinder's symphonic calm, with little evidence of Mellotron or piano (normally Moraz's instrument of choice). They would still be played on stage, however.

Pip Williams and Greg Jackman were retained as producer and engineer respectively, although a change of recording venue brought them to Strawberry Studios South in Dorking, south-west of London. A converted cinema, it was opened in 1976 by 10cc members Graham Gouldman and Eric Stewart. Strawberry Studios in Stockport (where 'Blue Guitar' was recorded) had become so popular, 10cc established an alternate location to record their own albums with 1977's *Deceptive Bends* being the first.

For the Moody Blues, sales were beginning to slip worldwide, and in the USA it was their first album not to enter the *Billboard* top twenty since 1968's *In Search of the Lost Chord*. They were still able to pique the interest of record buyers, however, and it did respectable business in most countries, especially Canada, where it achieved gold status. The October review in *Rolling Stone* magazine was mostly positive, awarding it three stars. Two singles, 'Blue

World' and 'Sitting at the Wheel', had a modicum of success in several regions, although the third, 'Running Water' (released in America only), disappeared without a trace. This was very much the video age and promotional films for TV were produced for all three singles.

For me, this is the best of the quartet of albums from the 1980s. Like *Long Distance Voyager*, the synth-pop tendencies are kept mostly under control, although the next album *The Other Side of Life* would be a different story. It combines radio-friendly tunes (the two most popular singles conspicuously front the album) with ballads and more adventurous songs. The latter is best represented by two sets of linked tracks that open and close side two of the vinyl LP. A fair proportion of the songs were performed on the subsequent tour but were dropped soon after. Hayward, however, felt that they did not carry over the successful formula from the last album and for the next, there would be a change of producer.

Album Cover
The cover artwork with its blue and yellow hues takes images from Maxfield Parrish's painting 'Daybreak' (the two figures, columns and trees) and adds sci-fi elements, especially on the rear cover which features a flying saucer and the ubiquitous Voyager space probe. The inside gatefold spread includes the song lyrics against a star field background and Voyager travelling through space. The design is credited to The Studio, adding the words 'With all respect for Maxfield Parrish'.

'Blue World' (Justin Hayward)
The album kicks off in memorable style with Hayward's bright, upbeat song which lyrically seems to echo the cover artwork. It's fronted by Lodge's prominent, twangy bass line and Edge's crisp beat, although Moraz's synth flourishes are a tad overripe. Hayward delivers a measured vocal for the verses accompanied by sweet electric guitar embellishments on his 1964 Stratocaster. The chorus doesn't appear until two minutes in, but it's memorable and worth the wait. This song was the album's most obvious single and the first to be released (albeit drastically edited to just over three and a half minutes). In the UK it appeared in tandem with the album in August that year before stalling at number 35 in the chart. During the subsequent tours, it was placed in the latter part of the set amongst some of the band's more established songs before being replaced by 'The Other Side of Life' in 1986.

'Meet Me Halfway' (Justin Hayward, John Lodge)
This, on the other hand, was not a single release but it certainly had all the right credentials, and at a little over four minutes, there was no need for any editing. It's a really engaging, mid-tempo song with a strong vocal from Hayward and a catchy chorus, benefiting from Lodge's striking countermelody. The rhythm really swings, and the keyboard strings are a delight, as are the

tasty Mark Knopfler-like guitar fills. It seems to me that the songs Hayward and Lodge write separately are often stronger than those they write together, but this is one of their better joint efforts. Listen with a discerning ear, and you can identify their individual compositional contributions.

'Sitting at the Wheel' (John Lodge)
To my ears, this is one of Lodge's most misjudged efforts. It's undeniably lively in a foot-tapping way, but it's a curious hybrid of synth-pop (the reverb-heavy drum sound and Eurythmics style synths) and rock 'n' roll (Lodge's energetic, echo-laden chorus and Moraz's Fats Domino-inspired boogie-woogie piano). The Steven Greenberg Remix included on the 2008 CD reissue is even more offbeat with rhythmic elements reminiscent of the Flying Lizards' cover of 'Money' and the Sensational Alex Harvey Band's 'The Faith Healer'. Like his 1977 solo album *Natural Avenue*, later band albums would feature the occasional rock and roll song from Lodge, inspired by his early heroes Jerry Lee Lewis, Little Richard and Buddy Holly. Despite my doubts as to its merits, it vied with 'Gemini Dream' as the opening song during *The Present* tours before being dropped in 1986. Another edited single, it did better than 'Blue World' in America, reaching number 27 in the *Billboard* chart.

'Going Nowhere' (Graeme Edge)
Call me old fashioned, but in comparison, this is a real Moody Blues song. Surprisingly, it's from the pen of Graeme Edge, who's usually responsible for the band's heavier songs. It's a lovely acoustic guitar ballad with Thomas' mature lead vocal (one of his very best) complemented by Hayward and Lodge's heavenly choral harmonies. Moraz's symphonic scoring and the inventive percussive textures strike exactly the right tone for this bittersweet tale of love lost. A lovely way to close side one of the original vinyl disc. It was also the B-side of the singles 'Blue World' in the UK and 'Sitting at the Wheel' in the USA. The title proved to be an omen, although performed live, it was soon jettisoned to make way for songs from the next album.

'Hole in the World' (John Lodge)
A rare, if short (under two minutes), instrumental from Lodge ceremoniously opens side two. It's the first of two linked tracks with a striking martial drum pattern and rhythmic synths. The spacey guitar and keys melody beautifully leads into...

'Under My Feet' (John Lodge)
One of the best songs on the album and one of Lodge's best, period. It boasts a lovely orchestral theme, beautifully fluid guitar lines and restrained but memorable verses. In the striking choral hook, the high harmonies sound like they've drifted in from the West Coast with a Beach Boys-like perfection. The trumpet-like keyboard bridge is stunning, leading to a triumphant reprise of

the chorus. Edge's martial drums return to wrap things up and bring this two-parter full circle. An excellent song and a riposte to anyone who claims the band were past their best at this point in their career. Justifiably, this couplet made its way into the setlist for the 1983 tour. This song was the B-side of the 'Running Water' single released in 1984.

'It's Cold Outside of Your Heart' (Justin Hayward)
A great title for a song, and a wonder no one thought of it before. The processed lead guitar gives the whole thing a country vibe. Strummed acoustic underpins the warm verses joined by Moraz's rippling synth lines and electric guitar for the memorable chorus. The title sums up the song perfectly and although its overly sentimental in a country and western style (one of my least favourite genres), Hayward's touching vocal and memorable tune carries the day.

'Running Water' (Justin Hayward)
Two back to back ballads from Hayward underlines his position as the band's principal songwriter by this stage of their career. Gentle acoustic guitar and atmospheric keyboard orchestrations underpin his poignant verses and heartfelt chorus. The keyboard refrain brings 'The Day We Meet Again' from *Octave* to mind. Even the trebly guitar breaks don't sound out of place. There's something reassuringly old fashioned about this song and one that strikes a chord with fans of a certain age. The chorus, with just a hint of echo, is simply gorgeous, and who can argue with the sentiment 'We live to love another day'. During *The Present* tours, this song featured in the second half of the set. It was perhaps too subtle as a single however and failed to chart.

'I Am' (Ray Thomas)
Another two-parter with a short introduction, this time to close side two. A haunting, ambient flute theme from Thomas underscores his impassioned vocal. It has an air of Indian flavoured mysticism with choral chants that hark back to the Moody Blues of the late 1960s, which is carried into...

'Sorry' (Ray Thomas)
Clocking in at five minutes, the concluding song on the album and despite the title, there is nothing to apologise for here. It's not too far removed from Thomas' 1970s ballads, given a 1980s makeover. The moving verses are accompanied by flute and rippling acoustic guitar, building to the rousing chorus with Queen-like layered harmonies (and Lodge's falsetto to the fore). For me, the instrumental bridge is the highlight with a galloping guitar riff reminiscent of Billy Joel's 1980 hit 'It's Still Rock and Roll to Me'. The extended coda features a superb and very proggy synth solo from Moraz to play out. This track was the B-side of the singles 'Sitting at the Wheel' in the UK and 'Blue World' in the USA.

Related Tracks:
None. The three singles 'Blue World' b/w 'Going Nowhere', 'Sitting at the Wheel' b/w 'Sorry' and 'Running Water' b/w 'Under My Feet' were all album tracks.

The Other Side of Life (1986)

Personnel:
Justin Hayward: vocals, guitar
John Lodge: vocals, bass
Ray Thomas: backing vocals, tambourine
Graeme Edge: drums, percussion
Patrick Moraz: keyboards
Additional personnel:
Barry Radman: additional programming & sampling
Produced by: Tony Visconti
Engineered by: Tony Visconti
Recorded at: Good Earth Studios, London, 1985 – 1986
UK and USA release date: April 1986
Highest chart places: UK: 24, USA: 9
Running time: 42:10

Nearly three years separate the release of this album and the previous *The Present*. It's the first since *The Magnificent Moodies* not to have a song or a lead vocal from Ray Thomas. His contributions are generally limited to backing vocals. Patrick Moraz, on the other hand, has his feet firmly under the table and receives his first writing credit (in partnership with Graeme Edge) for the song 'The Spirit'. Otherwise, it's very much the Justin Hayward and John Lodge show, who individually or jointly are responsible for all the other songs.

Renowned producer Tony Visconti was hired for the recording sessions which took place at his studios located in Soho, London. Visconti is probably best known for his work with Marc Bolan's T. Rex and David Bowie and oversaw several notable hit singles during the 1970s. Clearly, the band were hoping he would bring some of that success to the Moody Blues. Although the resulting sound is bright and clear in a compressed, radio-friendly way, his customary ingenuity and creativity are lacking here in my view. The band, and Hayward in particular thought otherwise, however.

The album's chart placing in the UK was the lowest since the 1967 release of *Days of Future Passed*, although it fared much better in America where it earned a platinum disc. It stalled at number 46 in Canada (a popular region for the band) but thanks to consistent sales it was also certified platinum. The edited single 'Your Wildest Dreams' released in tandem with the album went top ten in the USA, helped by an entertaining MTV friendly video. The title song 'The Other Side of Life' (also edited) released four months later also did respectable business Stateside. Although they were scorned by much of the music press throughout the '80s, it was a happy time for the band and Hayward was especially proud of 'Your Wildest Dreams' and its 1988 successor 'I Know You're Out There Somewhere'. *Rolling Stone* magazine, in particular, were won over by the song's commercial sensibilities.

Threshold Records was now under the auspices of Polydor Records who had taken over Decca in 1983. The label deemed that Hayward and Lodge's songs were the commercial way forward for the band. While they were able to keep their synth-pop tendencies under a tight rein on *Long Distance Voyager* and *The Present*, on this album such tendencies get the better of them. The opening song sets the tone and while its undeniably a classy pop song, sound and production wise it is firmly rooted in the early '80s. With a few exceptions (such as the title track), many of the songs, especially 'Talkin' Talkin'' and 'Running Out of Love' sound around five years out of date. The lyrics had also become more predictable compared with the songs of the '60s and '70s, with love and nostalgia now the common themes.

Along with 'Rock 'n' Roll Over You' and 'It May Be a Fire', the two singles made it into the band's concert setlist where they had a longevity that far outlived the album. Sell out concerts, especially in America, were attracting a younger audience (partly encouraged by the singles and videos) along with their legion of loyal fans. They spent a good deal of 1986 touring the States with UK new wave band The Fixx who had several US top twenty hits to their credit. Even though the Moodies had a one-man orchestra in Moraz, a second keyboardist Bias Boshell, who had also worked with Barclay James Harvest, was recruited to bolster their live sound. Whereas Moraz was from the progressive, jazz-fusion school, Boshell's background was more associated with the mainstream and folk-rock. Female backing singers were also introduced in 1986 and would become a staple of the stage line-up.

Album Cover

Once again, a new album brings a new logo. This time the band's name is set against a globe-like background being circled by a very small (and easy to miss) Concorde. Overall, the artwork is more contemporary than previous sleeves, and it works even though it's not a gatefold. The designer Alwyn Clayden had a string of album covers to his credit. The front cover features black and white photos of the band members floating in a darkened laboratory. On the back is a group photo, including individual headshots, track listing and album credits. The insert sheet is standard fare with the lyrics on one side and the same group picture from the cover on the reverse.

'Your Wildest Dreams' (Justin Hayward)

Reaching number nine, this was the band's best-selling single in the USA since the 1972 reissue of 'Nights in White Satin'. Its 21-week run on the *Billboard* chart was the longest of any Moody Blues single. The *Billboard* award-winning video is an enjoyable (if fictionalised) mini-history of the Moodies featuring the band Mood Six and a young Hayward lookalike. The director Brian Grant (a friend of Hayward) was one of the most successful of the MTV generation, directing videos for Tina Turner, Donna Summer, Peter Gabriel, Queen and Aretha Franklin. Hayward later said that as a result of his appearance in this and the video for the sequel 'I Know You're Out There Somewhere', he was recognised in the street for the first time in his career.

Ironically, given the nostalgic tone of the video, the song is awash with 1980s production techniques, including the guitar synth intro, the synth swirls, the slapped bass and synthetic Linn drum sound. The majority of the track was put together by Hayward (utilising a Yamaha DX7 digital synth) and Visconti with minimal involvement from the rest of the band. That aside, it's one of the Moodies' catchiest tunes ever and one of Hayward's best-known songs of lost love. The delightful, wordless harmonies capture the mood perfectly. It remained a permanent fixture within the band's setlist and regularly opened the second half of the show following the intermission.

'Talkin' Talkin'' (Justin Hayward, John Lodge)
This song ups the synth-pop ante by several ratchets. It moves at a breathless pace, with Lodge's lead vocal supported by Hayward, worming its way into your brain. Despite the joint songwriting credit, the style and rock and roll metaphors owe more to the style of the bassist than they do the guitarist. Moraz's whirling synth hook, Edge's prominent drum pattern (based on the *Top of the Pops* theme 'Yellow Pearl') and the guitar break, are all heavily influenced by Ultravox who had a run of successful UK singles in the early '80s. And you can dance to it.

'Rock 'n' Roll Over You' (John Lodge)
It may be the mid-'80s, but when it comes to song titles and lyrics, Lodge can't get his musical roots out of his system. Forget the title, however. This is another slice of '80s, synth-driven dance music. Again, it's vaguely infectious and there's a sterling synth solo at the halfway mark, but given the minimal guitar and programmed drum sound, the Moody Blues it ain't. The band thought differently, however, because it remained in the setlist for both *The Other Side of Life* and *Sur la mer* tours. It also featured on the soundtrack of the film *The Karate Kid, Part II*, a box office hit that same year.

'I Just Don't Care' (Justin Hayward)
A return to a semblance of normality with a welcome, and for this album rare, ballad from Hayward. Sparse acoustic guitar, a percussive pulse and keyboard orchestrations provide a sympathetic backing. The uplifting guitar bridge is Hayward's best contribution to the album thus far. Only the lacklustre chorus lets the side down and the closing line 'I just don't care, I love you' is unconvincing. This song aspires to be another 'Driftwood' (from *Octave*) but falls short of the mark.

'Running Out of Love' (Justin Hayward, John Lodge)
A mid-tempo and, by their standards, plodding song from Hayward and Lodge that would be better titled 'Running Out of Inspiration'. It seems little more than an excuse for producer Visconti to demonstrate the gated sound

techniques he adopted from Trevor Horn. Moraz's rhythmic keyboard fills, the synthesised bass parts and the Simmons electronic drum-beats all owe a debt to ABC's 1982 hit 'Poison Arrow' but without the same charm and energy. An uninspired close to side one.

'The Other Side of Life' (Justin Hayward)
The title track opens side two. As a single, it did reasonably well in the USA, especially in the contemporary and mainstream rock charts. Nudging seven minutes, it's by far the album's longest song, losing a full two minutes for the single edit. With the odd exception (the unnecessarily exaggerated drum fill before the chorus), the synthetic rhythms are more discreet and work for, rather than against, the song. The result is an atmospheric, radio-friendly offering that deserved its single success. Moraz's keyboard backdrop is superbly tasteful, and Hayward adds a scorching guitar solo. When it was first released, it had a fresh contemporary sound compared with many of the other songs here. In concert, it had an almost permanent place in the latter half of the band's setlist where it often followed 'Isn't Life Strange'.

'The Spirit' (Graeme Edge, Patrick Moraz)
Moraz's third Moody Blues album and his first (and last) songwriting credit. It's an up-tempo song with a choral hook that strains to be anthemic but falls a little short. Although it's not one of Edge's best songs (I believe Moraz's contributions were the keyboard parts), it's decent enough. Hayward's heavy riffs and Moraz's synth stabs complement each other, and the all too short organ solo is a highlight. The choral harmonies are basic (for the Moodies) but work well within the context of the song. Even the Trevor Horn style bass rumbles are kept to a minimum.

'Slings and Arrows' (Justin Hayward, John Lodge)
Like 'Sitting at the Wheel' on *The Present* album, this has a retro rock and roll vibe given a 1980s pop makeover. Edge lays down a lively beat over a drum loop with Hayward providing early '60s flavoured twangy guitar lines. The monosyllabic chorus is far from their best, but Hayward gives a spirited vocal performance ably supported by Lodge and Thomas. With guitar dominating, keyboards are kept very much in the background.

'It May Be a Fire' (John Lodge)
The closing song on the album seems to tip its hat to Rod Stewart's 1985 version of 'People Get Ready', but it's none the worse for that. Taken at a languid pace, Lodge and Edge lay down a solid rhythm with engaging keyboard orchestrations from Moraz. Vocally, Lodge is in contemplative mood with a measured but infectious chorus. What gives the song its edge, however, is Hayward's stunning, Jeff Beck-style guitar fills. It's some of his most impressive playing ever, and as a result, this is the best song on the album by several miles

(or kilometres if you prefer). Deservedly, it made its way into the band's setlist for *The Other Side of Life* tour.

Related Tracks:
None. The two singles 'Your Wildest Dreams' b/w 'Talkin' Talkin'' and 'The Other Side of Life' b/w 'The Spirit' were all album tracks.

Sur la mer (1988)

Personnel:
Justin Hayward: guitars, vocals, keyboards, drum sequencing
John Lodge: bass guitar, vocals, keyboards, drum sequencing
Graeme Edge: drums, percussion
Patrick Moraz: keyboards, synthesizers, arrangements
Produced by: Tony Visconti
Engineered by: Tony Visconti, Paul Cartledge, Sam Smith
Recorded at: Good Earth Studios, London, October 1987 – April 1988
UK and USA release date: June 1988
Highest chart places: UK: 21, USA: 38
Running time: 50:56

It being the late 1980s, *Sur la mer* was the band's first simultaneous vinyl and CD release. As a result, it was their longest album thus far. More significantly, it was the first Moody Blues album without Ray Thomas. Although he recorded backing vocals as he had done for *The Other Side of Life*, for reasons best known to the producer, they never made it onto the album. Also, for the first time since the *Blue Jays* album, Justin Hayward and John Lodge were fully in control of the songwriting. As a result, the overall structure lacks the scope and depth of previous albums, especially when five band members were contributing. Despite his lack of participation, Thomas continued to perform live with the band, where his flute, vocals and exuberant stage presence remained as vital as ever.

The album title *Sur la mer* is French for 'On the sea', a play on words, as according to Hayward, the songs are all in the key of 'C'. Despite being a virtuoso keyboardist, for this album, Patrick Moraz tempered his playing for a simpler, more synth-pop biased style. Tony Visconti is again at the production helm, and he adds his usual, overtly commercial sheen to the overall sound. He and Hayward, in particular, were utilising '80s technology to construct songs like 'I Know You're Out There Somewhere'. Released as a single two weeks before the album, it reaped the benefits and continued their run of USA hits. In the UK, sales for the album itself were consistent with *The Other Side of Life*, but it did less well in most other regions, especially America. In many parts of Europe, it didn't chart at all.

In keeping with the three previous 1980s albums, it opens with a Hayward hit song. Despite the rest of the tracks lacking the same commercial sensibilities, they all have a glossy, 1980s radio-friendly sound. As a result, the album hasn't dated particularly well. As songwriters, Hayward and Lodge spread themselves a little too thinly here. While all the songs have their merits, none really stand out. The rich musical textures and inventive vocal harmonies for which the band were renowned are conspicuously absent. Tellingly, only three songs from the album featured in the band's live setlist which increasingly was becoming more reliant on the older songs.

Album Cover
Another single, non-gatefold sleeve and another borrowed piece of art. The front cover is 'Le Fort d'Antibes', a 1955 painting by French artist Nicolas De Staël. The rear cover has a faded parchment look with a glowing tribute by the band's publicist Nick Massey. Continuing the theme of nostalgia, the lyric sheet is particularly good, featuring black and white photos of the band members from their childhood.

'I Know You're Out There Somewhere' (Justin Hayward)
This is one of the Moodies' best known, post-1970s songs and deservedly it was popular on American radio when released as a single in May 1988. It picks up from where 'Your Wildest Dreams' left off, with a ridiculously catchy chorus which Hayward uses to open the song. He also provides the counterpoint backing vocals in the latter part of the track. A simple but driving rhythm from Edge and Lodge, and an infectious keyboard hook from Moraz are the only other ingredients needed. The sluggish bridge that occupies the midsection seems superfluous to requirements and was rightly axed for the single. Using the Yamaha DX7 digital synth, Hayward recreated the same keyboard and bass sound from 'Your Wildest Dreams' and the same tempo.

It benefited from another entertaining promo video with actress Janet Spencer-Turner reprising her role from 'Your Wildest Dreams' as Hayward's lost (and now found) first love. The band had script control over both videos for the only time in their career and although the happy ending is fictional, Janet's character is based on a real person from Hayward's past.

It would become another permanent live favourite where along with 'The Story in Your Eyes' it usually closed the first half of the band's set. Hayward has stated on several occasions that this is his personal favourite of all his songs. The British Academy of songwriters, composers and authors agreed, and he received the 1988 Ivor Novello Award for Composer of the Year. While Hayward's choice of song is perhaps not surprising, more bizarrely, the 1980s is also his favourite period of the band's music. Lodge has also pointed out that he had his most fun in the '80s and that many of the band's current audience discovered the band during this period.

'Want to Be with You' (Justin Hayward, John Lodge)
In contrast to the opening song, this is a mellow and quite lovely ballad that has a distinctly old fashioned, nostalgic feel about it. The arrangement for the verses is sublime with acoustic guitar, percussion, piano and subdued keyboard strings. It breaks like a wave for the surging chorus with synth fanfares joined by lead guitar for the instrumental bridge. Although it's co-written and co-sung with Lodge, Hayward's voice is the more prominent, singing in the first person which gives it a more personal feel. Although the protagonist is in a struggling relationship, the song title ultimately reflects his true feelings.

'River of Endless Love' (Justin Hayward, John Lodge)
This, on the other hand, is a very different kettle of synth-pop. Sequencers are in action here with a rhythmic synth loop and pronounced drum-beat. It gives the song a hypnotic, driving pulse assisted by Hayward's heavy riff and bright choral harmonies. The chant-like vocals make the verses and chorus almost indistinguishable, and for the coda, Moraz creates a very convincing sax sound during his solo.

'No More Lies' (Justin Hayward)
This track is the other, less well-known single from the album, released in October 1988. It's a breezy acoustic and electric guitar-driven tune from Hayward and, although mildly memorable, it's the kind of song you feel he could dash off in his sleep. The drums and bass sound decidedly synthetic and Lodge is on hand for the sparse, counterpoint backing vocals. The song proper finishes around the four-minute mark, allowing ample space for Moraz's stirring keyboard strings to play out. Not surprisingly, its presence in the band's setlist was short-lived.

Ironically, although he isn't on the album, Ray Thomas appears on the picture sleeve for the single along with the rest of the band. He can also be seen in the promo videos for both this song and 'I Know You're Out There Somewhere' 'playing' tambourine.

'Here Comes the Weekend' (John Lodge)
A typically nostalgic offering from Lodge that harks back to the singalong UK pop songs of the early 1970s, but with a 1980s makeover. It moves at an energetic lick driven by frenetic acoustic guitar, a boogie-woogie rhythm and Moraz's exhilarating keyboard runs. File in the same category as Elton John's 'Saturday Night's Alright for Fighting'. When this song was performed on the subsequent tour, the extended 'sax' solo at the end allowed Moraz to go walkabout with his keytar just as he did with 'Veteran Cosmic Rocker', which was still in the setlist at the time.

'Vintage Wine' (Justin Hayward)
Another bright and breezy, acoustic guitar driven tune from Hayward to open side two of the vinyl LP. Compared with his many other contributions to the band over the years this may seem like a fairly inconsequential song, but it has an optimistic, joyful spring in its step that's hard not to like. Hayward's lead vocal is suitably upbeat and the wordless harmonies uplifting. Moraz enters into the spirit of things adding playful, flute-like keyboard fills.

This song continues the album's theme of nostalgia. It has an autobiographical subtext where the opening lines 'I remember the taste of the vintage wine, from '63 through to '69', and later, 'Oh I tell you, music set me free' alludes to Hayward's teenage groups The Whispers, All Things Bright and Marty Wilde's Trio as well the early Moody Blues.

'Breaking Point' (Justin Hayward, John Lodge)

The third of four joint Hayward and Lodge compositions on the album and it's surprising that Moraz doesn't also get a writing credit. Keyboards and electronic effects dominate the track and Moraz is probably responsible for the arrangements. Following an eerily atmospheric intro, rhythmic keyboards along with a skipping drum pattern underpin Lodge's unwavering lead vocal. The overall effect is quite hypnotic where mood, tempo and instrumentation remain constant throughout the song. Vocals aside, it's the closest the Moody Blues ever got to the sound and style of Jean-Michel Jarre.

'Miracle' (Justin Hayward, John Lodge)

If there was ever an indication that Hayward and Lodge were struggling to come up with enough ideas to fill a complete album, this is it. Once again, we're in synth-pop territory, even though by 1988 the genre was well past its sell-by date. Although it has a brisk pace, the song is lacking in dynamics and impact despite the unison singing for both the verses and chorus. Even the upfront bass line and Human League-style 'trumpet' synth stabs fail to lift this above the ordinary.

'Love Is on the Run' (John Lodge)

This track is much better and a welcome ballad from Lodge, which he didn't write nearly enough of in this period. That said, the choral hook 'Love is on the run from me' is not one of his most inspired. The song does, however, benefit from a lovely arrangement of rhythmic acoustic guitar and keyboard orchestrations. Best of all is the beautiful slide guitar playing and, as a result, the instrumental coda that follows the false ending is by far the most memorable part.

'Deep' (Justin Hayward)

To close the album, something very different from Hayward. Compared with the chaste romanticism of many of his songs, it's ripe with sexual implications, which is perhaps why it remains a favourite for many fans despite it never being played live. It has a slow burning quality with a synthetic drum pattern providing the repetitious beat and Hayward's measured vocal gradually building in intensity. It's atmospheric and very Peter Gabriel-ish, emphasised by the stark synth lines, gated drum sound and fat bass fills. Hayward cuts loose at the four-minute fourteen seconds mark with a vibrato-laden guitar solo of which David Gilmour would be proud. One of his best on any album, in my opinion, joined by Moraz's synths for the stirring coda. A fine way to conclude an otherwise patchy album.

Related Tracks:

None. The two singles 'I Know You're Out There Somewhere' b/w 'Miracle' and 'No More Lies' b/w 'River of Endless Love' were all album tracks.

Keys of the Kingdom (1991)

Personnel:
Justin Hayward: vocals, acoustic guitar, electric guitar
John Lodge: vocals, bass
Graeme Edge: drums, percussion
Ray Thomas: vocals, flute
Additional personnel:
Patrick Moraz: keyboards on 'Say What You Mean', 'Celtic Sonant' and 'Magic'
Bias Boshell: keyboards, drum machine
Paul Bliss: keyboards, drum machine
Guy Barker: trumpet
Jamie Talbot: alto saxophone
Nigel Hitchcock: tenor saxophone
Pete Beachill: trombone
Andy Duncan: drums on 'Is This Heaven?' and 'Magic'
Anne Dudley: arranger, conductor on 'Bless the Wings (That Bring You Back)' and 'Shadows On The Wall'
Orchestra: Pro Arte Orchestra of London on 'Bless the Wings (That Bring You Back)' and 'Shadows On The Wall'
Produced by: Tony Visconti, Christopher Neil, Alan Tarney
Engineered by: Tony Visconti, Pete Jones, Gerry Kitchingham
Recorded at: Olympic Studios and R.G. Jones Studios, London, October 1990 – May 1991
UK release date: July 1991, USA release date: June 1991
Highest chart places: UK: 54, USA: 94
Running time: 53:02

A new decade had begun, and this was album number fourteen from the band. It was the first of only two albums released in the 1990s. Recording began following the 1990 American tour which ended in September. During the recording, Patrick Moraz voiced his displeasure with the album and the band's reluctance to allow him to make any significant contributions. As a result, he was summarily dismissed before the subsequent tour which began in June 1991. The Moody Blues was now officially a quartet, although Moraz plays 'additional keyboards' on three tracks. Compared with previous albums, however, his contributions are muted. Also, on the album is Bias Boshell who was promoted to principal keyboardist for touring duties and Paul Bliss who would become the support keyboardist. Moraz didn't go quietly, however, and took legal action for unpaid royalties. The band vainly claimed that he had not been a fully-fledged member even though album sleeves, tour programmes and promotional material suggested otherwise. With other session musicians involved, Graeme Edge played on just three songs. He celebrated his 50th birthday in March 1991 and was finding it difficult to sustain two-hour-plus performances. As a result, Gordon Marshall was recruited as second drummer for live performances, and he would remain with the band until 2015.

On a more positive note, Ray Thomas was back, and he'd brought his flute. He contributed the elegiac 'Celtic Sonant' as well as co-writing the closing song 'Never Blame the Rainbows for the Rain'. Otherwise, Justin Hayward and John Lodge dominated, with the guitarist providing the obligatory two singles 'Say It with Love' and 'Bless the Wings (That Bring You Back)'. Sales for both were disappointing, however, despite a decent showing by the former in the American mainstream rock chart. The album was recorded and mixed in several studios with different backing musicians and three separate producers presiding. Indeed, the additional musicians involved in the album reads like a cast of thousands compared with previous records. The results are far more cohesive than one could reasonably expect and despite its occasional drawbacks, this for me was their best album since 1983's *The Present*. The music press didn't agree however with mostly negative reviews, no wonder the band would be in no rush to return to the studios.

As a sign of the times, in the USA the album was released on CD only, although a vinyl option was available in the UK and mainland Europe. It was also the first not to enter the top 50 in either the UK or the USA, although Canada remained loyal as it crept into the top 30. As was the norm by now, the two singles opened the album, followed by a mixed bag of styles including synth-pop, dance, mainstream rock, pop, funk, soft ballads and folk. Although there is no concept as such, many of the songs had a sentimental, nostalgic theme.

On the resulting 'Tour of the Kingdoms', 'Bless the Wings (That Bring You Back)', 'Lean on Me (Tonight)' and 'Say It with Love' were the only three songs from the album regularly played, and usually side by side in the first half of the set. The band performed at the 1991 Montreux Jazz Festival and in 1992 they made their legendary appearance at the Red Rocks Amphitheatre with the Colorado Symphony Orchestra. Under the direction of Larry Baird, the orchestra helped them recapture the magic of their earlier work including music from *Days of Future Passed*. The band's first with a full orchestra, it paved the way for similar concerts throughout the 1990s with Baird as arranger and conductor. Rather than taking an orchestra on tour, the band used regional ensembles to keep costs down. The 1992 concerts celebrated the 25th anniversary of *Days of Future Passed* and they co-headlined a tour with American band Chicago. In 2007, Hayward stated that the orchestrated songs of the '90s and beyond were more faithful to the originals than the performances in the '80s.

Album Cover

The front cover features a photo of the Alps which is rather ordinary in itself, although the 'flying' logo is very striking. The rear cover (or CD inlay) features a sunset sky credited to Satori that's similar to Phil Travers' artwork for *Blue Jays*. Ironically, Travers offered his services for this album, but they declined. The insert sheet with the vinyl album has the usual lyrics on one side and the album credits on the other enclosed by individual black and white headshots of the four band members (Hayward, Lodge, Edge and Thomas).

'Say It with Love' (Justin Hayward)

This song was released as a single in June 1991, a couple of weeks before the album and while it's not a bad song per se, it's pretty obvious why it wasn't a big hit. It would, however, feature in the band's live repertoire for most of the '90s. Paul Bliss' programmed drums and keyboards kick things off, joined by a basic bass riff and minimal chord progression. Hayward's vocal has a nostalgic yearning with verses like 'I remember a long time ago, when I heard those guitars that I worship so' harking back to 'Vintage Wine' on the last album. The chorus is decent enough, and the hook (and song title) has a disarming charm that makes criticism seem almost churlish. He also throws in a guitar solo which is quite memorable, if only for the ear piercing sustain. Hayward plays his recently acquired black Guild F-30 acoustic guitar on both this and the following song.

'Bless the Wings (That Bring You Back)' (Justin Hayward)

This track became another single attempt, released in August 1991 and although it's a quality song, it doesn't really smack of chart hit potential. A soaring guitar phrase opens the song, which has a welcoming and distinctive, old fashioned charm. This solo, coupled with the touching vocal, echoes some of Hayward's more lyrical tunes of the early 1970s. Delicate strings arranged and conducted by Anne Dudley are integrated sensitively into the overall mood of the song. As a bonus, Edge plays real drums on this song. It's one of their most lovingly crafted tracks for several albums, superbly produced by Alan Tarney. As a live song, it never made it far beyond the 'Tour of the Kingdoms', but it was performed at Red Rocks, Denver in September 1992 with the Colorado Symphony Orchestra.

In the '60s and '70s, Peter Knight had been the band's orchestrator of choice, but sadly he died in July 1985. Hayward met Dudley through Tarney and was impressed by her work on this song. She would work with Hayward again on his 2013 album *Spirits of The Western Sky*, in particular, the song 'One Day, Someday'.

'Is This Heaven?' (Justin Hayward, John Lodge)

Sung by both Hayward and Lodge, if the catchy melody is naggingly familiar, think back to the Beach Boys' 1964 ballad 'Don't Worry Baby'. In fact, the whole song and the arrangement, in particular, has a sunny Californian vibe, especially when you break it down to its constituent parts. The galloping rhythm guitar, finger snaps, exotic sitar embellishments and plucked violins echo Brian Wilson in his 1960s prime. Throw in Andy Duncan's sliding drum pattern, plus the whistling and the sound of tap dancing (credited to one Stephen Mear), and you have a delightful if a little quirky, confection.

'Say What You Mean (Parts I & II)' (Justin Hayward)
This track doesn't belong on a Moodies album, no matter how hip they wanted to sound. That said, as cod '80s style dance music goes, it's not a bad effort with Bias Boshell's drum machine and keys capturing the sound of New Order and the Human League. He's aided by funk basslines and a classy horn arrangement of saxophones, trumpet and trombone. Vocally, Hayward enters into the spirit of things, sounding reasonably convincing for a man in his mid-40s. Moraz is also in there somewhere, I suspect, providing the 'orchestral' embellishments.

Producer Visconti stops and restarts the song at the three-minute 48-second mark, which explains the parts one and two in the song title. It's a nod to '80s dance singles where different mixes of the same song would often feature on the A and B-sides. The second part replaces Hayward's singing (with the exception of the choral hook) with a spoken section.

'Lean on Me (Tonight)' (John Lodge)
This song is on more familiar ground, being an easy-going ballad that boasts a splendid, keyboard orchestral fanfare from Paul Bliss. His jaunty piano rhythm, on the other hand, distracts from, rather than adds to, the mood of the song. The instrumental bridge features a very agreeable, melodic guitar break from Hayward. It concludes what is, on the whole, a satisfying opening side of the vinyl album. This track was one of three songs from the album (the other two being 'Say It with Love' and 'Bless the Wings') performed at Red Rocks with the Colorado Symphony Orchestra in 1992. It would be performed throughout the '90s, with Lodge playing the rhythm part on 12-string acoustic, and following the turn of the millennium, it would become an almost permanent fixture in the band's setlist.

'Hope and Pray' (Justin Hayward)
Bliss is once again at the keyboards for this infectious opening to side two. The song moves at a lively but melodic pace, with a superb, breathy lead vocal from Hayward and an equally superb guitar solo at the halfway mark. The subject is simple but bittersweet, he's waiting (in vain?) for the return of his lost love. This is one of those songs in the band's canon that is easily overlooked, but it rewards repeat plays. Although the song itself is over five minutes long, the guitar fade ending seems to come too soon.

'Shadows on the Wall' (John Lodge)
This gentle ballad is Lodge's homage to the late John Lennon. His vocal is uncannily like the man himself, and the song's style, and tone (think 'Jealous Guy' and 'Woman') would fit comfortably on a Lennon album. The memorable choral hook 'Chasing shadows on the wall' paraphrases 'Watchin' shadows on the wall' from 'Watching the Wheels' on Lennon's 1980 *Double Fantasy* album, released just three weeks before his death. Enhancing the mood is Hayward's

delicious slide guitar, Dudley's melancholic string arrangement and Edge's tasteful drumming. In May 1990, Lodge and Hayward performed 'Across the Universe' as part of a John Lennon tribute concert in Liverpool.

'Once is Enough' (Justin Hayward, John Lodge)
At 53 minutes, the entire album was too much of a stretch for the vinyl version, and as a result, this song only appeared on the CD version. A heavy rock guitar lick sets the tone for this mid-tempo, funk rocker while Hayward's spirited lead vocal is sweetened by the layered harmonies. It's perhaps not surprising it was sacrificed, as – despite the enthusiastic treatment – this is the album's most obviously dispensable track.

'Celtic Sonant' (Ray Thomas)
This song was eagerly awaited by fans, being Thomas' first contribution in eight years. If Hayward and Lodge had restyled themselves for the late '80s/early '90s, Thomas has both feet firmly planted in the past. His voice had matured with age, sounding rich and full bodied for this evocative folk ballad which, as the title suggests, has a traditional Celtic flavour. It's like nothing else on the album and brings to mind the unofficial Scottish national anthem 'Flower of Scotland'. The beautiful arrangement is headed by Thomas' resonant flute against a lush keyboard backdrop with acoustic guitar, harp (played by Boshell on keyboards) and full-blooded choral voices. Close your eyes while listening to this and you're halfway to a remote island off the coast of Scotland or Ireland.

'Magic' (John Lodge)
This track is Lodge at his most direct. The song opens with keyboard strings (Moraz again) and strummed acoustic guitar before settling into a basic but solid guitar groove with a nimble bass line and Andy Duncan's articulate drumming. The song is mainstream rock of the old school variety and instrumentally, it is the album's least synthetic sounding track (and all the better for it). Hayward's guitar fills are a delight, and the ballsy horn arrangement is capped by a storming sax solo to play out. The similarly titled 'Simply Magic' appears on Lodge's second solo album *10,000 Light Years Ago*.

'Never Blame the Rainbows for the Rain' (Justin Hayward, Ray Thomas)
We arrive at easily one of the soppiest song titles in the band's catalogue, for this overly sentimental ballad. The arrangement is exactly what you would expect; fulsome acoustic guitar, light percussion, an understated bass motif and keyboard orchestrations (from Boshell). Hayward's chorus, however, is cloyingly sweet with overripe, multi-tracked harmonies and a flourish of weeping, steel guitar to close. It is a lacklustre and unimaginative conclusion to an otherwise fine album.

Related Tracks:

The two seven-inch singles 'Say It with Love' b/w 'Lean On Me (Tonight)' and 'Bless the Wings (That Bring You Back)' b/w 'Once Is Enough' were all album tracks.

'Highway' (Justin Hayward, John Lodge)

A leftover song from the sessions, this song originally appeared on the twelve-inch single version of 'Say It with Love'. It opens (and closes) with keyboards providing the authentic sound of bagpipes. It's a breezy, freewheeling song with a folky quality (I can imagine Lindisfarne singing this) and Hayward's lead vocal is doubled by Lodge for the strong chorus. It's a pity it wasn't included on the album, as it would have made a fitting closer. In 1994 this song was included in the *Time Traveller* box set and in 1998 it appeared on the two-disc compilation *Anthology*.

Strange Times (1999)

Personnel:
Justin Hayward: vocals, guitar
John Lodge: vocals, bass guitar
Graeme Edge: drums, percussion, vocals
Ray Thomas: vocals, flute, tambourine
Additional personnel:
Danilo Madonia: keyboards, programming, orchestrations
Produced by: The Moody Blues
Engineered by: Alberto Parodi
Recorded at: Mulinetti Studios, Genoa, Italy, December 1997 – June 1999
UK and USA release date: August 1999
Highest chart places: UK: 92, USA: 93
Running time: 57:33

After an eight-year gap, the longest between any successive Moody Blues' albums, this is the band's penultimate studio recording. 'Strange Times' indeed. To maintain their profile, the interim period had been filled with a succession of compilation albums, reissues, concerts (often with an orchestra) and live recordings. In the absence of any new studio product, the tours often promoted a compilation album. Significantly, the core seven albums, from *Days of Future Passed* to *Seventh Sojourn* had been remastered and reissued on CD in 1997. They included new liner notes from individual band members, although at the expense of the lyrics. They had perhaps left it too late for this album, however; it barely scraped into the top 100 on both sides of the Atlantic. The critics, however, generally treated it more kindly than they did *Keys of the Kingdom*. The only single from the album, Justin Hayward's 'English Sunset' was released the same day and fared even worse. Sales of their back catalogue remained impressive, however, averaging around half a million albums a year.

It would be Ray Thomas' last recording with the band, and the short but sweet 'My Little Lovely' was his sole compositional contribution. It is, however, a justifiably poetic ending to a recording career spanning nearly 35 years. Graeme Edge also had a track included (his first in thirteen years) in 'Nothing Changes' which fittingly concludes the album.

The band produced the album at the Mulinetti Studios, Genoa where Hayward recorded his 1996 solo album *The View from the Hill*. It had become his preferred location for recording, and he convinced Lodge and Edge to work there. Here, they were introduced to the multi-talented Danilo Madonia who makes a significant contribution to the recording, as he would on two American tours. Five out of the fourteen songs on the album were played during the *Strange Times* tours which typically concentrated on America for the most part. They were 'English Sunset', 'Haunted', 'Words You Say', 'Strange Times' and 'Nothing Changes'. 'English Sunset' had the most staying power, remaining in the setlist until the mid-noughties.

Free from the constraints of vinyl, Hayward and Lodge contribute no less than twelve songs between them, more than any other Moody Blues album. Despite the potential of the CD format, there are no attempts at ambitious length songs, with only two songs exceeding the five-minute mark. They did, however, overextend themselves in my view and several songs, Lodge's ballads especially, sound a little samey. That's despite the superb orchestrations, with the album boasting some of the lushest arrangements since *Seventh Sojourn*. Madonia, in particular, does a superb job throughout, although the now familiar programmed drums were becoming irksome, especially when they have a skilled musician like Edge in the band.

That same year the band made their infamous appearance in the animated TV show *The Simpsons* where they voiced themselves in the episode 'Viva Ned Flanders'. In 2001, excerpts from several Moodies standards were included in the IMAX film *Journey into Amazing Caves* and the corresponding soundtrack album. They were recorded by Hayward with studio musicians and worked into new songs written and arranged by Steve Wood and Daniel May. They included 'Nights in White Satin', 'Question', 'I Know You're Out There Somewhere' and 'Your Wildest Dreams'. Two original Moody Blues tracks, 'Water' and 'We Can Fly' also feature on the soundtrack.

Album Cover

A simple but effective CD booklet cover with a vivid beach and surf scene overlaid with an image of the Earth in what looks like a transparent shell. The back of the booklet is a mirror image of the front minus the Earth and shell. Compared with the previous cover, the band name is almost minuscule, and like the album title, it's in standard, non-stylised lettering. The CD inlay (and the inside of the booklet) has the same picture but this time with clock images and the usual song titles. In addition to the familiar Threshold logo, the Universal Records logo makes its first appearance.

'English Sunset' (Justin Hayward)

An intro of bubbling synths and electronic effects is overlaid with a synthetic rhythm (we've been here before) and Hayward's urgent (but always melodic) vocal. Following constant world tours, this is a celebration of his home country with light-hearted, spoken interjections from Lodge and Thomas that require an old fashioned, British sense of humour to appreciate. It's a lively tune with few distractions but ultimately a tad too uneventful for the singles market, despite a memorable, rhythmic guitar hook and a typically strong middle-eight. As well as being their first in eight years, 'English Sunset' was the band's penultimate single. It was performed at the Royal Albert Hall, London in May 2000 with an orchestra and is included on the *Hall of Fame* CD and DVD.

'Haunted' (Justin Hayward)

Hayward again, and an appropriate title for this bittersweet tale of lost love.

The distinctive 'Doo doo doo doo doo' choral hook brings to mind Lou Reed's 'Walk on the Wild Side'. Admittedly, this is not one of his most memorable ballads, but the tasteful arrangement of piano, guitar, delicate percussion and strings pulls the listener in and gives them a warm and comforting embrace. As a stage song, it lasted for the 1999/2000 *Strange Times* tours and was performed at the Albert Hall in May 2000.

'Sooner or Later (Walkin' on Air)' (Justin Hayward, John Lodge)
This song is perhaps most notable for the fact that Thomas, Hayward and Lodge share lead vocals, but it has more going for it than that. Driven by guitar, piano, organ and a lively rhythm, It's a bright and breezy song with a sprightly spring in its step. The verses (sung in turn by the trio) and the chorus are equally catchy and uplifting. The optimistic mood is typified by lines like 'Live for the moment' and 'Love is out there waiting for you', along with Hayward's Mark Knopfler-style guitar picking to close.

'Wherever You Are' (John Lodge)
A return to their psychedelic past for the Middle Eastern flavoured intro, but the prominent, programmed drums put a different spin on things. Led by piano, it's taken at a leisurely pace with Lodge's expressive vocals affirming that the future is more important than the past. Danilo Madonia provides keyboard 'strings' and atmospheric effects in the instrumental bridge, with a touch of flute and electric guitar to remind us that Hayward and Thomas were also involved.

'Foolish Love' (Justin Hayward)
Hayward's late period songs continue a preoccupation with love, and while the evocative chorus is more than decent, again it's the arrangement that carries the day. Madonia is again at the centre of things, providing some of the band's best keyboard orchestrations since Moraz's work on *The Present*. Not to be outdone, Hayward contributes jangly acoustic guitar while Edge's skipping drum pattern and Lodge's warm bass line play their part. Hayward is also in fine vocal form throughout.

'Love Don't Come Easy' (John Lodge)
The gentle, strummed acoustic guitar intro is reminiscent of 'Driftwood', but overall it's the Beatles circa the *Let It Be* album that seems to be the conspicuous role model for Lodge's ballad. His emotive lead vocal is particularly good, as is Madonia's piano and lush 'strings', and Hayward's melancholic slide guitar. Although it treads a thin line, it stays just the right side of saccharine sentimentality.

'All That Is Real Is You' (Justin Hayward)
And the ballads keep coming. It's also a return to one of Hayward's recurring (and autobiographical) themes of returning home from his world travels to

his true love. The vocal and melody are mellow but full of yearning and the arrangement is sparse, but far from simplistic. There are the familiar acoustic guitar, piano and keyboard strings, but around the two-minute mark, it surges to a blissful high with soaring lead guitar before subsiding for the reflective close.

'Strange Times' (Justin Hayward, John Lodge)

Halfway into the album and we arrive at the title song. With a sing-along chorus, created deliberately, it has all the hallmarks of a potential single, but perhaps due to the lack of success with 'English Sunset', it was never released in that format. It bowls along at a lively, mid-tempo pace with sprightly lead guitar, organ and a staccato acoustic guitar rhythm. Hayward's vocal raises several octaves to his upper register during the uplifting chorus, joined by a ringing guitar hook. Madonia's keyboard strings riff delightfully and I know I've said it before but once again it's the memorable middle-eight that stands out. This song first appeared in the setlist as early as 1997, but not surprisingly, it was dropped after the 1999/2000 tours.

'Words You Say' (John Lodge)

At five and a half minutes, this is the album's longest song and benefits from a sweeping orchestral arrangement that harks back to the *Blue Jays* album and *Days of Future Passed*. Lodge is, once again, in emotive vocal form regarding a strained relationship, supported by delicate flute and strings. Until the halfway mark it sounds like it belongs on a solo album, but discreet drums, tambourine, acoustic guitar and a warm bassline enter as a reminder that it's a Moody Blues song after all. Hayward also weighs in with a stately guitar bridge. The verses, vocal and arrangement are all undeniably gorgeous, but the flat, repetitive chorus doesn't fully justify all the pomp and splendour. It remained in the setlist until 2003 however and is one of three songs from the album included on the *Hall of Fame* CD and DVD released in 2000.

'My Little Lovely' (Ray Thomas)

Compared with the previous track, this sweet little song from Thomas, his last on a Moodies album, sounds almost stripped down. That said, it does feature a beautiful orchestral arrangement, acoustic guitar and accordion to elevate his familiar and wistful, child centred lyrics. It was written for Thomas' grandson who was newly born at the time. At well under two minutes, this song may seem much too short, but it says all it wants to say without outstaying its welcome. Sadly, before his untimely death in 2018, Thomas never produced that much-hoped-for third solo album.

'Forever Now' (John Lodge)

This is another song from Lodge that owes a debt to John Lennon, with a side order of George Harrison. Like 'Words You Say', it has a lush orchestral intro of flute and strings. For the sensitive verses, Lodge's plaintive vocal is accompanied by delicate piano, swelling strings and harp. Acoustic guitar, drums and bass weigh in at the one-minute mark. One of Lodge's typically jaunty sections follows where, on this occasion, he mirrors Lennon's vocal mannerisms. The choral hook is a delight thanks to Edge's inventive drum pattern and Hayward's overarching steel guitar. Like all of Lodge's songs on this album, it sounds very personal, and it's a surprise that he didn't get around to releasing a second solo album until 2015.

'The One' (Justin Hayward, John Lodge)

This is a contender for the album's strongest offering in my opinion, partly because it's so different from what's gone before. It combines mainstream pop-rock sensibilities (a driving rhythm, full-on guitar and a catchy chorus) with prog-rock tendencies (clever keyboard and guitar fills and lush vocal harmonies) to delightful effect. It put me in mind of 10cc back in their mid-'70s prime. Worthy of special mention is the tumbling 12-string guitar and synth hook during the chorus, which is ridiculously infectious, reaching a stunning peak at the two-and-a-half-minute mark. Lodge sings the verses, doubled by Hayward for the chorus, who also provides the cutting guitar break.

'The Swallow' (Justin Hayward)

Hayward's final song on the album is notable for the inclusion of an acoustic guitar solo as opposed to his customary acoustic rhythm playing. He makes good use of guitar harmonics along with a backing of strings. This is so engrossing that when the rhythm track enters, it seems almost intrusive. Lovely flute playing and orchestral embellishments support the chorus which, like the bird in question, soars skywards. The song almost fades around the three-minute mark before guitar, bass and drums bring it back into focus, overlaid by the acoustic playing that opened. It concludes with a short but sweet classical flourish.

'Nothing Changes' (Graeme Edge)

A return to the good old days with a combined poem and song from Edge. This time Edge narrates his own words with his distinct 'Brummie' accent still evident after more than 30 years of globetrotting with the band. Following a suitably spacey intro, the words are solemnly delivered over a sparse piano backing. Full-bodied acoustic guitar, strings and flute enter to accompany the final verses. Finally, Hayward brings in his soaring electric guitar and voice to sing the payoff lines 'Nothing changes, and nothing stays the same, and life is still a simple game' against the lush orchestral backdrop. It's a touching tribute to Mike Pinder before the fade to bring both the song and the album to a serene conclusion. Like 'Words You Say', this song remained in the setlist until 2003.

Related Tracks:

'This Is the Moment' (Frank Wildhorn, Leslie Bricusse)
This is a rare cover version, and the song's show tune origins are not hard to detect. The track is from the Broadway musical *Jekyll & Hyde,* and this version first appeared on *Soccer Rocks the Globe*, the official compilation album for the 1994 FIFA World Cup. In certain regions, including Japan, it was a bonus track on *Strange Times* along with 'Highway' (see *Keys of the Kingdom*). Hayward makes the most of this beautiful, show-stopping song. His performance is heartfelt with a stylish backing of lush keyboard orchestrations, piano and choir. Even allowing for the fact that it's a cover version, it doesn't sound like the Moody Blues, being more a throwback to Hayward's 1989 *Classic Blue* album.

'Water' (Justin Hayward, John Lodge)
This is the first of two original Moody Blues tracks included in the 2001 IMAX film *Journey into Amazing Caves* and the corresponding soundtrack album. It's also a rare instrumental from the band, the first since 'Hole in the World' on the 1983 album *The Present*. The mellow, atmospheric vibe is reminiscent of early '70s Pink Floyd dominated by Hayward's spacey lead guitar and ethereal wordless harmonies. I'm sure it's very effective in the film, but as a standalone piece, it's fairly inconsequential.

'We Can Fly' (Justin Hayward, John Lodge)
The second original song from *Journey into Amazing Caves*. This track is better, a breezy pop song with a memorable choral hook augmented by engaging harmonies, strummed acoustic rhythm and electric guitar fills. This time it's Hayward's breathy vocal in the verses that brings to mind Pink Floyd, or more specifically David Gilmour's singing style.

December (2003)

Personnel:
Justin Hayward: vocals, guitar
John Lodge: vocals, bass guitar
Graeme Edge: drums, percussion
Additional personnel:
Danilo Madonia: programming, keyboards, orchestrations
Norda Mullen: flute
The Orchestra of Carlo Felice, Genoa
Produced by: Justin Hayward, John Lodge
Engineered by: Alberto Parodi
Recorded at: Mulinetti Studios, Genoa, Italy, November 2002 – August 2003
UK and USA release date: October 2003
Highest chart places: UK: Did not chart, USA: Did not chart
Running time: 42:08

A new millennium and, of all things, a Moody Blues Christmas album. More significantly, it was also their last studio album. Under different circumstances, this could have been a novel diversion before the next album proper. But that wasn't to be, and as such, it stands as a mostly failed attempt to recapture the imagination of the general record-buying public. In a recording career spanning 39 years, it was the first album since 1965's *The Magnificent Moodies* to include non-original songs. It's therefore ironic that after four decades of producing inventive, original songs the band's recording career (as of time of writing) should be bookended by two albums reliant upon cover versions.

They had been reduced to a trio at the end of 2002 with the official retirement of Ray Thomas. This was well-earned, given that he had been with the Moody Blues since the very beginning in 1964. American session musician Norda Mullen had the unenviable task of replacing Thomas for touring purposes. She proved to be a major asset and plays flute on several tracks here. In 2001, Paul Bliss had been promoted to principal keyboardist, following Bias Boshell's departure, and Bernie (Bernadette) Barlow was recruited to provide keyboard support and backing vocals for live work. From what had previously been an all-male domain (with the exception of the backing singers), the Moody Blues had taken on a whole new, female-friendly look.

Like *Strange Times*, the album was recorded in Italy with the band producing. Danilo Madonia is again on hand for keyboard duties, and he does an absolutely superb job. They also make excellent use of an orchestra on several tracks. All the songs have a festive theme with Justin Hayward and John Lodge's compositions sprinkled with seasonal favourites. Appreciation of this album is very much dependent upon two things; a fondness for sentimental Christmas songs and a tolerance of cover versions. It's a pity that Thomas wasn't involved, the childlike wonder conveyed in many of his songs would have been ideal for this album. Although involved, Graeme Edge wisely abstained from songwriting. That said, it's not a bad album by any stretch of the imagination. The original songs are all quite memorable, complemented by a selection of tastefully chosen and mostly sympathetically performed covers. There's no raucous 'Merry Xmas Everybody' or 'I Wish It Could Be Christmas Every Day' here.

December failed to chart in any region, although in America it did reach number ten in *Billboard*'s 'Top Holiday Albums'. The only single from the album, 'December Snow', released in November, failed to raise record buyer's Christmas spirit. In the UK to boost sales, the album was re-packaged as a bonus disc with the compilation *Ballads* released the same year. As an indicator of the album's potential in terms of sales and playability you really had to look no further than the title. Following its initial release, as each Christmas rolled around the band hoped that the season of goodwill would stimulate renewed interest in the album and single. A quartet of songs from the album 'Don't Need a Reindeer', 'The Spirit of Christmas', 'December Snow' and 'White Christmas' were played back to back during the 2003 autumn/winter tour. With the exception of 'December Snow', they were soon dropped once the holiday season was over.

In many ways, *December* is an appropriate title for a final album. The last month of the year, it marks the ending of one chapter in our lives before the start of another. When questioned on the subject of another album in later years, neither Hayward nor Lodge ruled out the possibility, saying that they would be willing if approached by a sympathetic record company. Time will tell.

Album Cover

The cover and CD booklet artwork by Luccio De Giuseppe is not particularly inspired. A blue-tinged picture of a boy with his sledge in a snowy landscape resembles a scene from a bland Christmas card. The booklet includes an overexposed photo of the three band members, album credits and the lyrics to all songs including the covers. In the repackaged version, *December* and *Ballads* are housed in a slipcase with the sticker 'Includes the new Moody Blues Christmas Album December' on the front.

'Don't Need a Reindeer' (Justin Hayward)

This is a rather sweet, child-friendly opening song with a catchy, upbeat chorus. It features the usual Christmas trimmings of chiming keyboards, acoustic guitar, sleigh bells and choral voices. The programmed drums are a sign of the times, but a disappointment nonetheless. As is often the case in a Hayward song, the middle-eight is the most uplifting section, especially the acapella part at the three-minute mark.

'December Snow' (Justin Hayward)

Of the original songs on the album, this is the best by some distance and harks back to Hayward's plaintive songs of old. For the verses, the arrangement is sparse and restrained with Edge's drum fills and strings elevating the surging chorus. Hayward's melodic guitar embellishments are an absolute joy, as is Madonia's tasteful and deceptively laid-back piano solo, underpinned by organ, and if I'm not mistaken, a Mellotron sample. This was justifiably chosen as the single, despite the subsequent lack of success. It was also the only song from the album to have a respectable life span in the band's concert setlist where it remained throughout most of the noughties. In an interview in 2005, Hayward stated that this, along with the inevitable 'I Know You're Out There Somewhere' was one of his favourite songs.

'In the Quiet of Christmas Morning (Bach 147)' (J. S. Bach, Justin Hayward, John Lodge)

Hayward and Lodge add words to Bach's famous cantata 'Jesus, bleibet meine Freude' ('Jesu, Joy of Man's Desiring') and the results are much better than you might expect. Hayward's vocal (backed by Lodge) is suitably reverent, and the delightfully baroque orchestral arrangement remain respectful to the original. The lyrical flute soloing is courtesy of the classically trained Norda Mullen.

'On This Christmas Day' (John Lodge)

Lodge's opening verses are typically melancholic with gentle acoustic guitar, swelling strings and a discreet rhythm section. The chorus has a haunting beauty, and the instrumental bridge features a beautifully fluid solo from Hayward. Despite the rich arrangement, the instrumental trappings normally associated with Christmas songs are kept mostly at bay. This song is a close runner-up to 'December Snow' as the album's best offering.

'Happy Xmas (War Is Over)' (John Lennon, Yoko Ono)

Given Hayward and Lodge's admiration for John Lennon, it's not surprising this song was included. While I applaud the message, I never found the 1971 original wholly convincing, especially the tacked-on children's choir. This is as good as any cover version could be, given the song's inherent limitations, and I like the way Hayward and Lodge exchange the verses. The strings and piano arrangement are inspired without being overblown and thankfully there's no children's choir (or Yoko Ono). In fact, at just over two and a half minutes it fades all too soon.

On 5 May 1990, Hayward and Lodge performed 'Across the Universe' on acoustic guitars backed by an orchestra as part of the 'John Lennon Memorial Concert' held in Liverpool. In an interview before the performance, Hayward stated that Lennon was his number one British rock and roll hero.

'A Winter's Tale' (Mike Batt, Tim Rice)

Hayward worked closely with Mike Batt on the 1989 *Classic Blue* album, so this is another unsurprising inclusion. The song's style and melancholic tone are perfect for the band. Hayward does a credible vocal job here, displaying a tad more emotion than David Essex did on the 1982 original. The arrangement is crisp and airy with prominent (keyboard) flute and acoustic guitar with a sprinkling of strings. Only the synthetic rhythm track lets the side down.

'The Spirit of Christmas' (John Lodge)
Lodge reminds us of the true meaning of Christmas and does it in typically heartfelt fashion. References to 'The star of Bethlehem' and 'The Church of the Nativity' are wrapped up in a sympathetic arrangement of flute (Norda Mullen once again), acoustic guitar, orchestra and piano. A gospel choir makes a brief and unexpected appearance in the middle-eight and Hayward's ringing guitar soloing elevates the otherwise so-so, singalong chorus above the ordinary.

'Yes I Believe' (Justin Hayward)
Hayward's opening line 'The spirit of Christmas is the spirit of love' references Lodge's previous song, but otherwise, he manages to avoid the 'C' word for the rest of the track. The words are still full of optimism however and the song itself suitably upbeat with echoing drums (ala 'Bridge over Troubled Water') punctuating the uplifting chorus. It concludes with a memorable guitar break and a short but sumptuous orchestral flourish.

'When a Child Is Born' (Zacar, Fred Jay)
Johnny Mathis' 1976 version is so quintessential, one has to wonder why anyone bothers covering this song, although many have had a go. Hayward and Lodge make a pretty good fist of it, sharing the verses and combining for the heavenly chorus. The wordless harmonies are lush and, with the exception of flute-like keys and strings, Hayward's guitars, acoustic and electric, provide the stylish instrumental backdrop.

'White Christmas' (Irving Berlin)
A Christmas perennial dating back to the 1940s, everyone who sings this song will always be measured against Bing Crosby's legendary original. Because of its age, we can even excuse the song's sickly-sweet sentimentality. Once again, the lead vocals are evenly shared, and the mellow first half remains faithful to the original with discreet orchestrations. A change of tempo however for the second half which features a full band arrangement with twangy lead guitar and sprightly bass, drums and piano. It was performed in the subsequent autumn/winter tour, a rare occurrence of a cover version in the band's setlist.

'In the Bleak Midwinter' (Christina Rossetti, Gustav Holst)
This must qualify as one of the saddest, most bittersweet songs ever written, especially when you consider that it's a Christmas carol. Holst's 1906 music perfectly captures the essence of Rossetti's original poem, which dates back to 1872. The piano backing here is a tad too lethargic and the trebly guitar soloing totally out of place, but Hayward's thoughtful vocal and the solemn

strings do it justice. This song is best performed by a church choir, in my view, although Annie Lennox sang a stirring version on her 2010 Christmas album *A Christmas Cornucopia*.

Related Tracks:
None.

Live Albums and Videos

When it comes to official live albums, the Moody Blues have been poorly served, especially compared with other bands of their ilk. They were also late starters. The first album *Caught Live + 5* wasn't released until 1977, and the recording was more than seven years old. The long delay was partly due to the band's belief that the recording was substandard. It was their only live release during the 1970s, no wonder bootlegs were popular during this era. Although live albums and DVDs appear with common frequency these days, even the more popular artists averaged just one or two throughout the '70s.

An absence of live releases during the 1980s bypassed the Patrick Moraz era and again made it open season for bootleggers. The second official live album *A Night at Red Rocks with the Colorado Symphony Orchestra* appeared in 1993, sixteen years after the first. The flow of live releases improved following the turn of the millennium with CDs, DVDs (and more recently Blu-rays), no doubt to compensate for the absence of studio albums. These were generally contemporary recordings although several were from the archives, dating back to the 1960s.

Sadly, there is very little to show from the concerts of the 1970s (arguably when the band were at their peak) or the 1980s. The occasional live song has popped up as a bonus track on album reissues, but these are few and far between. The seventeen-disc *Timeless Flight* box set released in 2013 helped bridge the gap with concert recordings from December 1975 (the *Blue Jays* tour), May 1979 (the *Octave* tour) and December 1983 (*The Present* tour). It also includes an April 1970 concert on DVD which features songs from *A Question of Balance*. The 2014 boxset *The Polydor Years: 1986-1992* includes a July 1986 recording from *The Other Side of Life* tour.

In most cases, however, these recordings are not the complete concert. In 2013, the 25 May 1979 concert on *Timeless Flight* also surfaced as *Live in Seattle 1979,* and although it's an unofficial release, it's an excellent soundboard recording. Recordings from the *Every Good Boy Deserves Favour* and *Seventh Sojourn* tours (the author's favourite period) remain scarce, however. There are also no official filmed concerts from the Patrick Moraz era, which is a shame; the 1992 court case received more attention.

Caught Live + 5 (2 LP: 1977)

The band's first live album, the sound quality and performances are a little rough around the edges, especially when compared with the polished studio originals. It's the place to go however if you want to hear the band in all their raw, formative glory. The remastered CD has also improved the sound somewhat. In addition to regular producer Tony Clarke and engineer Derek Varnals, there were several other engineers involved, including Elton John's producer Gus Dudgeon and Queen's producer Roy Thomas Baker.

It was recorded at the Royal Albert Hall, London on 12 December 1969, and as such there were no songs from the three most recent 1970s albums. There is however a balanced selection from the 1960s, including stage favourites 'Gypsy', 'Tuesday Afternoon', 'Nights in White Satin' and 'Ride My See-Saw' alongside the three-part 'Have You Heard' suite. The live recordings occupy three sides of the double vinyl LP with the fourth given over to five previously unreleased studio tracks that date back even further to 1967 and 1968. These are discussed elsewhere in the book, and they're worth the price of admission alone.

Released three years into the band's mid-'70s hiatus, this package was clearly a compromise to appease fans that had been waiting patiently for new material. It was welcomed by American fans who placed it at number 26 in the *Billboard* chart, although UK record buyers were mostly happy to wait for the next studio album.

A Night at Red Rocks with the Colorado Symphony Orchestra (CD & VHS: 1993, 2 CD: 2003)
The Other Side of Red Rocks (VHS: 1999, DVD: 2000)

This album is very popular with fans and has been released in various guises over the years. In 1993 it was released both as a single CD and a video, with four additional songs on the latter. In 1999, a behind the scenes documentary video *The Other Side of Red Rocks* was released. Finally, in 2003 a two-disc 'Deluxe Edition' featuring the entire concert was released. The DVDs are also included in the 2014 *The Polydor Years: 1986-1992* box set.

Recorded on 9 September 1992, it was originally broadcast on American TV and celebrated the 25th anniversary of *Days of Future Passed*. In addition to a sprinkling of songs from that album, they played all their most popular tunes up to and including 'Say It with Love' from the *Keys of the Kingdom* album. This rates highly on every level. It's a generous selection of songs (23 in total on the 2003 edition) and one of the best ever group and orchestra recordings in a live setting. The latter is under the direction of conductor, arranger (and Moodies fan) Larry Baird. Everyone involved gives a spirited performance, and the American crowd love every minute of it. It also paved the way for a series of orchestral concerts throughout the 1990s and beyond.

Hall of Fame (CD: 2000)
Hall of Fame – Live from the Royal Albert Hall (VHS/DVD: 2000)

On 1 May 2000, the band returned to the Royal Albert Hall, London, this time with the World Festival Orchestra in tow conducted by Larry Baird. Unlike *Caught Live + 5* however, it took only three months between recording and release. It's the last recording to feature Ray Thomas who retired two years later. The regular backing musicians include Paul Bliss and Bias Boshell on keyboards, Gordon Marshall on drums with Susan Shattock and Tracy Graham on backing vocals. Many of the songs from *A Night at Red Rocks* are included here although at 70 minutes this is a shorter set (on disc at least).

Again, both the orchestra (who open proceedings) and the band are in fine form throughout. In addition to the CD, it was their first simultaneous DVD release. The artwork also provided the cover for the 2001 'Hall of Fame' tour programme.

The Lost Performance – Live in Paris '70 (DVD: 2004)

To call this DVD a live recording is a bit of an exaggeration. ORTF filmed the 60-minute performance for French TV at La Taverne de L'Olympia, Paris on the 14 April 1970, four months before the release of *A Question of Balance*. The video footage is intimate, and it's nice to see the band in a relaxed, nightclub setting. Although the sound is palatable, clearly the band are miming (and not particularly well at times) to playbacks with occasional live playing. It is probably best avoided, particularly as much of it can be seen on the internet.

Lovely to See You: Live (2 CD: 2005, DVD: 2005)

Recorded at the Greek Theatre, Los Angeles on 11 June 2005, this is the band without Ray Thomas or an orchestra. The one-hour 40-minute setlist is a pretty solid representation of their career across five decades (minus Thomas and Pinder's songs of course), ranging from 'Tuesday Afternoon' to 'December Snow'. Even 'Forever Autumn' gets an airing (for which the band had to obtain permission). The performances are polished and energetic (even if Edge does get a little carried away) with excellent backing from Paul Bliss and Bernie Barlow (keyboards), Gordon Marshall (drums) and Norda Mullen especially, providing flute, rhythm guitar and backing vocals. The DVD extra features a 30-minute interview with Hayward, Lodge and Edge.

Live at Montreux 1991 (DVD: 2005)

On 3 July 1991, during the 'Tour of the Kingdoms', the band stopped off at the 25th Montreux Jazz Festival. Along with the customary favourites, they played three songs from the current album during the 90-minute set. The line-up is mostly the same as on *Hall of Fame* except for one change of backing singer. They obviously had a few gremlins that evening, the sound balance isn't perfect, especially during the opening songs, and neither is Hayward's voice at times. There are some solid performances however and things improve by the time they get to 'Nights in White Satin', which benefits from Sue Shattock and June Boyce's strong backing vocals.

Live at the BBC: 1967–1970 (2 CD: 2007)

If you don't mind multiple versions of the same songs, this is a valuable two-CD package. It brings together the band's BBC radio sessions and TV show recordings from this period and a 'BBC Live in Concert' recorded on 17 December 1969. Collectively, they capture the Moodies 'Mark Two' in their early prime and provide a pretty comprehensive overview of their 1960s output. Be mindful, however. Several of the sessions are almost too perfect and suspiciously close to the originals, so clearly backing tracks and overdubs have been utilised. As you would expect from the BBC, the sound quality is mostly good. When it was released, Hayward commented that he didn't realise these recordings still existed and how pleased he was to see them out. In April 2019, it was re-released as a stylish triple coloured vinyl set.

Live at the Isle of Wight Festival 1970 (CD: 2008)
Threshold of a Dream: Live at the Isle of Wight Festival 1970 (DVD: 2009)

This was recorded on 30 August 1970 during the band's second, historic appearance at the annual Isle of Wight Festival. At a little over 60-minutes, it's one of their best known live recordings, filmed in front of a 600,000 strong crowd. The inclusion of songs from *A Question of Balance* is the most significant difference between this and the *Caught Live + 5* setlist recorded eight months earlier. Overall, it's also a better performance with the band in their prime. 'Tuesday Afternoon', 'Nights in White Satin' and 'Legend of a Mind' are especially tight. Both sound and picture are pretty decent given the vintage. It's well worth catching the DVD (or Blu-ray), especially the sight of Pinder behind his bulky Mellotron looking out onto a sea people, perfectly capturing the festival atmosphere. The individual personalities at the time also come across; from Thomas' restless energy to Hayward's wary reserve. Although the full set was recorded, it wasn't all filmed, so some songs are accompanied by separate footage, but it works well enough. The interviews with Lodge, Hayward, Edge and Pinder that flesh out the DVD were recorded in 2008. Director, producer Murray Lerner was also responsible for the two-hour documentary film *Message to Love: The Isle of Wight Festival 1970* from which some of the footage here is taken.

Days of Future Passed Live (2 CD/2 LP: 2018, DVD/Blu-ray: 2018)

Although no strangers to orchestral concerts, this is the Moody Blues with bells and whistles. They perform *Days of Future Passed* in its entirety, backed by the Toronto World Festival Orchestra conducted by Elliot Davis with British luvvie Jeremy Irons narrating Edge's poems. The backing band comprises Norda Mullen, Julie Ragins, Alan Hewitt and Billy Ashbaugh. The set opens with the band's 'hits' and closes with the usual 'Question' and 'Ride My See-Saw' encore. It was recorded at the Sony Centre for the Performing Arts, Toronto in July 2017 to celebrate the album's 50th anniversary. Hayward sings Pinder's 'Dawn Is a Feeling', Lodge sings 'The Sunset' and they combine for Thomas' 'Another Morning' and 'Twilight Time'. As was now the norm for live performances, 'Late Lament' is placed before 'Nights in White Satin' but the orchestral finale is intact. The whole show is very polished and the sound reproduction, in particular, is stunning. Vocally, Hayward and Lodge can be excused for sounding more sedate these days given that they are both in their

70s. This recording is unique, and there are no plans to repeat the process for any of the other core albums even though this year (2019) marks the 50th anniversary of both *On the Threshold of a Dream* and *To Our Children's Children's Children*.

Compilation Albums

Once upon a time, compilations were budget priced LPs that you came across by accident in your local record shop. Although they often contained minimal information, back in the early 1970s, I was introduced to several bands this way. These days compilations vary dramatically in terms of format, content, quality and price. They range from the inexpensive CDs that can be picked up in the local supermarket to the lavish box sets which, with the scarcity of record shops, can often only be purchased over the internet.

When it comes to the Moody Blues, prospective buyers are spoilt for choice. Released in 1974, *This Is The Moody Blues* has the distinction of being their first, although the floodgates didn't fully open until 1978. A plethora of compilations followed, occasionally fuelled by bouts of inactivity by the band. With the onset of CDs in the mid-'80s, compilations became cheaper to produce, and the new format allowed more material to be included on fewer discs.

Given the band's extensive output, for newcomers to the Moodies or anyone with a passing interest, I would recommend at least a two-disc or ideally a three-disc set. As their last studio album was released in 2003, in theory, anything from the past fifteen years should be comprehensive enough. Box sets, on the other hand, are more likely to appeal to diehard fans and completists. At one time, the excellent five CD *Time Traveller* released in 1994 was the one to have, but in 2013 this was usurped by the seventeen disc 'Deluxe edition' of *Timeless Flight*. Even the latter, however, excludes the Denny Laine era (1964-1966) material.

At the last count, there were around 30 Moody Blues compilations, and that doesn't take into account regional variations. More often than not, the majority are simply recycling the same familiar songs. There is also plenty of unofficial material out there, often overpriced (on the basis that it's a rare item) and of poor quality. In this section, I've tried to be as comprehensive as possible although there may be one or two that have slipped through the net. The band has also featured on numerous 'Various artists' compilations including *Brum Beat – Midlands Beat Groups of the '60s* (1993) and *The Psychedelic Scene* (1998).

This Is The Moody Blues (2 LP: 1974)

This was released in October 1974 during the band's sabbatical so clearly, the purpose was to maintain their profile in the absence of any new product. The seven previous albums are depicted on the cover, and there is a representative selection of songs from each, although they are not in chronological order. Highlights include the 'Have You Heard' suite and the combined 'Nights in White Satin' and 'Late Lament' from *Days of Future Passed*. Breaching the top twenty on both sides of the Atlantic and reaching number two in Canada, this was an essential purchase for every self-respecting 1970s rock fan. When my wife and I first met, with different tastes in music we had just two albums in common, *Simon and Garfunkel's Greatest Hits* and *This Is The Moody Blues*.

The Great Moody Blues (2 LP: 1978)
Released by Deram in Europe, this is basically a combined package of the first two Moodies 'Mark Two' albums *Days of Future Passed* and *In Search of the Lost Chord* in their entirety.

Out of This World (LP: 1979)
This album was a single LP 'greatest hits' package released by the budget label K-tel. The band clearly endorsed it because the uninspired artwork was also used for the cover of their 1979 European tour programme. Advertised on TV at the time, it did very good business in the UK reaching number fifteen in the album chart.

Eternity in an Hour: A Collection of the Best of The Moody Blues (LP: 1981)
Released in Australia amongst other regions by Threshold, this includes the singles from the period of *Days of Future Passed* to the (then current) *Long Distance Voyager* album. The title and the artwork which depicts an hourglass against a sky background continues the theme of time as featured in several Moody Blues album titles, including the compilations *Time Traveller* and *Timeless Flight*.

Voices in the Sky: The Best of The Moody Blues (UK LP: 1984, USA LP: 1985)
This is where it gets a little confusing. Different versions were released in the UK and the USA. The UK version has twelve tracks with a plain blue cover while the North American version has ten tracks with more colourful artwork. The track sequencing is also different. A strange inclusion on the UK version is the A and B-sides of the 1981 'Talking Out of Turn' single which didn't chart in the UK. The blue artwork also provided the cover for the 1984 European tour programme.

Prelude (LP: 1987)
This was an indispensable release back in October 1987, containing a roundup of singles, B-sides and rarities from the 1967 *Days of Future Passed* and 1968 *In Search of the Lost Chord* period. It also includes the five studio tracks from the *Caught Live + 5* album recorded in the same period. Its significance has been somewhat negated in more recent years due to the myriad of bonus tracks included on CD reissues of the original studio albums.

Greatest Hits (LP/CD: 1989)
This album is notable for the 'symphonic' versions of 'Isn't Life Strange' and 'Question' with the London Symphony Orchestra arranged by Anne Dudley. Otherwise, it contains the usual '60s and '70s suspects, updated with the 1980s hits 'Your Wildest Dreams', 'The Voice', 'Gemini Dream' and 'I Know You're Out

There Somewhere'. The orchestra sounds quite spectacular (or overblown, depending upon your tastes) on 'Isn't Life Strange', especially during the instrumental bridge. 'Question' is less effective and does nothing to enhance the original. Both LSO versions resurfaced on the 2014 box set *The Polydor Years: 1986-1992*.

The Story of The Moody Blues: Legend of a Band (VHS: 1990, DVD: 2005)

Originally released on VHS video, this is a one-hour twenty-minute documentary. It includes interviews with the four band members (excluding Patrick Moraz) interspersed with promotional videos of their more popular songs. There is also some concert footage, although these are only fragments. The helicopter sequence where John Lodge revisits the location of the 1970 Isle of Wight Festival was reused in the 2009 *Threshold of a Dream* DVD. It's OK as a historical record, but like all documentaries, it dated very quickly. Confusingly, *Greatest Hits* (see above) was re-released in 1990, adopting the same title and cover artwork as this documentary.

Time Traveller (5 CD: 1994)

Like *Prelude*, this boxset was a desirable item in its time. The first four discs include a decent selection of tracks from *Days of Future Passed* through to *Keys of the Kingdom*, although some albums (*On the Threshold of a Dream* for example) are favoured more than others. Surprisingly, there's a generous selection from *Blue Jays*. 'Blue Guitar', 'Forever Autumn', the occasional single and the previously unreleased 'Highway' are thrown in for good measure. The 'bonus' disc, perhaps the most interesting, includes songs recorded during *A Night at Red Rocks* but not included on the original 1993 release of that album. While the song selections are subjective, back in 1984 I would have rated this five stars. The artwork also provided the cover for the band's 1996 tour programme.

True Story (CD: 1996)

At less than 30 minutes, this is a meagre collection of ten previously released album tracks and singles from the Denny Laine era circa 1964-1966. Surprisingly, 'Go Now' isn't included.

The Very Best of The Moody Blues (CD: 1996)
The Best of The Moody Blues (CD: 1997)

This album is one of the band's best-selling compilations in the UK, reaching number thirteen in the album chart and achieving platinum status. With a generous seventy-seven minutes, it also makes full use of the CD format. With the exception of 'Go Now', included for the first time on a Moodies compilation, there's nothing new or surprising here with all the obvious hits and the now obligatory 'Blue Guitar' and 'Forever Autumn'. The artwork also provided the cover for the 1997 USA summer tour book.

Anthology (2 CD: 1998)
This release is basically an expanded version of *The Best of The Moody Blues* with similar artwork. Whereas that collection went no further than 1988s 'I Know You're Out There Somewhere', this brings things up to date (or at least 1994). It also includes a few more choice tracks from the 1960s and '70s, including 'Remember Me My Friend' from the *Blue Jays* album.

Classic Moody Blues: The Universal Masters Collection (CD: 1999)
Released in Europe only, this is an ad hoc seventeen track collection of singles, album and non-album tracks, including 'Highway' which seems to crop up on every other compilation. The tracks are placed in no particular order, and it has a rushed, thrown together feel about it.

The Best of The Moody Blues: 20th Century Masters – The Millennium Collection (CD: 2000)
A 53-minute collection of the A-sides from ten singles, ranging from 'Nights in White Satin' to 'I Know You're Out There Somewhere'. It is a pointless release, given the other compilations available.

The Singles+ (2 CD: 2001)
This is much better. Disc one includes many of the early singles from both the Moodies 'Mark One' and 'Two'. It also mixes album tracks (the plus part of the title) with the more popular singles. Disc two is more standard fare, concluding with 'I Know You're Out There Somewhere' (again).

The Collection (2 CD: 2001)
This collection is essentially *Anthology* with a different title and artwork (which is borrowed from the *Time Traveller* box set).

Say It with Love (CD: 2003)
The clue is in the title. Amongst the ballads, there are a few of the more obvious up-tempo tunes – mainly the hit singles.

Ballads (CD: 2003)
Again, the title says it all. It's similar to *Say It with Love* with a few song variations. In the UK it was bundled with the final studio album *December* as a two-disc package. The two albums proved to be a compatible listening experience, especially for a romantic, winter's night in by the fire.

Gold (2 CD: 2005)
And they keep coming. That said, with 34 tracks spanning 155 minutes,

this is an excellent starter pack. It's part of Polydor's 'Gold' series, and the remastering is superb. Opening with 'Tuesday Afternoon' and closing with 'December Snow', this could be all that the casual listener needs.

An Introduction to The Moody Blues (CD: 2006)

A good place to start if you want to revisit the Denny Laine era. With eighteen songs, it's a comprehensive overview of the first album and singles. It has been somewhat overshadowed by Esoteric Recordings' 2014 two CD edition of *The Magnificent Moodies* album.

Classic Artists: The Moody Blues (2 DVD/CD: 2006)

This package is part of the 'Classic Artists' series of DVDs which focused on several artists including Jethro Tull and Yes. DVD one is a two and a half hour documentary from director/producer Jon Brewer including interviews with band members and associates, plus excerpts from concert footage and promos. Recorded in 2005, Moraz is absent, and Thomas talks only briefly. DVD two features another 90 minutes of promo videos and interviews. The 22-minute bonus CD includes songs from the archives performed by pre-Moodies bands like the Saints & Sinners and El Riot and the Rebels. Also included are two 1964 Moody Blues songs, the previously unreleased 'You Better Move On' and 'Lose Your Money'. Justin Hayward's 1965 single 'London Is Behind Me' also makes a rare appearance. Like many collections of this kind, the interviews are occasionally illuminating but the real interest lies in the all too brief snippets of concert footage. It begins well with a detailed account of the 'Brumbeat' scene and the band's early years, but then skips haphazardly through the core seven albums and later work.

Collected (3 CD: 2007)

The cover of this boxset tells all, with three CDs and 54 tracks. The artwork is also an imaginative fusion of all the original album covers. It contains few surprises, and although much of it is in chronological order, three songs from the Denny Laine era and three early 'Mark Two' non-album tracks are stuck on at the end, almost as an afterthought.

Playlist Plus (3 CD: 2008)

While *Collected* was released by Universal, this three-disc set is released by Polydor. It contains pretty much the same selection of songs only without the very early stuff. It also throws in a *Blue Jays* song (and the obligatory 'Blue Guitar') for good measure.

Icon (CD: 2011)
Icon 2 (2 CD: 2011)

From Polydor, the eleven-track single disc version is the absolute bare essentials. The 23-track two-disc version is better, containing all the singles and a few choice songs up to and including 'December Snow'. Strictly for newbies and casual listeners as well as completists.

Nights in White Satin: The Collection (CD: 2012)
A mixed bag of eighteen songs covering the 1967-1991 period. Some of the tracks, like 'Nights in White Satin', are live recordings, but this is not made obvious on the cover.

Timeless Flight (2013)
This is available in a standard two-disc version, a four-disc version and a seventeen-disc 'Deluxe edition' boxset. If you're a diehard fan – and your wallet and shelf can stand the strain – the latter is the one to have in your collection. It includes eleven remastered CDs with choice tracks from each album and singles, previously unreleased mixes, out-takes and concert recordings. The six DVDs include 5.1 surround sound mixes of six of the core seven albums (*In Search of the Lost Chord* is conspicuously absent) plus assorted TV performances, promo videos, etc. The icing on the cake is a 120-page hardback book, although this came in for a lot of criticism due to typo errors. Although the sound is excellent, the video images on the DVDs are a little underwhelming. The four-disc version contains album tracks and singles while the two-disc version is the bare essentials. You pays your money, and you takes your choice.

The Polydor Years: 1986-1992 (6 CD/2 DVD: 2014)
This eight-disc boxset is another desirable collector's item. As the title suggests, the albums *The Other Side of Life*, *Sur la mer* and *Keys of the Kingdom* are included in remastered form, along with bonus tracks and a 1991 BBC radio session. Better still is a July 1986 concert recorded in Cleveland, Ohio, during *The Other Side of Life* tour. There is also a remastered edition of the September 1992 *A Night at Red Rocks* concert. DVD one contains the same concert and DVD two has 'The Other Side of Red Rocks' documentary. Also included is a 64-page hardback book and a rather nice 7" blue vinyl single of 'Al Fin Voy A Encontrate' ('I Know You're Out There Somewhere' for those that don't speak Spanish).

Time Is on My Side (CD: 2015)
Like *True Story*, this is another sparse collection of ten songs from the Denny Laine era. 'Go Now' is included this time along with the song that provides the album title. With just 28 minutes of music and one of the worst covers since *Out of This World*, your money is better spent elsewhere.

5 Classic Albums (5 CD: 2015)
This package is part of the '5 Classic Albums' series from Universal. Other artists in the series include ELO, Fairport Convention and Steve Hackett. If you

simply want to replace your vinyl versions of *On the Threshold of a Dream*, *To Our Children's Children's Children*, *A Question of Balance*, *Every Good Boy Deserves Favour* and *Seventh Sojourn* then this budget package of CDs may do the trick. Be advised, however. They have not been expanded or remastered and, like others in the series, there have been quality issues with the wrong tracks on the wrong discs.

Nights in White Satin: The Essential (3 CD: 2017)

I like this, if only for the kitsch cover photo of the band in their 1960s prime. Released by Decca at a very modest price, the 51 tracks begin with the pre-*Days of Future Passed* singles and runs through to the 1999 *Strange Times* album, but surprisingly stops short before *December*. All the singles – with the exception of 'December Snow' – are included along with a sprinkling of album tracks. Under different circumstances, the inclusion of Pinder's 'The Voyage' would have been welcome, but the opening and closing 'Have You Heard' sections are missing, and it doesn't sound quite right somehow.

Tribute Albums and Bands

Compared with bands like Pink Floyd and Genesis, the Moody Blues have been the subject of very few tribute albums. They can be a mixed blessing for any band and are often met with scepticism, especially by fans who consider the originals sacrosanct. Those I've included here do at least convey a degree of integrity rather than exploiting the source material. The stylistic interpretations are certainly diverse, ranging from orchestral to bluegrass to prog-rock. Members of the band feature on two of these albums. As both Justin Hayward and John Lodge include Moodies songs in their solo concerts, in a sense they themselves are paying tribute to the band (even though they wrote the songs).

In addition to tribute albums, not surprisingly the band has been favoured with cover versions of their more popular songs. These include 'Nights in White Satin' by Bettye LaVette, Procol Harum, Eric Burdon, Percy Faith, Nancy Sinatra, Il Divo, Elkie Brooks, Giorgio Moroder, Deodato, Les Jelly Roll, The Dickies and Sandra; 'Question' by Vicky Leandros, Nina and Fish; 'A Simple Game' by the Four Tops; 'Tuesday Afternoon' by David Lanz, Neal Morse and Doughboys; 'Ride My See-Saw' by Bongwater; 'The Story in Your Eyes' by Stiv Bators and Fountains of Wayne and 'I'm Just a Singer (In a Rock and Roll Band)' by James Last. These are just a few, and as you can imagine, each version varies dramatically in both style and quality.

Although the band still exists as a touring unit, unsurprisingly there are several Moody Blues tribute bands out there. They include Time Traveller who promote themselves as 'North America's #1 Moody Blues Tribute Show' and perform with an orchestra. In August 2017 at a show in St. Charles, Illinois, Denny Laine appeared on stage and performed 'Go Now' with the band. Other American acts include The Lost Chord, Gemini Dream ('The Midwest's premier Moody Blues Tribute Band') and Tuesday Afternoon. The most high-profile UK band is Go Now! who play theatres throughout the UK and was formed by Gordon Marshall who toured with the Moody Blues as second drummer for 25 years. Other notable UK bands are Legend of a Band and Blue Onyx, although the latter folded in the Summer of 2013. Considering that the Moodies as a band tour less frequently these days, especially outside America, clearly tribute acts are providing a valid service.

Justin Hayward and Friends Sing the Moody Blues Classic Hits (CD: 1994)

This is not a Justin Hayward solo album, although it's often listed as such. Inspired by the band's orchestral concerts of the 1990s, he covers a selection of Moody Blues standards, backed by the Frankfurt Rock Orchestra (with members of the Prague Philharmonic Orchestra). He shares lead vocals with Michael Sadler of Saga and Shaun Williamson of the Atlanta Rhythm Section. Despite the album raising the question as to whether the world really needs another version of 'Nights in White Satin' or 'Forever Autumn', it's not without its merits. The orchestra (conducted by Leon Ives) is full of pomp and splendour, although the quality of the singing is variable. Sadler is in fine vocal form during 'Nights in White Satin' and 'New Horizons', but Williamson's strained, rock histrionics do neither 'Question' or 'Isn't Life Strange' any favours. Hayward is as good as you would expect, but he sounds exactly as he did on the originals, so really what was the point? It's been reissued under a variety of different titles and even more varied cover artwork.

Moody Bluegrass: A Nashville Tribute to The Moody Blues (CD: 2004)

Cards on the table, I'm not a fan of bluegrass or country music. My idea of American roots music is Aaron Copland and Leonard Bernstein. That said, this is an album that's hard not to like. It features the cream of Nashville musicians and singers including Alison Krauss, John Cowan and the late Harley Allen. They take a selection of Moodies songs and inject the sound of the American south, utilising traditional instruments like fiddle, dobro and banjo. The focus is on the more popular tunes like 'I'm Just a Singer (In a Rock and Roll Band)' and 'Your Wildest Dreams', and while it's tongue in cheek at times, it's done with style, taste and panache.

Higher and Higher – A Tribute to The Moody Blues (3 CD: 2006)

This album was released by Italian label Mellow Records who specialise in progressive rock. With 41 songs over three discs, it's certainly the most comprehensive Moodies tribute to date. The International array of performers include many lesser known, but still notable prog acts like Mystery, Spirits Burning, Elegant Simplicity, Flamborough Head and Roz Vitalis. If you are familiar with any of these bands, then you will know that the musicianship is excellent. The vocals, on the other hand, are variable. You know they've done their homework when disc one opens with 'London Is Behind Me' (Justin Hayward's 1965 pre-Moodies single). Other less familiar songs amongst the better-known tunes include 'Twilight Time', 'The Best Way to Travel' and 'I Never Thought I'd Live to Be A Hundred'. While the occasional song is slavishly reproduced, there are significant departures to make this a worthwhile venture.

Moody Bluegrass TWO... Much Love – A Nashville Celebration of The Moody Blues (CD: 2011)

This album repeats the formula of the first album, but the song selections are less obvious this time around. Additional singers include Vince Gill and Ricky Skaggs. More significantly, it features the five members of the classic-era Moody Blues on the same album (if not the same tracks) for the first time in 33 years. Hayward and Lodge sing 'It's Cold Outside of Your Heart' and 'Send Me No Wine' respectively, Thomas and Pinder add flute and Mellotron to a superb

'Dear Diary' and Edge narrates 'Higher and Higher'. The highlight, however, is probably the original instrumental 'Lost Chord' performed on a variety of acoustic instruments by David Harvey and Tim May.

Solo Albums

Although the Moody Blues as a band went into hibernation from 1974 to 1977, the individual members did not. Worldwide record sales of around twenty million had given them the financial stability to pursue their individual ambitions. After seven years of constant touring and recording, the decision to put the band on hold provided the ideal environment for solo projects. Mike Pinder released one album while Justin Hayward, John Lodge, Ray Thomas and Graeme Edge were each represented by two albums during this period. The unifying factor was Threshold Records, which released all the albums.

With the exception of the *Blue Jays* project, Thomas guesting on Edge's first album, and Pinder and Thomas performing on one song on Lodge's 2015 *10,000 Light Years Ago* album, they have avoided each other's solo work. They have also excluded solo material (with the exception of 'Forever Autumn') from the Moody Blues concerts. Clearly, for all of them, the band and their solo activities were two separate entities. Musically, the albums are all very individual with Edge's partnership with Adrian Gurvitz being the most obvious departure from the Moody Blues sound.

Surprisingly, with the exception of Hayward, whose solo output has remained fairly constant, very few solo albums have been released outside the 1970s hiatus period. Even after leaving the band in 1978, Pinder released just one further album of original songs in 1994 (which is included here). Patrick Moraz, on the other hand, released several albums before and after his time with the Moodies, but it's his 1978-1991 output while a band member that's discussed here. Denny Laine's extensive output following his tenure with the Moody Blues warrants a book on its own.

Justin Hayward

If you put Justin Hayward's solo albums alongside his body of work with the Moody Blues, there is ample evidence that in terms of pure melody he is one of the best singers and songwriters the UK has ever produced. Except Moraz, he is by far the Moodies' most prolific solo artist, which is not surprising given his track record with the band. From 1978 onwards, he established himself as the band's principal songwriter for both album tracks and singles.

Following the 1975 *Blue Jays* partnership with John Lodge, Hayward released his debut album *Songwriter* in 1977, just two weeks after Lodge's debut. While the title is not particularly original, it's certainly appropriate. It would be the first of six studio albums spanning 36 years. None of the other band members have appeared on any of his solo albums. Surprisingly, given his success with the Moody Blues, none of his solo compositions have been hits.

To fill the gaps between the band albums of the 1980s, in addition to solo albums Hayward kept himself busy writing and performing songs for UK TV and the occasional film. These include the 1984 remake of *She* and the 1988 franchise sequel *Howling IV: The Original Nightmare*. In 1985, his song 'The Angels Cry' was performed by former ABBA member Agnetha Fältskog on her album *Eyes of a Woman*. He is also proud of his involvement with Alan Simon's 2003 *Gaia* environmental project, performing the song 'On the Road'.

Since 1974, Hayward and Lodge have received several accolades including awards from the ASCAP (American Society of Composers, Authors and Publishers) and Ivor Novello awards for their achievements as songwriters.

'London Is Behind Me' b/w 'Day Must Come' (Single: December 1965)

Released on the PYE label, this is the single Hayward played to Mike Pinder in 1966 that secured him a place in the Moody Blues. If you've never heard these songs before, be prepared for a surprise. Very much of their time, they give very little indication of his later work. 'London Is Behind Me' is a lively, foot-tapping song with Hayward's convincing American hillbilly drawl. It's very much in the skiffle style of producer Lonnie Donegan, one of Hayward's early heroes. Donegan recorded his own version of this song in 1978. Hayward's original appears on the 2006 *Classic Artists: The Moody Blues* compilation. 'Day Must Come' is better, in a bubbly pop style with both Hayward's echo-laden vocal and the drum slaps prominent. The string arrangement sounds cheesy and very mid-'60s, but Hayward's rapid, carefully pronounced delivery displays bags of confidence.

In August 1966, Hayward released a second single 'I Can't Face the World Without You' b/w 'I'll Be Here Tomorrow' on the Parlophone label. These were self-penned songs, produced by Alan A. Freeman.

Songwriter (LP: February 1977)

Hayward's debut album was recorded with keyboard player Ken Freeman and members of rock band Trapeze: Mel Galley (bass), Terry Rowley (guitar) and Dave Holland (drums). He doesn't step completely out of his comfort zone, however, enlisting producer Tony Clarke, arranger/conductor Peter Knight and the string trio from the *Blue Jays* album. Hayward plays a variety of instruments, including guitars, drums, bass, violin, cello, flute and tambourine. The songs range from comfortably familiar ballads 'One Lonely Room', 'Stage Door' and 'Raised on Love' (featuring his daughter Doremi) to the six and a half minute closer 'Nostradamus'. This is the album's standout song with world music rhythms, exuberant and inventive orchestrations and great production from Clarke. The two-part title song is also notable with solid piano and synth from Freeman although the disco rhythm during the instrumental bridge has dated it somewhat.

The 2004 re-release features four bonus tracks, including the 1979 non-album single 'Marie'. I, however, prefer 'Heart of Steel', with a typically emotive vocal from Hayward, and Buddy Holly's 'Learning The Game' which remains true to the spirit of the original with an infectious guitar hook.

The arrangements on *Songwriter* bear little resemblance to the Moody Blues with Hayward's voice and guitar being the only obvious connection. Overall, although some of the songs are not as strong as they might be and the lyrics occasionally lapse into cliché, it remains a solid album. It reached number 28 in the UK album chart and 37 in the *Billboard* chart and remains his best-selling album on both sides of the Atlantic. Three singles were released from the album, although none charted.

Jeff Wayne's Musical Version of The War of the Worlds (2 LP: June 1978)

This needs no introduction, the album and concerts have been a huge commercial success. Hayward sings on two tracks, the opening 'The Eve of the War' (along with Richard Burton's spoken prose) and the token ballad 'Forever Autumn'. Although other notable singers like David Essex and Chris Thompson were involved, Hayward's performance is the most convincing. It also helps that 'Forever Autumn' is by far the best song in the musical. He sings the role of the 'Journalist' and at the time, it was for him, a rare instance of performing someone else's songs. He remains very appreciative of the song stating that it was one of the easiest he ever recorded. The wordless backing harmonies during 'The Eve of the War' are (intentionally) reminiscent of 'Nights in White Satin' while the melancholic 'Forever Autumn' is closer to 'Tuesday Afternoon'. Released as a single, in August 1978 it peaked at number five in the UK chart. Not only would it occasionally be performed live by the Moodies, but it also became a staple of their compilation albums. Hayward reprised his role for Wayne's 2006 to 2010 *The War of the Worlds* tours.

That same year he also guested on the album *Eye of Wendor: Prophecies* by prog-rock band Mandalaband. Rick Wakeman no doubt had 'Forever Autumn' in mind when he chose Hayward to sing the listless ballad 'Still Waters Run Deep' on the 1999 *Return to the Centre of the Earth* album. Like *The War of the Worlds*, it features several prominent guest vocalists and an actor (Patrick Stewart) as the narrator.

Night Flight (LP: June 1980)

Most of Hayward's second album was recorded in 1979 in between touring commitments with the band and released in 1980 while they were working on *Long Distance Voyager*. He had been impressed by Jeff Wayne's production on 'Forever Autumn' so he seemed like the obvious choice for this album. Six out of the ten songs are non-Hayward compositions and this album distances him even further from the sound of the Moody Blues. The title song (written by Wayne and Paul Vigrass) was released as a single and is very late '70s pop. It does, however, provide an uplifting start, buoyed by Hayward's enthusiastic vocal and a spirited orchestral arrangement similar to 'The Eve of the War'. Of the other covers, Hall and Oates soul-pop 'I'm Sorry' doesn't suit Hayward at all while the title 'It's Not On' is an appropriate reaction to Wayne and Gary Osborne's insipid MOR ballad.

Hayward's four songs vary in style and quality. 'Suitcase' is perhaps the best, beginning in 'New Horizons' ballad territory before concluding with a memorable choral and orchestral coda. 'Nearer to You' on the other hand with its cod disco rhythm, synth swirls and girlie backing voices is dangerously close to Bee Gees territory. Two singles were released from the album to no success. That same year Hayward also released a single with Marti Webb titled 'Unexpected Song'.

Moving Mountains (LP: September 1985)

The third album was recorded in 1984 and 1985 between band albums. Moodies' producer Tony Visconti oversees one track, as does Jeff Wayne, but Martin Wyatt produces the rest, and he does an excellent job. This time Hayward is solely responsible for all but two of the nine songs (ten on the 1989 CD reissue) and it was his strongest collection thus far. Highlights are many, but I would single out the lilting title song that would have sat comfortably on a Moodies album with dexterous guitar picking and Chris White's gorgeous sax playing echoing 'Driftwood'. Hayward is playing his 1964 Stratocaster here which features strongly on both this album and *Night Flight*. 'Lost and Found' is a beautifully constructed ballad with an infectious chorus and inventive drum fills. 'Goodbye' is a breezy, acoustic song with a double-tracked vocal and a catchy instrumental hook.

The only missteps are the heavy-handed keyboard bridge during the reggae-infused 'One Again' (produced by Visconti) and 'Silverbird' (co-written with Wayne). While it boasts a lively flamenco guitar hook and rich choral backing from P.P. Arnold and Vicki Brown, at a little under eight minutes, it's four minutes too long. The closing 'The Best Is Yet to Come' is one of my all-time favourite ballads and although it doesn't match the sincerity of Clifford T. Ward's original, Peter Knight's tasteful orchestral arrangement and Hayward's heartfelt vocal work their charm.

Classic Blue (October 1989)

The fourth album is a personal favourite, thanks to the presence of the London Philharmonic Orchestra under the direction of Mike Batt, who also produced the album. Clearly, this is a nod to *Days of Future Passed*, although the songs are mostly cover versions, sprinkled with a few of Batt's own tunes. The album certainly lives up to its title with an impeccable selection of classic songs. With the exception of Batt's 'As Long as the Moon Can Shine' from 1986, the original songs were all released between 1965 and 1979.

The arrangements are suitably tasteful for the most part, and apart from the occasional triumphant surge, the orchestrations allow Hayward's sensitive, reverb-heavy vocal (occasionally backed by Batt's falsetto) to carry the songs. Some, like 'God Only Knows', 'A Whiter Shade of Pale' and 'Man of the World', work better than might be expected, although 'Stairway to Heaven' takes Hayward outside his vocal comfort zone. No such problems with 'MacArthur Park' however; in my view, it's better than the 1968 Richard Harris original (which takes some doing) and is worth the price of admission alone. 'The Tracks of My Tears' b/w 'Railway Hotel' was released as a single.

The View from the Hill (CD: October 1996)

Another album and another producer, this time it's respected session guitarist Phil Palmer who provides a bright, razor-sharp sound. It was recorded at Mulinetti Studios, Genoa, Italy where the final two Moody Blues albums would be produced. Palmer and touring keyboardist Paul Bliss wrote two of the songs and both play on the album. Hayward wrote or co-wrote the other nine. It was recorded in 1995 and 1996, mostly during the summer months when the band weren't touring. The results for me is Hayward's best collection of solo songs that rank alongside some of his best work with the band. He also extends his vocabulary beyond the love themes that have been prevalent in much of his recent work.

Several songs including 'The Promised Land', 'Something to Believe In', 'Shame' and 'Billy' have a social conscience theme, but the music is by no means downbeat. They all combine beautiful melodies with a memorable chorus and 'The Promised Land' is particularly uplifting (with a hint of Bruce Hornsby). Hayward's vocals are suitably emotive with strong support from layered acoustic and electric guitars, piano and keys, strings and gorgeous backing harmonies. Other standout songs are the upbeat opener 'I Heard It' with a catchy choral hook that's on a par with the Moodies' hits of the 1980s, the haunting 'Broken Dream' (probably my favourite) with delicate classical guitar and sustained keys, and to close, 'Children of Paradise' a sweet acoustic ballad with a delightful string arrangement and tender vocal.

The album was recorded and released in the eight-year gap that separated the *Keys of the Kingdom* and *Strange Times* albums. As a mark of his faith in the album, it formed the basis of Hayward's 1996-1998 solo tours. Despite being an artistic success, *The View from the Hill* was the least successful in terms of chart performance and fans would have to wait more than sixteen years for his next studio album.

Live in San Juan Capistrano (CD: 1998, VHS: 1998, DVD: 2002)

This live album followed in the wake of *The View from the Hill* album and the 1996-1998 tours which saw Hayward performing in small venues and bookstores across America. At the end of the tour he played three dates in San Juan Capistrano, California and two of those, on the 3 and 4 April 1998, were recorded and filmed. The DVD, in particular, captures the warmth and intimacy of the performances, including Hayward's modest, softly spoken introductions. Moodies regulars Paul Bliss (keyboards) and Gordon Marshall (drums, flute) along with Mickey Feat (bass, vocals) provide solid support. The audio was edited to fit onto a single CD, but the video and DVD are the full, near two-hour show with excellent sound and decent picture quality. The balance between Hayward's solo material and Moody Blues standards (plus

'Blue Guitar' and 'Forever Autumn') is spot on, performed both acoustically and electrically. We can even forgive the drum solo at the end of 'The Story in Your Eyes'.

Spirits of the Western Sky (CD: February 2013)

For his sixth and most recent studio album, in 2012 Hayward returned to Mulinetti Studios, Genoa. Several years earlier, he and his wife Marie had moved to an apartment in Monaco in the South of France so that he could be close to the Italian border and Genoa. He also recorded in Nashville with the musicians he worked with on the 2011 tribute album *Moody Bluegrass TWO... Much Love*. He handles the majority of the production, aided by Albert Parodi, while Anne Dudley, who worked on the *Keys of the Kingdom* album, provides the orchestral arrangements. Kenny Loggins adds guitar fills and vocal support to 'On the Road to Love' which he co-wrote with Hayward.

It begins strongly with the breezy 'In Your Blue Eyes' featuring some fine lead and rhythm guitar. The standout song, however, is the slow-burning 'The Western Sky' featuring a basic but infectious chord progression and beautiful vocal support from Tracey Ackerman. It's a supremely crafted song that doesn't waste a second of its seven minutes. It's complemented by 'The Eastern Sun', a pastoral ballad with a sparse but inventive arrangement of two acoustic guitars playing counterpoint rhythm. The folky vibe reminded me of early Simon & Garfunkel. The album begins to sag around the halfway mark, however. The three Nashville songs certainly have an authentic country sound with Dobro, fiddle, banjo, mandolin and Hayward's vocal inflection, but it's not for me I'm afraid. That said, Glen Duncan's violin solo and coda during the reworked 'Broken Dream' is simply sublime. The final four tracks smack of filler material, including two techno versions of 'I Know You're Out There Somewhere' (retitled 'Out There Somewhere') and to be honest the album would have been better off without them.

Spirits... Live (CD: August 2014, DVD: 2014)

The title sums this up succinctly, and like *Live in San Juan Capistrano*, it was recorded at the end of an American tour. This time the venue was the Buckhead Theater, Atlanta on 17 August 2013. The tour did, however, continue in 2014, in between the Moody Blues' *Timeless Flight* tour dates. Backup comes from Moodies keyboardist Alan Hewitt and vocalist, keyboardist Julie Ragins along with guitarist Mike Dawes (the latter two are still supporting Hayward in 2019).

Again, the DVD captures the full concert and also features a one-hour documentary 'On the Road to Love', with behind the scenes footage from the 2013 US tour. Although the staging is basic, we get to see Hayward and his band up close and personal. Both picture and sound are superb with a satisfying balance of acoustic and electric performances. The DVD sales in America were particularly good and on 28 February 2015, the concert footage was broadcast on TV by PBS.

Live in Concert at the Capitol Theatre (DVD: 2016)
One aspect of solo touring, in particular, that appeals to Hayward, is the freedom to play acoustic guitar which is again evident here. Like *Spirits... Live*, this near two-hour disc was filmed by filmmaker and composer David Minasian, and the band line-up remained the same. It was recorded at the Capitol Theatre in Clearwater, Florida in 2015. The DVD includes a bonus music video for a new song, 'The Wind of Heaven', written by Hayward and Minasian. Clocking in at eight and a half minutes, it's a laid-back and pleasant enough song, although Minasian's organ solo is the most arresting part.

All the Way (CD: 2016)
This is a fifteen-track compilation culled from studio and live albums. Personally, my song selections would have been a little different, but as an introduction to Hayward's solo work, this is as good as any place to start. A 'Tour Edition' includes a bonus disc with previously unreleased tracks.

John Lodge
From the 1967 *Days of Future Passed* album onwards, John Lodge's contributions to the Moody Blues have been immense. He also has the distinction of being the composer of the song that closes all their concerts. Arguably, he was at the peak of his songwriting powers in the 1970s and the *Seventh Sojourn* album, in particular, proved that he could write both ballads and rockers and turn them into hits. His songs, along with Justin Hayward's, both individually and collectively, would dominate the band's albums and setlists. Although he's often labelled as the band's resident rock and roller, based on songs like 'Ride My See-Saw' and 'I'm Just a Singer (In a Rock and Roll Band)', he's also responsible for sensitive ballads like 'Emily's Song' and the expansive 'One More Time to Live'. As a result, his solo work was open to all possibilities.

Like Hayward, following the *Blue Jays* project he released his debut album *Natural Avenue* in early 1977. Unlike Hayward however, he surprisingly failed to capitalise on its success. It would be a lengthy 38-year wait before his second album, the aptly titled *10,000 Light Years Ago* (released just two months before his 70th birthday). It was a reunion of sorts with Mike Pinder and Ray Thomas playing on one song. Like the other Moodies solo projects, however, he generally chose to work with session musicians and later, members of the touring band.

Regular Yes artist Roger Dean's superb cover and logo for *Natural Avenue* is his only artwork for a Moody Blues related studio album. He also designed the cover for the 2017 *Live from Birmingham: The 10,000 Light Years Tour*, reusing the same logo.

Natural Avenue (LP: January 1977)
This record was released just two weeks before Hayward's *Songwriter* album, and the contrast between the two as writers and performers is apparent.

With Tony Clarke producing, Lodge is backed by seasoned musicians and his rhythm partnership with Kenney Jones, in particular, is extremely tight. Several songs have a retro sound including the title track with its energetic rock and roll shuffle, harmonica (from Lodge himself) and both soprano and alto saxes to the fore. There's also a superlative sax solo from Jimmy Jewel during 'Summer Breeze'. Chris Spedding's guitar soloing, on the other hand, is uncharacteristically sloppy at times, especially during 'Piece of My Heart'.

The album has its fair share of anthemic ballads, including 'Who Could Change', 'Carry Me (a song for Kristian)' and 'Rainbow', where Lodge's singing has a fragile vulnerability. During the penultimate 'Say You Love Me' even his falsetto strains to reach the high notes. And although I have a penchant for lush orchestrations and harmonies, the Brian Rogers Orchestra and the backing vocals are too sugary sweet for my tastes. 'Broken Dreams, Hard Road' boasts the album's best instrumental hook and while the concluding 'Children of Rock 'n Roll' has a nimble bass line, it's let down by the song's overt sentimentality.

The album reached number 38 in the UK album chart but failed to breach the *Billboard* top 100. The 1996 CD reissue includes the 1980 single 'Street Café' (where Lodge seems to be aping Bryan Ferry) and B-side 'Threw It All Away' which features fine piano from Patrick Moraz and soulful female backing vocals. Both tracks are superbly produced by Pip Williams.

10,000 Light Years Ago (CD, LP: May 2015)

When Lodge returned to the recording studio in 2014, he took Chris Spedding with him along with the Moody Blues touring musicians and, on one song, a couple of surprise guests. At less than 32 minutes and just eight songs, it's pretty short (even by vinyl standards) but the material and performances are strong, especially the first half of the album. It was produced by Lodge and keyboardist Alan Hewitt who co-wrote three of the songs.

The opening song 'In My Mind' wears its Pink Floyd influences on its sleeve with a sprawling, bluesy guitar intro, Gordon Marshall's tasteful drum fills and Lodge's echo-drenched vocal. It was nominated for "Rock Anthem of the Year" by *Prog Magazine*. The nostalgic 'Those Days in Birmingham' is a superb mid-tempo song with a memorable chorus and blistering guitar soloing. The understated 'Simply Magic' (written for Lodge's grandson) features lovely acoustic guitar picking backed by flute and Mellotron strings from Messrs Thomas and Pinder respectively. 'Get Me Out of Here' shows that Lodge hasn't lost his edge as a songwriter with inventive rhythm work, superb slide guitar and another strong chorus.

The second half is less consistent, ranging from the whimsical, vaudeville style of 'Love Passed Me By' to the inevitable rock and roll pastiche '(You Drive Me) Crazy' and the token piano ballad 'Lose Your Love'. The title song, on the other hand, is a suitably rousing closer with full-blooded riffs, soaring guitar fills and an anthemic choral hook.

As well as retailing as a single CD, the album was packaged as a limited two-disc edition with a DVD which includes an interview with Lodge, session footage and a promo video.

Live from Birmingham: The 10,000 Light Years Tour (Deluxe DVD/CD Box Set, 2 LP: 2017)

In September 2016, Lodge embarked on his first-ever solo tour and this superb live recording is from the last night. Filmed at the Town Hall in his hometown of Birmingham, both sound and picture are excellent. From the 'Light Years Overture' and the energetic opening song 'Steppin' in a Slide Zone' to a storming 'Ride My See-Saw', Lodge and band are in stunning form. The line-up includes Alan Hewitt (keyboards), Gordon Marshall (drums), Tim Maple (guitars), Norda Mullen (flute) and Gemma Johnson (cello). Along with a decent selection of songs from the last album and 'Saved by the Music' from *Blue Jays*, it includes several Moodies tunes (penned by Lodge naturally).

Ray Thomas

Ray Thomas' songs for the Moody Blues contrasted with the more commercial and contemporary styles of Justin Hayward and John Lodge. Never predictable, they encompassed sentiment, romance, nostalgia and humour. When he retired at the end of 2002, it was hoped that without the pressure of touring, he would one day find the inspiration and energy to record another solo album, but that wasn't to be. During the band's hiatus in the 1970s however, he seized the opportunity with both hands, recording two back to back albums *From Mighty Oaks* (1975) and *Hopes, Wishes and Dreams* (1976). The songs were mostly co-written with singer, songwriter (and one-time Denny Laine & The Diplomats member) Nicky James, who had signed to Threshold Records in 1972. A core line-up of musicians feature on both albums, including brothers John and Trevor Jones on guitar and bass respectively, from '70s prog band Jonesy and Mike Moran on keyboards. Phil Travers provided the evocative artwork for both albums and *Hopes, Wishes and Dreams* would be his final Moody Blues related cover. Another familiar name, engineer Derek Varnals assisted Thomas with the production.

A four-disc box set combining both albums was released in 2010 which concludes with a new song 'The Trouble with Memories', co-written by Thomas and keyboardist Bias Boshell. Additionally, Esoteric Recordings remastered and reissued both albums in 2011. Following retirement, Thomas continued to do occasional session work which included work for contemporary prog-rock bands and several album tracks for The Pinder Brothers (Mike Pinder's sons Michael Lee and Matt). He remained in touch with Pinder over the years, and as co-founders of the Moody Blues (and born just two days apart), they often reminisced about the early days and reflected on the band's achievements.

From Mighty Oaks (LP: July 1975)

While Hayward and Lodge were launching the *Blue Jays* project, and the

Graeme Edge Band were finalising their first album, Thomas entered Threshold studios in 1974 with a collection of new songs. This album sees him dabbling in several genres and is bookended by two standout tracks. The title track is a sweeping overture for full orchestra arranged and conducted by Richard Hewson, harking back to *Days of Future Passed*. The concluding 'I Wish We Could Fly' (the only song written by Thomas alone) features an uplifting chorus delivered with passion, supported by a dramatic orchestral and choral backing. In between, it's a fusion of pop-rock ('Hey Mama Life' which features a strong melody and soaring coda), country ('Rock-A-Bye Baby Blues'), big band swing (the single 'High Above My Head'), MOR ('Love Is the Key') and sentimental ballads ('Play It Again' and 'Adam and I'). The latter provided the inspiration for the album title and Travers' splendid artwork which forgoes his usual fantasy imagery for the naturalistic landscape style of John Constable.

While the songs brim with confidence, for me they all too often take the safe, mainstream pop-rock route. Lyrically, however, it's Thomas as we know him. Even when he sings in the third person, his down to earth, homespun philosophising is almost autobiographical.

Hopes, Wishes and Dreams (LP: June 1976)

In terms of style and quality, this album is another mixed bag. The opening 'In Your Song' incongruously combines the Eagles' crisp guitar and harmonies with a limp disco beat. 'Friends' is better with fine piano and guitar exchanges between Mike Moran and John Jones. They give the album that all important lift while bassist Trevor Jones and drummer Graham Deakin do a solid, workmanlike job. 'We Need Love' has power ballad pretensions while 'Within Your Eyes' is a melancholic acoustic ballad. 'One Night Stand' (released as a single) is a victim of the mid-'70's disco craze, and the pop-gospel influenced 'Keep On Searching' seems to be modelled on the Rolling Stones' 'Tumbling Dice'. 'Migration', on the other hand, benefits from the absence of an obvious rhythm track with lush piano and flute providing all that's needed to give the song its beauty and grace. 'The Last Dream' attempts to end the album on a high but the uninspired melody and extravagant arrangement lack the requisite grandeur.

One has to admire Thomas for the courage of his convictions and displaying a different side to his work with the Moody Blues. Like *From Mighty Oaks*, vocally Thomas is on top form throughout and the production and arrangements on both albums are immaculate.

Mike Pinder

From 1964 to 1978, Mike Pinder was for many the heart and soul of the Moody Blues. He was certainly one of the chief architects in terms of shaping the post-Denny Laine sound and identity. His distinct Mellotron tones were present on virtually every song. As a composer, his individualistic style and lyrics steeped in spiritualism and mysticism set him apart from Justin Hayward and John

Lodge in particular. If any of the band members were going to have a busy solo career, you would have put your money on Pinder, but it didn't turn out that way. When he left the band in 1978, he effectively retired as a professional musician.

His debut album *The Promise* was recorded at his Indigo Ranch studio in Malibu during the band's 1970's hiatus. He had relocated from the UK to California in 1974, and following the divorce of his first wife that year, he married an American girl. It was a healthy musical environment; he had his own studio and was free from the distractions of recording and touring with the band. His second, and most recent album of original songs, *Among the Stars*, did not appear until eighteen years later, however. Although he was inactive professionally, in the interim he was still writing and recording demos. In 2013, Esoteric Recordings combined the two albums in a three-disc set which also included an interview on DVD, recorded in June 2012.

In 1995 he released *A Planet with One Mind* featuring children's stories recited by himself, backed by ambient world music. *A People with One Heart* followed in 1996. As yet, however, he has shown no sign of releasing a third album of songs. When he joined the other band members for the April 2018 Rock & Roll Hall of Fame ceremony, he was in very good spirits, and there was no hint of the animosity that reputedly clouded his departure in 1978.

The Promise (LP: April 1976)

On its initial release, this surprised many, especially those expecting a Mellotron-fest. Instead, it's an eclectic collection of songs, featuring no less than fifteen session musicians and singers. He does, however, use the Mellotron Mark V for the first time on this album. Ironically, Patrick Moraz played the same instrument on the *Octave* tour after he replaced Pinder in 1978.

He had certainly soaked-up the musical language of the West Coast, resulting in a laid-back but optimistic album, and vocally Pinder had never sounded better. Several songs have a distinct mid-'70s, soul-pop vibe, aided by the gospel-tinged backing voices of Maxine Willard, Jeanne King and Julia Tillman. The musicianship is exemplary, especially Flynn J. Johnson's nimble bass on 'Free as a Dove' and 'Carry On' and Jim Dillon's slide guitar during 'You'll Make It Through', a song he co-wrote with Pinder. The smooth jazz 'Someone to Believe In' features superb impromptu tenor sax and flute soloing from Tom Peterson.

'Air' is a rare instrumental with a memorable melody and lively flute, trumpet and sax playing, but it's the concluding three songs that epitomise Pinder. The understated 'Message' features classical guitar, piano, ARP synth and sitar, while 'The Seed' is a throwback to the Moodies with Pinder's spoken verse over an ambient backing. The lyrics to the title song are typically personal, 'It's been my goal for nine long years to write this song', and Mellotron comes into its own for the symphonic coda.

Among the Stars (CD: 1994)

This album takes the soul-pop elements of *The Promise* and refines and updates them, resulting in a very polished (and American) pop-rock sound. For the most part, Pinder turns his mind to love, and there's nothing wrong with that. In addition to the impressive line-up of musicians and singers (more than twenty in total), it's a family affair with no less than five Pinder's (including Mike himself) credited. The musicianship throughout is faultless with excellent guitar, sax, bass and drumming. All the songs – with the exception of the title track, a poem – have a sunny, upbeat vibe. Even the final song 'The World Today', which takes a political, socially aware stance, has an uplifting tone before concluding with a haze of swirling acoustic guitar and Mellotron strings.

I'll leave the final words to Pinder himself, taken from the sleeve notes: 'To all my listeners: I dedicate this music to you, with thoughts of the past, and hopes for the future, always evolving, in the here and now, my gratitude as love, grows within.'

Graeme Edge

Of the five band members, Graeme Edge, being a non-singer, was the only one who formed his own band (albeit studio-bound) in the Graeme Edge Band. The group featured Adrian Gurvitz and brother Paul. Edge and Gurvitz had equal input, and as such the two albums released, *Kick Off Your Muddy Boots* and *Paradise Ballroom*, were the least like the Moody Blues. The Gurvitz brothers had recently been involved in a similar project, the Baker Gurvitz Army with Ginger Baker. The former Cream drummer also guests on *Kick Off Your Muddy Boots,* and Ray Thomas adds backing vocals to the same album. To introduce the band, a non-album single 'We Like to Do It' produced by Tony Clarke, was released in 1974. It eventually found its way onto the 2009 CD reissue of the first album.

On *Kick Off Your Muddy Boots*, Edge and Adrian Gurvitz wrote half the songs each, whereas on the second album they co-wrote all the songs. They were also responsible for the impeccable production on both albums. Adrian supplied guitar and vocals while Paul handled bass and backing vocals. The end results can best be described as blues flavoured rock with a touch of soul-funk and a glossy veneer. Artist Joe Petagno (noted for his work for Motorhead amongst others) was responsible for the distinctive sci-fi meets fantasy covers for both albums.

These albums would be Edge's only significant recordings outside the Moody Blues, although he did contribute to the 2011 bluegrass tribute album *Moody Bluegrass TWO ... Much Love* along with Hayward, Lodge, Thomas and Pinder.

Kick Off Your Muddy Boots (LP: September 1975)

This album is a strong and confident collection of rock songs with Adrian Gurvitz's soulful singing and guitar to the fore. The blues-inflected soloing and solid riffs on songs like 'Bareback Rider', 'In Dreams' and 'Lost in Space' would not sound out of place on an Eric Clapton album. On the other hand, the lyrical slide guitar playing on the ballad 'Have You Ever Wondered', and up-tempo 'Shotgun' owe more to George Harrison. Martyn Ford's lush orchestral arrangements provide the sweetener on several songs including the closing 'Somethin' We'd Like to Say', which includes inventive drumming from Edge. Ginger Baker joins him for the swing rhythm on 'Gew Janna Woman' and another guest, Brian Parrish, adds his distinctive vocal to the rhythmic 'My Life's Not Wasted'. The lively string arrangements on both these songs are superb. The only minor blemish is the instrumental 'The Tunnel', a pastiche of Isaac Hayes' 'Theme from Shaft' (the clue is in the title) complete with a syncopated funk rhythm and wah-wah guitar. The aforementioned 'We Like to Do It' is a cross between the playful tone of Lovin Spoonful's 'Daydream' (including the opening riff) and the boogie rock of Status Quo and has not dated particularly well.

Paradise Ballroom (LP: April 1977)

Although the title song clocks in at nearly ten minutes, this is no prog-rock mini-epic. Blue-eyed soul-funk is the name of the game, complete with Earth, Wind & Fire-style horns. Adrian's lively guitar work on this track is a joy, as it is throughout the album. 'Human' is more laid-back with a pleasant acoustic guitar and flute motif that bears some resemblance to 'Forever Autumn'. 'Everybody Needs Somebody' is based around a compelling riff that has danceability written all over it. The prominent guitar soloing in the mid-tempo rocker 'All Is Fair in Love' is straight from the Eric Clapton school of licks. 'Down, Down, Down' is a melodic diversion with sweet harmonies and steel guitar from B.J. Cole that sounds uncannily like Gallagher & Lyle. 'In the Light Of Night' is fairly bland soft funk but the album ends on a high with the engaging 'Caroline', a catchy ballad with great sax playing from Bill Easley. Other musicians on the album include Blue Weaver and Tony Hymas on keyboards augmented by strings and brass.

The 2009 Esoteric Recordings remastered reissue includes the bonus track 'Be My Eyes' which was the B-side of the single 'Everybody Needs Somebody' released five weeks after the original album.

Patrick Moraz

With only one songwriting credit during his thirteen years with the Moody Blues (for 'The Spirit', co-written with Graeme Edge), Patrick Moraz maintained a steady output of solo projects during his time in the band. He released several solo albums during this period and toured with his own band. As one half of the Moraz-Bruford partnership, he also recorded two jazz albums, *Music for Piano and Drums* (1983) and *Flags* (1985) and toured both albums with drummer Bill Bruford. Two Moraz-Bruford live albums, *Live in Tokyo* recorded at Laforet Museum, Akasaka in July 1985 and *Music for Piano and Drums: Live in Maryland* recorded in November 1984, were released in 2009 and

2012 respectively. If you can track them down, Moraz also released the solo performances *Future Memories Live on TV* (1979) and *Moraz Live / Abbey Road* (2012), recorded in 1987.

The contrast between the Moody Blues and his work outside the band couldn't be more acute. Like Vangelis, Moraz is a very individualistic musician and personality with a penchant for jazz, prog, Brazilian rhythms and solo piano. His acrimonious departure in 1991 mirrored his premature dismissal from Yes in November 1976. Despite compositional contributions to Yes' *Going for The One* album, released following his departure, he was never credited.

Although the solo material between 1978 and 1991 does not represent Moraz at his best, there is still evidence of his prestigious talents as a composer and musician. Although it falls outside the scope of this book, his debut solo album *The Story of I* is highly recommended. It was recorded when he was a member of Yes, who like the Moody Blues took time out in the mid-'70s to pursue solo projects. There are also some beautiful solo piano pieces on the albums *Resonance* (2000) and *ESP* (2003).

Patrick Moraz (LP: September 1978)
This is the album Moraz was preparing in Brazil when he received a call to go to London to meet the Moody Blues. His third solo album, it doesn't scale the heights of *The Story of I* (1976) and *Out in The Sun* (1977) but still contains elements of Moraz at his progressive best. It crackles and sizzles with stunning flights of keyboard virtuosity that effortlessly combine showmanship with melody. Except for two songs, including 'Keep the Children Alive', it's fully instrumental, and track titles like 'Jungles of the World' and 'Temples of Joy' reflect the tone of the music. Latin flavours, prog, jazz-fusion and world music rhythms are all part of the intoxicating brew. The longest piece, 'The Conflict', in particular, brings to mind Emerson, Lake & Palmer's 'Tarkus'. Only during the more experimental, avant-garde moments (and these are few) does he perhaps lose a sense of perspective. Otherwise, this is an album that deserved wider recognition. The 2006 CD remaster contains a ten-minute, improvised bonus track.

Coexistence (LP: 1980)
This album is actually a collaboration with Syrinx, aka pan pipe flute player Simion Stanciu. Confusingly, it was reissued with a different title, *Libertate*, in 1989. It's a not altogether successful fusion of jazz, new-age, classical and world music where Syrinx has the upper hand for the most part, instrumentally. The original cover artwork is superb, though.

Timecode (LP: November 1984)
This album is probably Moraz's most disparaged, by prog-rock fans at least. Despite the presence of singer John McBurnie from his first two albums and Bill Bruford's distinctive electronic drums on the track 'Life in the

Underworld', it remains a product of its time. Utilising 1980s production techniques, it combines synth-pop and dance music influences with all too brief elements of prog. With vocals dominating, this is song based and, with the exception of the instrumental 'Black Brains of Positronic Africa', his customary keyboard showmanship is kept firmly on a tight leash.

Future Memories II (1984)

Recorded live for Swiss TV at the Aquarius Studios, Geneva in April 1982. It features Moraz performing solo and spontaneously with elements of jazz and classical music. Track titles like 'Video Games (How Basic Can You Get?)' gives a rough idea of what to expect. It was remastered and reissued on CD in 2006 with bonus tracks.

Future Memories I & II (LP: 1985)

More of the same, this time incorporating longer pieces 'Eastern Sundays' and 'Metamorphoses' from 1979 as featured on *Future Memories Live on TV*. Although the performances were improvised, Moraz did two takes of the longer pieces, the first take to show the cameras the movements and the second take for the actual recording.

Human Interface (LP: 1987)

After the disappointment of *Timecode*, this is a return to form for Moraz. It's a purely instrumental solo album and contains several glorious flights, including the opening 'Light Elements' with its beautifully rich synth orchestrations. It brings Vangelis to mind and is the album's standout track. 'Beyond Binary' is more dramatic and is reminiscent of Keith Emerson's solo work. The triumphant 'Cin-A-Maah' is closer to Rick Wakeman territory and another memorable piece. As the title would suggest 'Modular Symphony (First Movement)' is in a baroque, classical vein, albeit with a Moraz twist. Although the rest of the album has its moments, it's more ambient and doesn't maintain the promise of the opening tracks. The 2007 remastered CD contains no new music but has two extended live versions.

Seventeen (Almost) Forgotten Songs

To round off the book, this is a personal selection of Moody Blues songs that are often overlooked or rarely performed but should not go unsung. With so many songs worthy of inclusion, I narrowed the choices by restricting it to one song from each album. These are not necessarily my favourite songs, but they are all worth revisiting. I've again taken the liberty of including the *Blue Jays* album. And if there seems to be an abundance of ballads, I make no apologies for that.

'Let Me Go' – *The Magnificent Moodies* (1965). This soulful, piano-led ballad is the best Denny Laine / Mike Pinder composition on the album.

'Day Begins' – *Days of Future Passed* (1967). The sumptuous orchestral introduction, incorporating the album's principal tunes. It would have to wait many years before being performed live.

'Visions of Paradise' – *In Search of the Lost Chord* (1968). A heavenly, underrated song from Hayward and Thomas that did not feature in the band's setlist.

'Are You Sitting Comfortably?' – *On the Threshold of a Dream* (1969). A gorgeous evocation of the Arthurian legend. This song would be played live in later years, in an acoustic setting.

"Out and In' – *To Our Children's Children's Children* (1969). Pinder's often overlooked, other-worldly view of the universe with sumptuous Mellotron orchestrations.

'And the Tide Rushes In' – *A Question of Balance* (1970). Thomas' sincere evocation of a failing marriage. Another neglected song as far as live performances were concerned.

'Emily's Song' – *Every Good Boy Deserves Favour* (1971). A beautiful lullaby for a baby girl. The song was first performed by the band in 1992 with the Colorado Symphony Orchestra.

'The Land of Make-Believe' – *Seventh Sojourn* (1972). A soaring ballad resurrected by Hayward for his solo concerts.

'Who Are You Now' – *Blue Jays* (1975). Hayward & Lodge meet Simon & Garfunkel, and the end result is pure poetry. It was performed on the subsequent UK tour.

'Had to Fall in Love' – *Octave* (1978). Despite the walking bass line, there's nothing pedestrian about Hayward's haunting ballad.

'Nervous' – *Long Distance Voyager* (1981). Typically atmospheric verses and an anthemic chorus from Lodge. It was performed on his 2016 solo tour.

'Hole in the World' / 'Under My Feet' – *The Present* (1983). Another splendid melody from Lodge, this time in two parts.

'It May Be a Fire' – *The Other Side of Life* (1986). This may be another Lodge song, but the honours go to Hayward for his stunning guitar playing.

'Deep' – *Sur la mer* (1988). More superb guitar soloing and despite it being Hayward's most sexually-charged song, it was never attempted live.

'Celtic Sonant' – *Keys of the Kingdom* (1991). An evocative folk ballad from Thomas. Close your eyes and you can almost smell the sea air.

'The Swallow' – *Strange Times* (1999). A lovely, late period song from Hayward with tasteful acoustic guitar picking.

'On This Christmas Day' – *December* (2003). The title says it all, Lodge's best tune on the band's final album.

Top Twenty Moody Blues Songs

I thought it would be fun to conclude the book with my personal top twenty Moody Blues songs. In the interest of diversity and fair play, I've excluded songs that appear in the 'Seventeen (Almost) Forgotten Songs' section of this book and limited my selection to no more than two from each album. Despite a lengthy shortlist, choosing the songs wasn't too difficult, the hard part was placing them in order of preference. No doubt every reader will have their own list of favorites, and as such you may consider compiling your own top twenty.

Thirteen of these top twenty songs were released as singles, although that didn't influence their inclusion. For the record, there are eight tracks from the 1960s, seven from the 1970s, three from the 1980s, one from the 1990s and one from the 2000s. With a total playing time of around 102 minutes, as a physical compilation album, that would equate to two CDs or three vinyl LPs.

1. 'Nights in White Satin / Late Lament' - *Days of Future Passed* (1967).
2. 'Question' - *A Question of Balance* (1970).
3. 'Have You Heard / The Voyage' - *On the Threshold of a Dream* (1969).
4. 'New Horizons' - *Seventh Sojourn* (1972).
5. 'One More Time to Live' - *Every Good Boy Deserves Favour* (1971).
6. 'Driftwood' - *Octave* (1978)
7. 'The Story in Your Eyes' - *Every Good Boy Deserves Favour* (1971).
8. 'Tuesday Afternoon' - *Days of Future Passed* (1967)
9. 'Go Now' - *The Magnificent Moodies* (1965).
10. 'Legend of a Mind' - *In Search of the Lost Chord* (1968)
11. 'Ride My See-Saw' - *In Search of the Lost Chord* (1968)
12. 'I Know You're Out There Somewhere' - *Sur la mer* (1988)
13. 'The Day We Meet Again' - *Octave* (1978).
14. 'Isn't Life Strange' - *Seventh Sojourn* (1972).
15. 'December Snow' - *December* (2003).
16. 'Nothing Changes' - *Strange Times* (1999).
17. 'Your Wildest Dreams' - *The Other Side of Life* (1986).
18. 'Watching and Waiting' - *To Our Children's Children's Children* (1969).
19. 'Running Water' - *The Present* (1983).
20. 'From the Bottom of My Heart (I Love You)' - *Go Now – The Moody Blues #1* (1965).

Bibliography

If this book has whetted your appetite, here is a selection of others that may be of interest.

Cushman, M., *Long Distance Voyagers: The Story of The Moody Blues 1965-1979* (Jacob Brown Media Group, 2018)

Grayson, C., *Wildest Dreams: A biography of the Moody Blues* (Independently published, 2018)

Whitfield, C., Whitfield B., *Timeless Troubadours: The Moody Blues Music and Message* (Muse House Press, 2013)

Randolph, A., *I'm Just Beginning to See: A Story in the Songs of Justin Hayward* (CreateSpace Independent Publishing Platform, 2013)

Edge, G., Marshall G., *The Written Works of Graeme Edge* (CreateSpace Independent Publishing Platform, 2012)

Wincentsen, E., *The Moody Blues Companion* (Wynn Publishing Company, 2001)

Online Resources

moodybluestoday.com – Official Moody Blues website
justinhayward.com – Official Justin Hayward website
johnlodge.com – Official John Lodge website
raythomas.co.uk – Official Ray Thomas website
mikepinder.com – Official Mike Pinder website
patrickmoraz.net – Official Patrick Moraz website

Also available in Sonicbond's On Track series

On Track series

AC/DC – Chris Sutton 978-1-78952-307-2
Allman Brothers Band – Andrew Wild 978-1-78952-252-5
Tori Amos – Lisa Torem 978-1-78952-142-9
Aphex Twin – Beau Waddell 978-1-78952-267-9
Asia – Peter Braidis 978-1-78952-099-6
Badfinger – Robert Day-Webb 978-1-878952-176-4
Barclay James Harvest – Keith and Monica Domone 978-1-78952-067-5
Beck – Arthur Lizie 978-1-78952-258-7
The Beat, General Public, Fine Young Cannibals – Steve Parry 978-1-78952-274-7
The Beatles 1962-1996 – Alberto Bravin and Andrew Wild 978-1-78952-355-3
The Beatles Solo 1969-1980 – Andrew Wild 978-1-78952-030-9
Blue Oyster Cult – Jacob Holm-Lupo 978-1-78952-007-1
Blur – Matt Bishop 978-178952-164-1
Marc Bolan and T.Rex – Peter Gallagher 978-1-78952-124-5
David Bowie 1964 to 1982 – Carl Ewens 978-1-78952-324-9
David Bowie 1963 to 2016 – Don Klees 978-1-78952-351-5
Kate Bush – Bill Thomas 978-1-78952-097-2
The Byrds – Andy McArthur 978-1-78952-280-8
Camel – Hamish Kuzminski 978-1-78952-040-8
Captain Beefheart – Opher Goodwin 978-1-78952-235-8
Caravan – Andy Boot 978-1-78952-127-6
Cardiacs – Eric Benac 978-1-78952-131-3
Wendy Carlos – Mark Marrington 978-1-78952-331-7
The Carpenters – Paul Tornbohm 978-1-78952-301-0
Nick Cave and The Bad Seeds – Dominic Sanderson 978-1-78952-240-2
Eric Clapton Solo – Andrew Wild 978-1-78952-141-2
The Clash (revised edition) – Nick Assirati 978-1-78952-325-6
Elvis Costello and The Attractions – Georg Purvis 978-1-78952-129-0
Crosby, Stills and Nash – Andrew Wild 978-1-78952-039-2
Creedence Clearwater Revival – Tony Thompson 978-1-78952-237-2
Crowded House – Jon Magidsohn 978-1-78952-292-1
The Damned – Morgan Brown 978-1-78952-136-8
David Bowie 1964 to 1982 – Carl Ewens 978-1-78952-324-9
David Bowie 1964 to 1982 – Carl Ewens 978-1-78952-324-9
Deep Purple and Rainbow 1968-79 – Steve Pilkington 978-1-78952-002-6
Deep Purple from 1984 – Phil Kafcaloudes 978-1-78952-354-6
Depeche Mode – Brian J. Robb 978-1-78952-277-8
Dire Straits – Andrew Wild 978-1-78952-044-6
The Divine Comedy – Alan Draper 978-1-78952-308-9
The Doors – Tony Thompson 978-1-78952-137-5
Dream Theater – Jordan Blum 978-1-78952-050-7
Bob Dylan 1962-1970 – Opher Goodwin 978-1-78952-275-2
Eagles – John Van der Kiste 978-1-78952-260-0
Earth, Wind and Fire – Bud Wilkins 978-1-78952-272-3
Electric Light Orchestra – Barry Delve 978-1-78952-152-8
Emerson Lake and Palmer – Mike Goode 978-1-78952-000-2
Fairport Convention – Kevan Furbank 978-1-78952-051-4
Peter Gabriel – Graeme Scarfe 978-1-78952-138-2
Genesis – Stuart MacFarlane 978-1-78952-005-7
Gentle Giant – Gary Steel 978-1-78952-058-3
Gong – Kevan Furbank 978-1-78952-082-8
Green Day – William E. Spevack 978-1-78952-261-7
Steve Hackett – Geoffrey Feakes 978-1-78952-098-9
Hall and Oates – Ian Abrahams 978-1-78952-167-2
Peter Hammill – Richard Rees Jones 978-1-78952-163-4
Roy Harper – Opher Goodwin 978-1-78952-130-6
Hawkwind (new edition) – Duncan Harris 978-1-78952-290-7
Jimi Hendrix – Emma Stott 978-1-78952-175-7
The Hollies – Andrew Darlington 978-1-78952-159-7
Horslips – Richard James 978-1-78952-263-1
The Human League and The Sheffield Scene – Andrew Darlington 978-1-78952-186-3
Humble Pie –Robert Day-Webb 978-1-78952-2761
Ian Hunter – G. Mick Smith 978-1-78952-304-1
The Incredible String Band – Tim Moon 978-1-78952-107-8
INXS – Manny Grillo 978-1-78952-302-7
Iron Maiden – Steve Pilkington 978-1-78952-061-3
Joe Jackson – Richard James 978-1-78952-189-4
The Jam – Stan Jeffries 978-1-78952-299-0
Jefferson Airplane – Richard Butterworth 978-1-78952-143-6
Jethro Tull – Jordan Blum 978-1-78952-016-3
J. Geils Band – James Romag 978-1-78952-332-4

Also available in Sonicbond's On Track series

Elton John in the 1970s – Peter Kearns 978-1-78952-034-7
Billy Joel – Lisa Torem 978-1-78952-183-2
Journey – Doug Thornton 978-1-78952-337-9
Judas Priest – John Tucker 978-1-78952-018-7
Kansas – Kevin Cummings 978-1-78952-057-6
Killing Joke – Nic Ransome 978-1-78952-273-0
The Kinks – Martin Hutchinson 978-1-78952-172-6
Korn – Matt Karpe 978-1-78952-153-5
Led Zeppelin – Steve Pilkington 978-1-78952-151-1
Level 42 – Matt Philips 978-1-78952-102-3
Little Feat – Georg Purvis – 978-1-78952-168-9
Magnum – Matthew Taylor – 978-1-78952-286-0
Aimee Mann – Jez Rowden 978-1-78952-036-1
Ralph McTell – Paul O. Jenkins 978-1-78952-294-5
Metallica – Barry Wood 978-1-78952-269-3
Joni Mitchell – Peter Kearns 978-1-78952-081-1
The Moody Blues – Geoffrey Feakes 978-1-78952-042-2
Motorhead – Duncan Harris 978-1-78952-173-3
Nektar – Scott Meze – 978-1-78952-257-0
New Order – Dennis Remmer – 978-1-78952-249-5
Nightwish – Simon McMurdo – 978-1-78952-270-9
Nirvana – William E. Spevack 978-1-78952-318-8
Laura Nyro – Philip Ward 978-1-78952-182-5
Oasis – Andrew Rooney 978-1-78952-300-3
Phil Ochs – Opher Goodwin 978-1-78952-326-3
Mike Oldfield – Ryan Yard 978-1-78952-060-6
Opeth – Jordan Blum 978-1-78-952-166-5
Pearl Jam – Ben L. Connor 978-1-78952-188-7
Tom Petty – Richard James 978-1-78952-128-3
Pink Floyd – Richard Butterworth 978-1-78952-242-6
The Police – Pete Braidis 978-1-78952-158-0
Porcupine Tree (Revised Edition) – Nick Holmes 978-1-78952-346-1
Procol Harum – Scott Meze 978-1-78952-315-7
Queen – Andrew Wild 978-1-78952-003-3
Radiohead – William Allen 978-1-78952-149-8
Gerry Rafferty – John Van der Kiste 978-1-78952-349-2
Rancid – Paul Matts 978-1-78952-187-0
Lou Reed 1972-1986 – Ethan Roy 978-1-78952-283-9
Renaissance – David Detmer 978-1-78952-062-0
REO Speedwagon – Jim Romag 978-1-78952-262-4
The Rolling Stones 1963-80 – Steve Pilkington 978-1-78952-017-0
Linda Ronstadt 1969-1989 – Daryl O. Lawrence 987-1-78952-293-8
Roxy Music – Michael Kulikowski 978-1-78952-335-5

Rush 1973 to 1982 – Richard James 978-1-78952-338-6
Sensational Alex Harvey Band – Peter Gallagher 978-1-7952-289-1
The Small Faces and The Faces – Andrew Darlington 978-1-78952-316-4
The Smashing Pumpkins – Matt Karpe 978-1-7952-291-4
The Smiths and Morrissey – Tommy Gunnarsson 978-1-78952-140-5
Soft Machine – Scott Meze 978-1078952-271-6
Sparks 1969-1979 – Chris Sutton 978-1-78952-279-2
Spirit – Rev. Keith A. Gordon – 978-1-78952- 248-8
Stackridge – Alan Draper 978-1-78952-232-7
Status Quo the Frantic Four Years – Richard James 978-1-78952-160-3
Steely Dan – Jez Rowden 978-1-78952-043-9
The Stranglers – Martin Hutchinson 978-1-78952-323-2
Talk Talk – Gary Steel 978-1-78952-284-6
Talking Heads – David Starkey 978-178952-353-9
Tears For Fears – Paul Clark – 978-178952-238-9
Thin Lizzy – Graeme Stroud 978-1-78952-064-4
Tool – Matt Karpe 978-1-78952-234-1
Toto – Jacob Holm-Lupo 978-1-78952-019-4
U2 – Eoghan Lyng 978-1-78952-078-1
UFO – Richard James 978-1-78952-073-6
Ultravox – Brian J. Robb 978-1-78952-330-0
Van Der Graaf Generator – Dan Coffey 978-1-78952-031-6
Van Halen – Morgan Brown – 9781-78952-256-3
Suzanne Vega – Lisa Torem 978-1-78952-281-5
Jack White And The White Stripes – Ben L. Connor 978-1-78952-303-4
The Who – Geoffrey Feakes 978-1-78952-076-7
Roy Wood and the Move – James R Turner 978-1-78952-008-8
Yes (new edition) – Stephen Lambe 978-1-78952-282-2
Neil Young 1963 to 1970 – Oper Goodwin 978-1-78952-298-3
Frank Zappa 1966 to 1979 – Eric Benac 978-1-78952-033-0
Warren Zevon – Peter Gallagher 978-1-78952-170-2
The Zombies – Emma Stott 978-1-78952-297-6
10CC – Peter Kearns 978-1-78952-054-5

... and many more to come!

Would you like to write for Sonicbond Publishing?

At Sonicbond Publishing we are always on the look-out for authors, particularly for our two main series:

On Track. Mixing fact with in depth analysis, the On Track series examines the work of a particular musical artist or group. All genres are considered from easy listening and jazz to 60s soul to 90s pop, via rock and metal.

On Screen. This series looks at the world of film and television. Subjects considered include directors, actors and writers, as well as entire television and film series. As with the On Track series, we balance fact with analysis.

While professional writing experience would, of course, be an advantage the most important qualification is to have real enthusiasm and knowledge of your subject. First-time authors are welcomed, but the ability to write well in English is essential.

Sonicbond Publishing has distribution throughout Europe and North America, and all books are also published in E-book form. Authors will be paid a royalty based on sales of their book.

Further details are available from www.sonicbondpublishing.co.uk. To contact us, complete the contact form there or email info@sonicbondpublishing.co.uk

www.ingramcontent.com/pod-product-compliance
Lightning Source LLC
Chambersburg PA
CBHW072157100526
44589CB00015B/2266